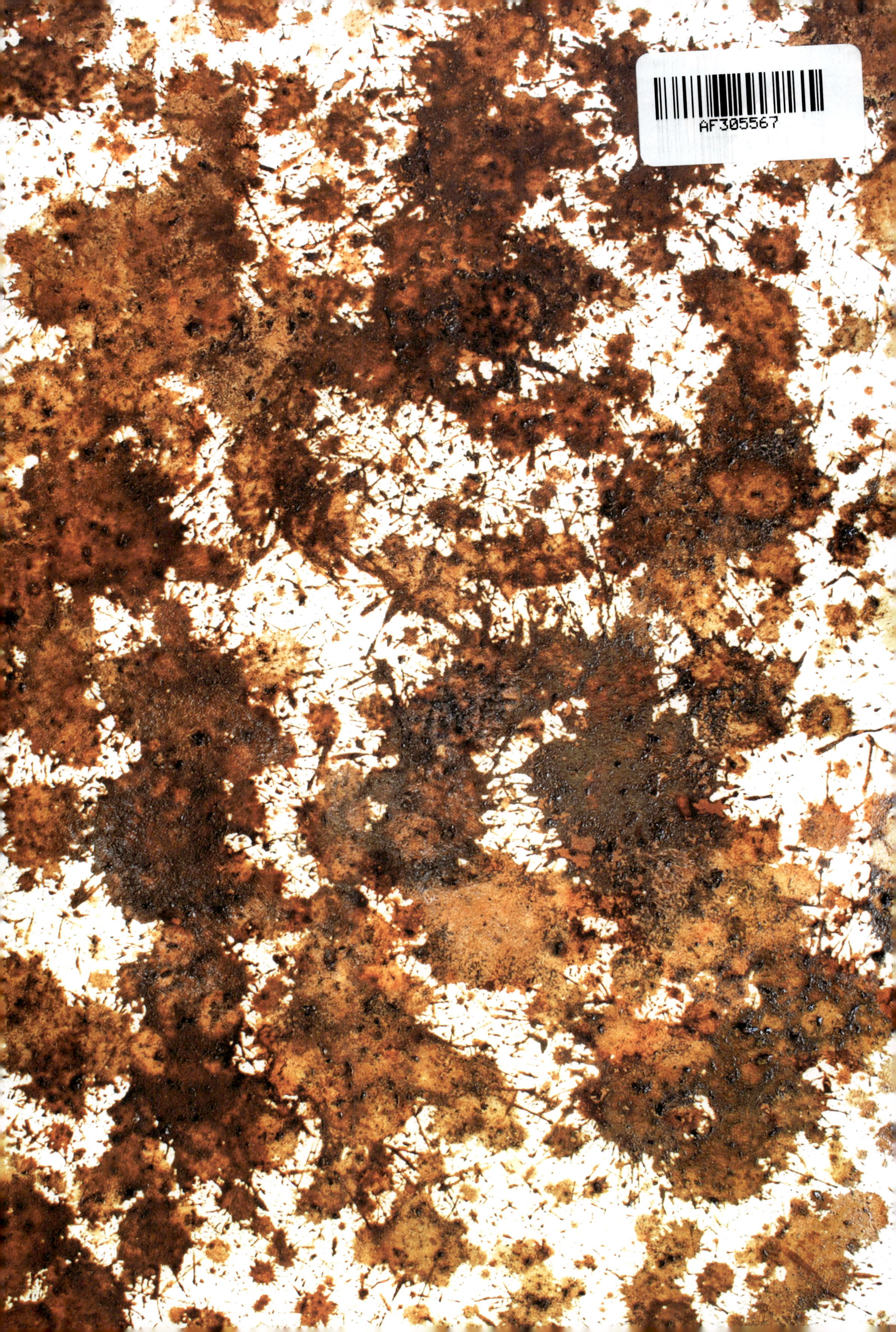

AF305567

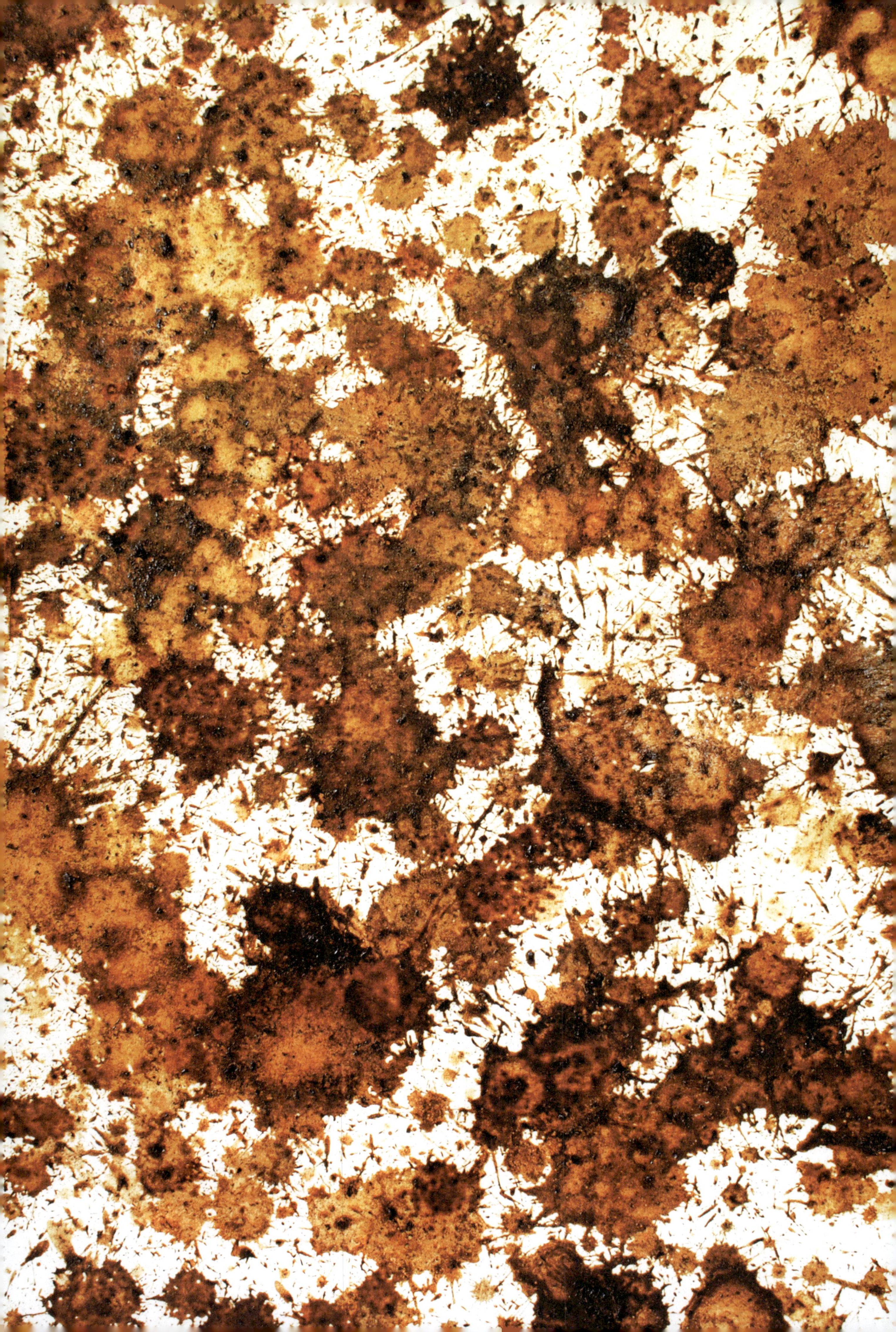

MARIA MADEIRA

KISS AND DON'T TELL

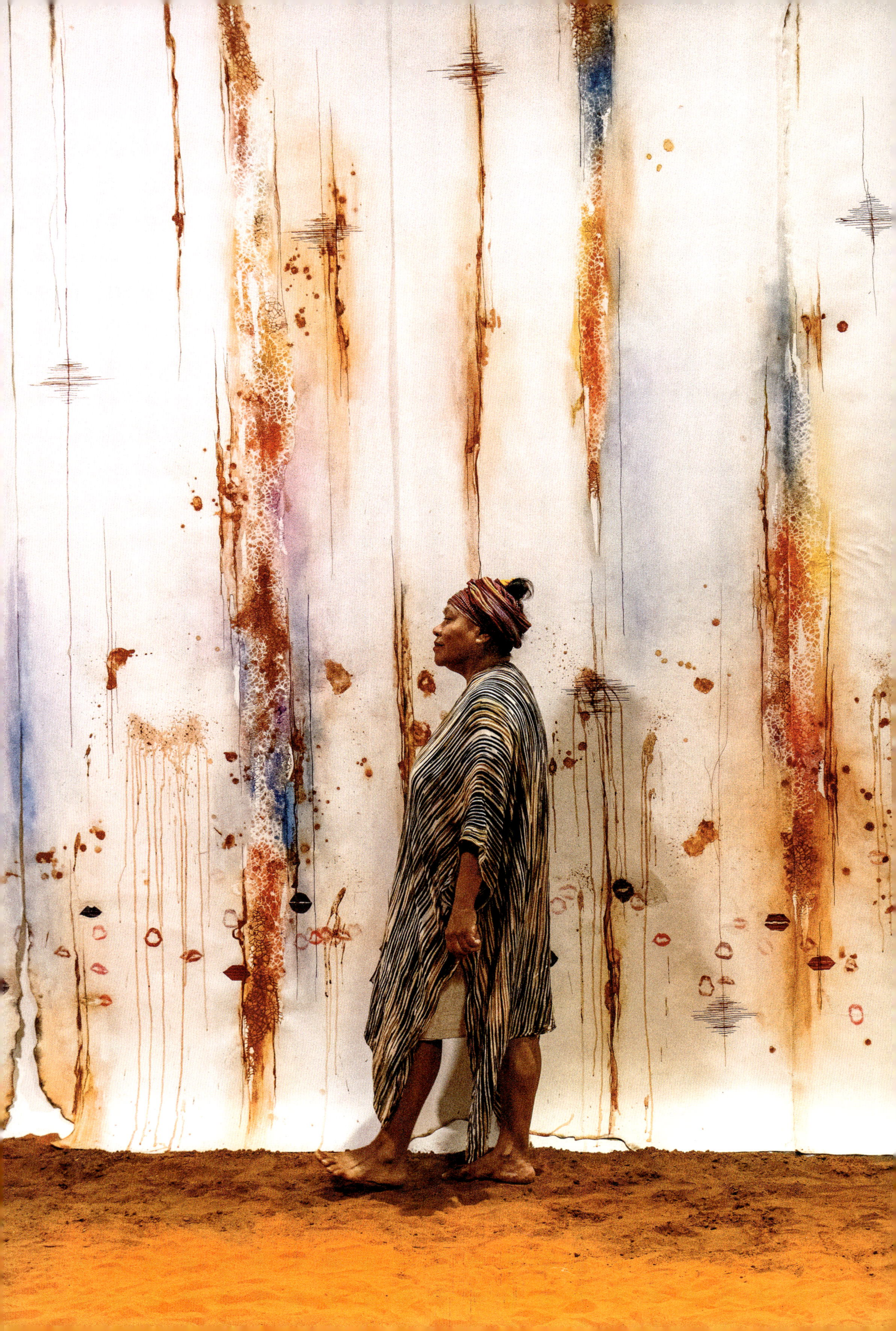

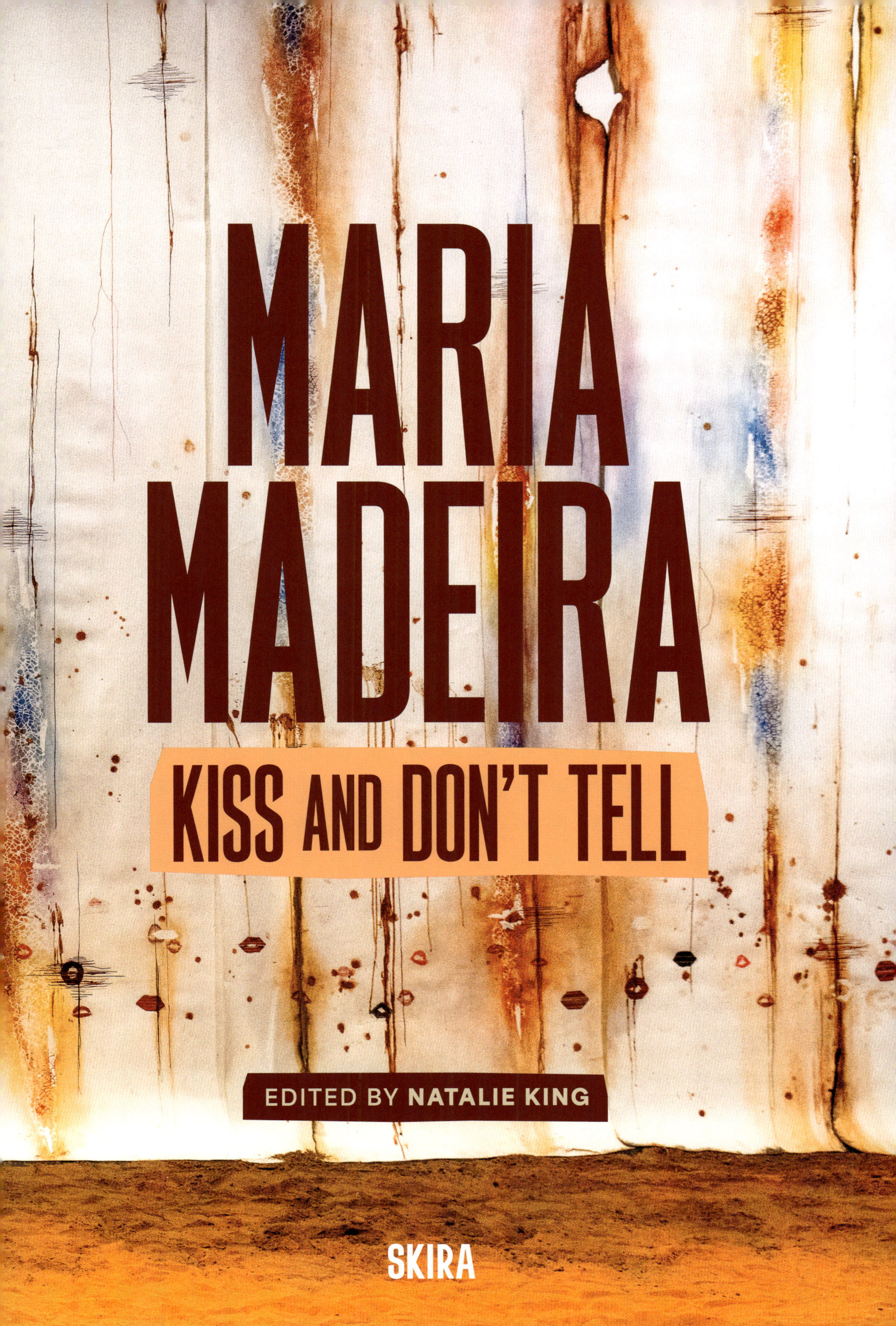

MARIA MADEIRA

KISS AND DON'T TELL

EDITED BY NATALIE KING

SKIRA

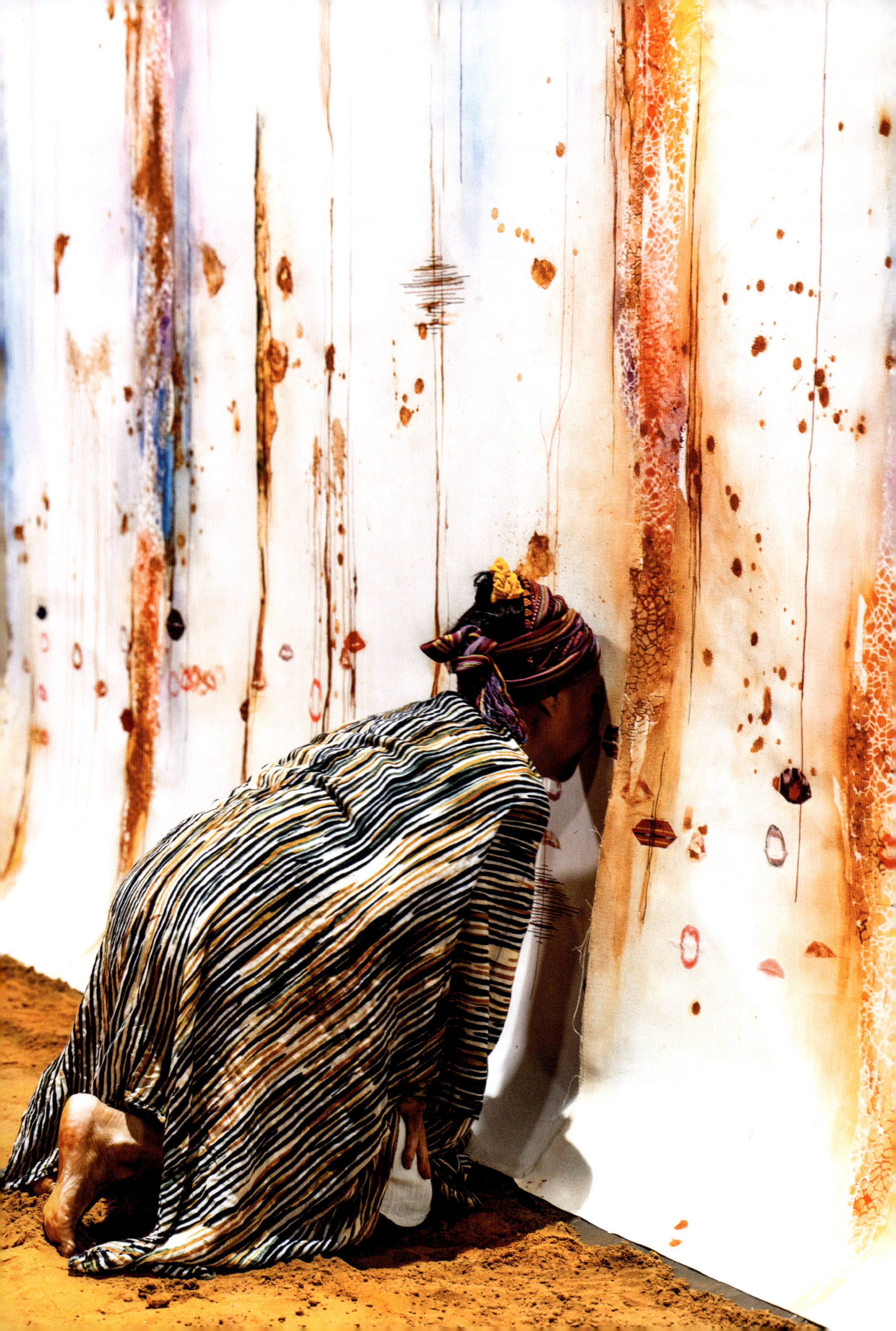

CONTENTS

OPPOSITE
Kiss and Don't Tell, 2024

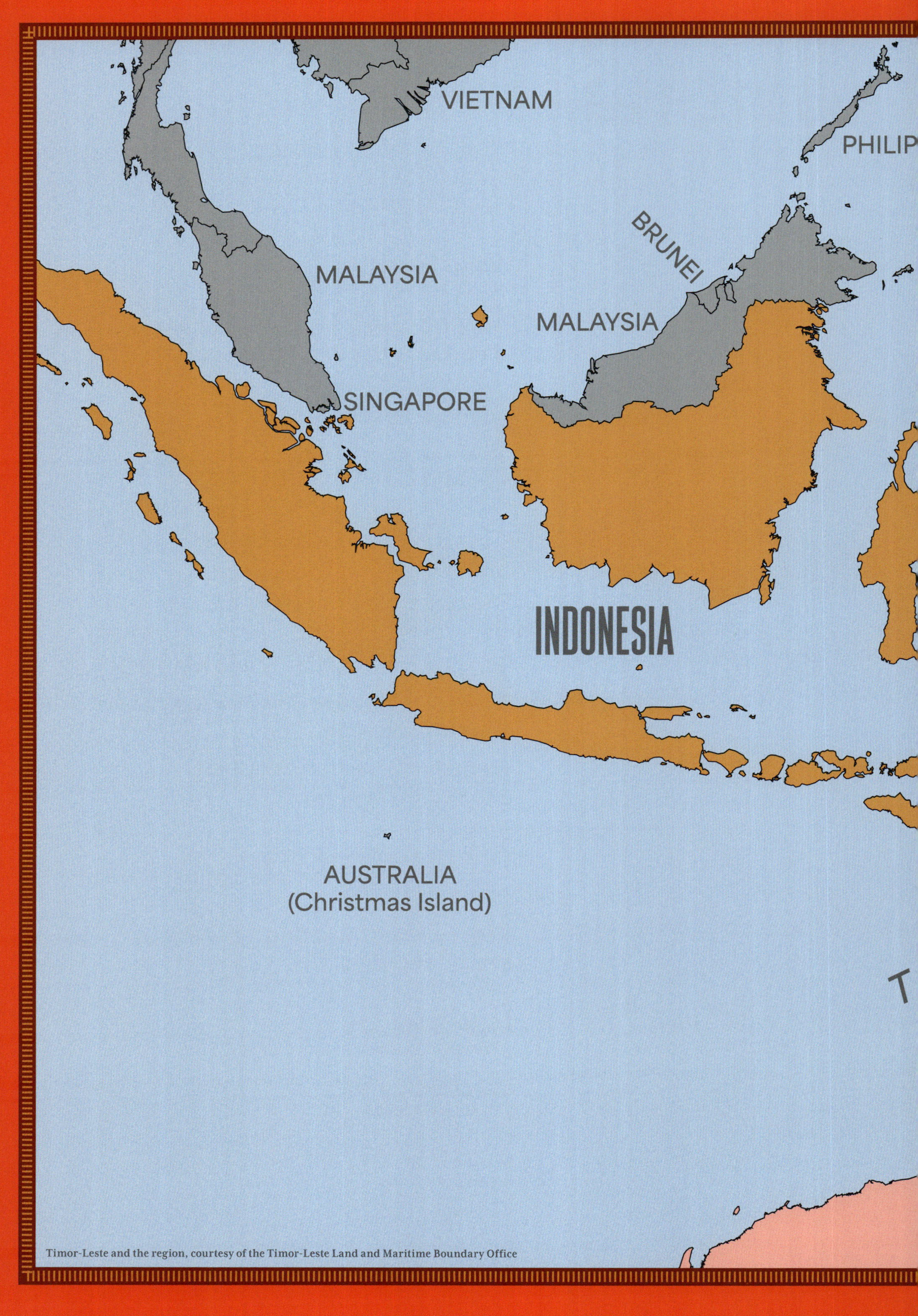

Timor-Leste and the region, courtesy of the Timor-Leste Land and Maritime Boundary Office

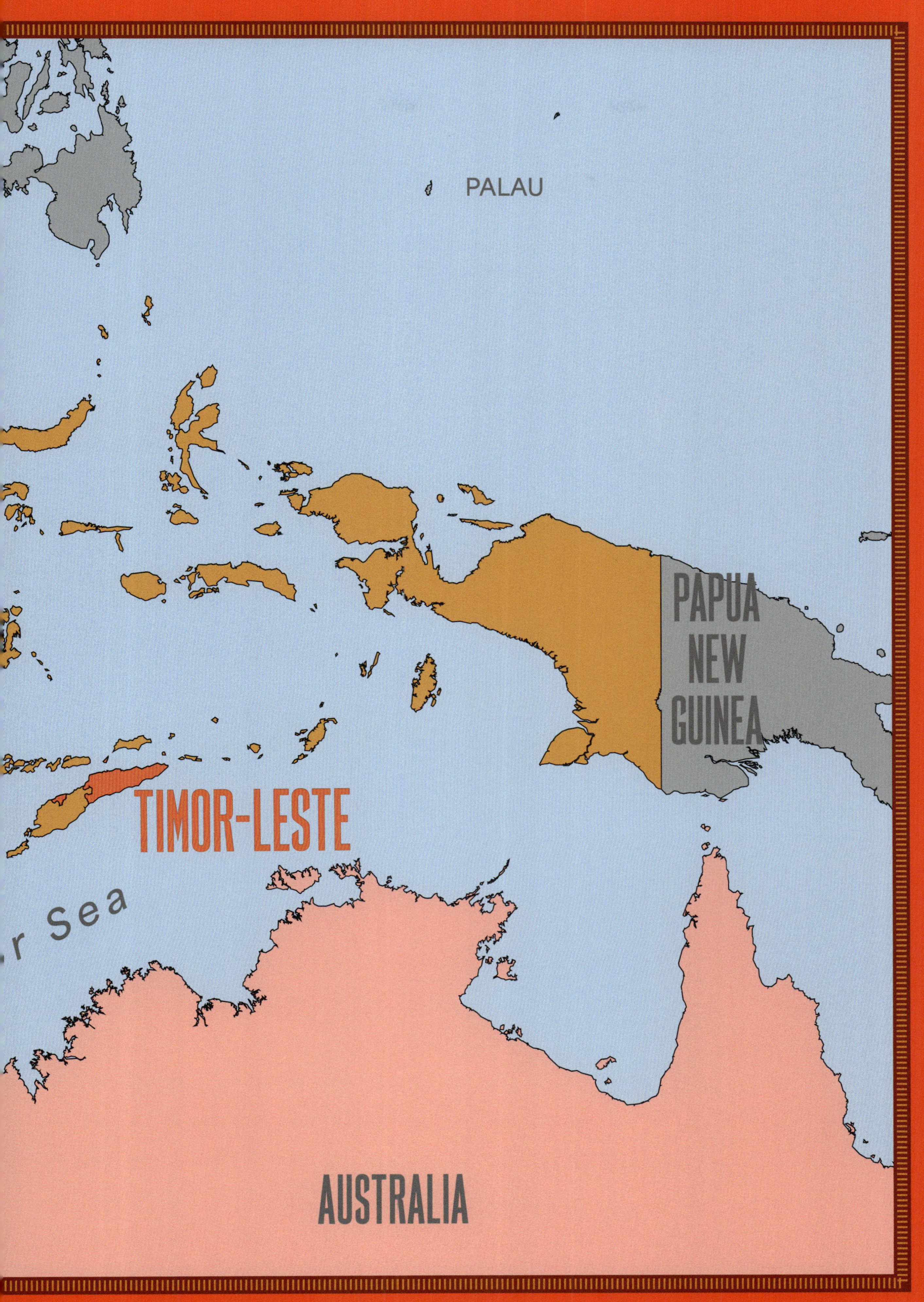

PALAU
PAPUA NEW GUINEA
TIMOR-LESTE
r Sea
AUSTRALIA

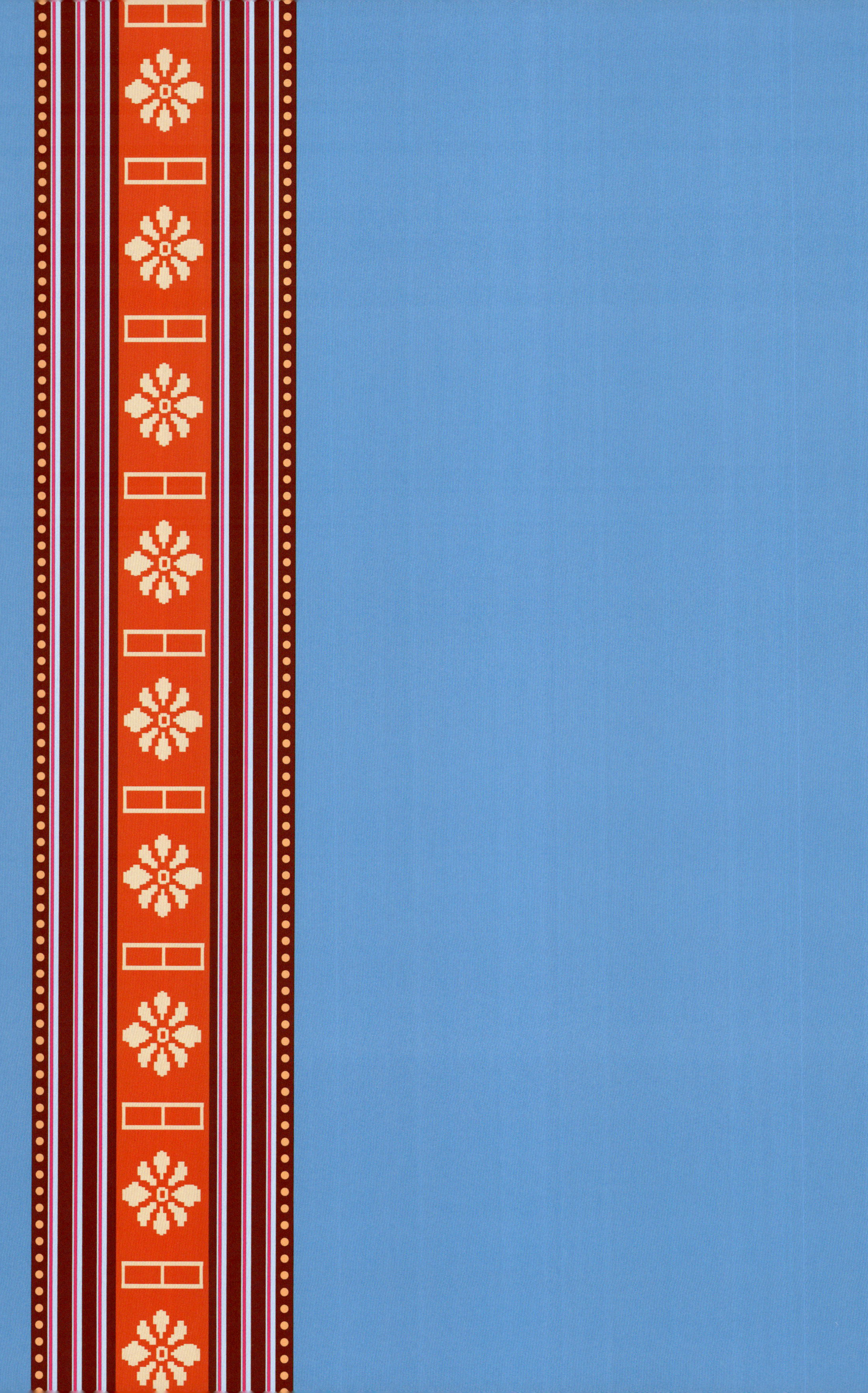

COMMISSIONER'S FOREWORD

Jorge Soares Cristovão

The first ever participation of Timor-Leste at the Venice Biennale is an extraordinary and momentous achievement for our small country. Throughout our tumultuous history, we have preserved our own distinctive culture in song, dance, ritual and visual arts and we are proud to share it on the world stage.

Dr Maria Madeira is the perfect artist to represent Timor-Leste at our first pavilion at the Venice Biennale. Madeira was born in Timor-Leste, lived as a refugee in Portugal, studied art, and achieved a Doctor of Philosophy in Australia. Her artistic practice is a bridge between our past and our future. She uses our traditional cloth 'tais', betel nut, and the red earth of her village to tell a story that speaks to the world today. Her work has been exhibited in Australia, Brazil, Indonesia, Macau, Portugal and Timor-Leste. Her recent exhibition at Fundacão Oriente in Dili, *Flowery Talk*, celebrated her belief that art and culture are the spirit and soul of a nation.

The journey of our people to independence and peace was possible because we chose the path of reconciliation and truth-telling. Timor-Leste's presence at the 60th Venice Biennale is an opportunity to demonstrate that forgiveness is the pathway to peace.

I sincerely thank the father of our nation, Prime Minister Kay Rala Xanana Gusmão for trusting me with the responsibility of being Timor-Leste's first Venice Biennale Commissioner. I also thank him for leading us on the pathway of reconciliation and peace. I am grateful for the support of the Minister of Youth, Sports, Art, and Culture, Nelyo Isaac Sarmento. I also thank the Prime Minister's Chief of Staff, Elizabeth Exposto, for her guidance and support. Lastly, I thank the team in the ministry, particularly Dr Nidio Pinto and Claudio Marques Cabral, M.ICP, L.Ed, for their professional support.

Prime Minister Gusmão's Government was only formed after a national election in May 2023. Conceiving and delivering the Timor-Leste Pavilion has been a whirlwind group effort led by our peerless Curator and Editor, Professor Natalie King OAM. I thank her and her incredibly talented and committed team for making our dream a reality. I particularly want to thank our Venice-based Exhibition Manager Diego Carpentiero for helping us engage with the Biennale and the city of Venice, and project Advisers Anna Schwartz AM, Simon Fenby and Dr Kim McGrath who helped drive the project forward.

Thank you also to Robert Connolly and his production crew for generously directing the film of Maria's performance on a pro bono basis. Finally, this beautiful catalogue would not have been possible without funding from a long-term friend and supporter of Timor-Leste, Peter McMullin AM, thank you Peter.

Timor-Leste is proud to share our story of courage and resilience on the world stage at the 60th Venice Biennale. I am hopeful that our presence in Venice will inspire our young people to explore their creativity and aspire to represent our nation at future biennales.

JORGE SOARES CRISTOVÃO
Commissioner, Timor-Leste at the 60th International Art Exhibition, La Biennale di Venezia, 2024

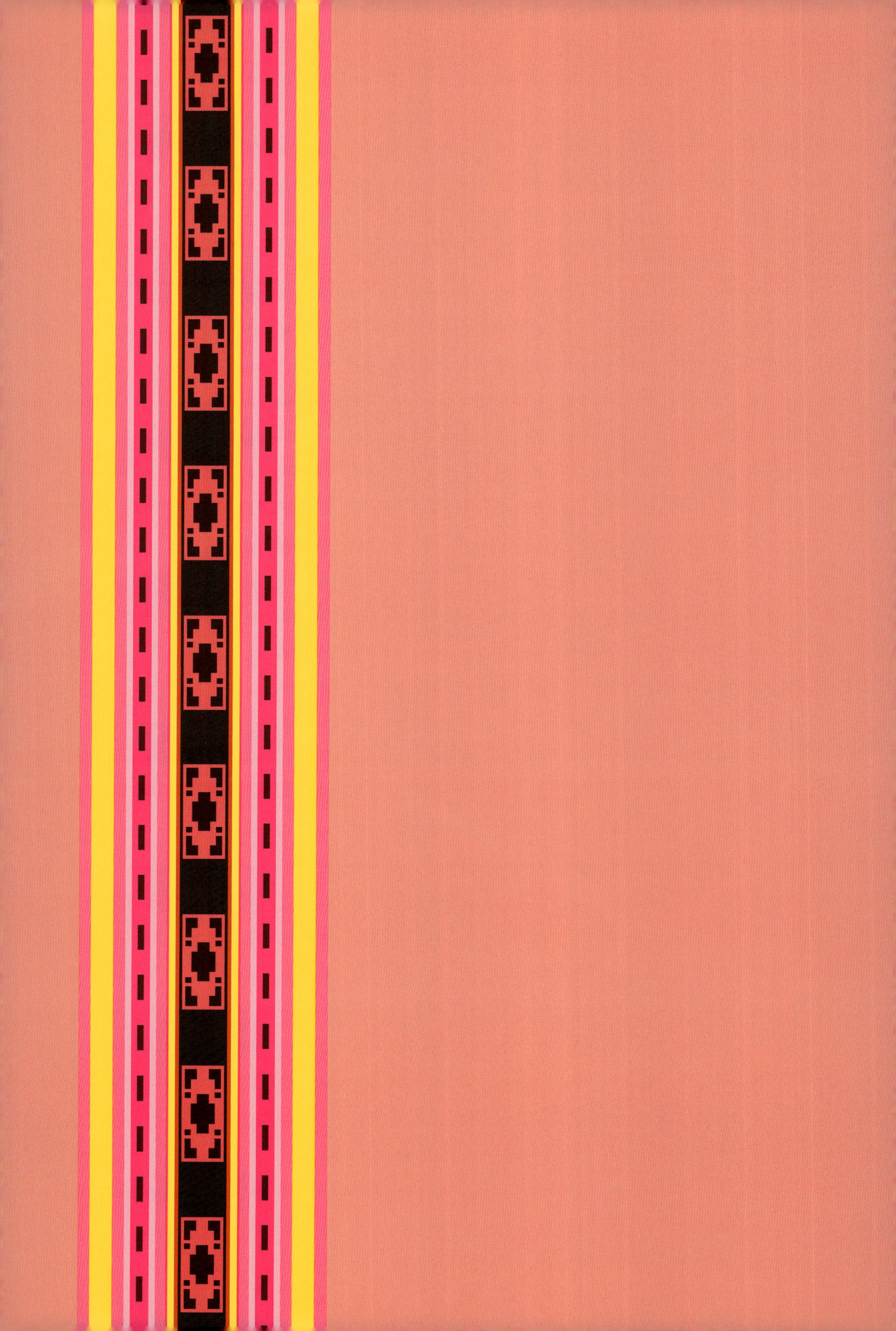

INTRODUCTION

Xanana Gusmão

It is of great significance to our nation that twenty-five years after the Timorese people voted in a United Nations-sponsored referendum to restore our independence, Timor-Leste is participating in the world's premiere visual arts event – la Biennale di Venezia.

Our path to independence was full of sacrifice and tragedy. Our distinct history, culture and heritage sustained us in our struggle for self-determination and fuelled our dreams of freedom.

Our shared cultural identity sustained us during our struggle and shaped our approach to building a peaceful nation. Despite the suffering we endured, Timor-Leste is now a thriving, free, open and democratic nation.

We maintained and honoured our unique culture and traditions and emerged stronger as a people. Importantly, we have not carried hatred in our hearts. We have instead given priority to reconciliation and peace. We look ahead and seek to expand the possibilities of our young nation. We proudly share our story of hope and inspiration.

After the Restoration of our Independence, we recognised the critical role of our culture in building solidarity and the importance of art in healing and expressing a vision for our future. We established an arts school, Arte Moris (Living Art), to support our young artists. Arte Moris is now located in the grounds of the Presidential Palace where it enjoys the unwavering support of our President, His Excellency, Dr José Ramos-Horta. Arte Moris is a vibrant centre for creativity and expression and many of our artists have spent time at the school, including Maria Madeira, who volunteered as a teacher there for many years.

Timor-Leste has risen from the ashes and emerged a place of hope. Maria Madeira's work tells this story. She incorporates the timeless traditions of our people in contemporary works of truth telling and beauty. She uses materials that define our land and our heritage, red earth, betel nut and tais – our traditional woven cloth – to present a narrative of resistance, resilience and renewal.

And in our troubled times she speaks to a universal experience of women in war. Madeira's work captures the power of reconciliation and the possibilities of hope.

Timor-Leste is proud to be able to showcase our art and culture. We are working to develop our creative economy by nurturing our traditions – our weaving, carving, drawing and painting, dance, design, film and music – to create jobs and opportunities for our people. While this is the first time our country is participating in La Biennale di Venezia, we look forward to many more exhibitions to celebrate our homeland and share our story with the world.

Finally, I want to thank Timor-Leste's inaugural Venice Biennale Commissioner, the Secretary of State for Arts and Culture, Jorge Soares Cristóvão and his team for making Timor-Leste's participation in La Biennale di Venezia a reality.

HIS EXCELLENCY KAY RALA (XANANA) GUSMÃO
Prime Minister, Democratic Republic of Timor-Leste

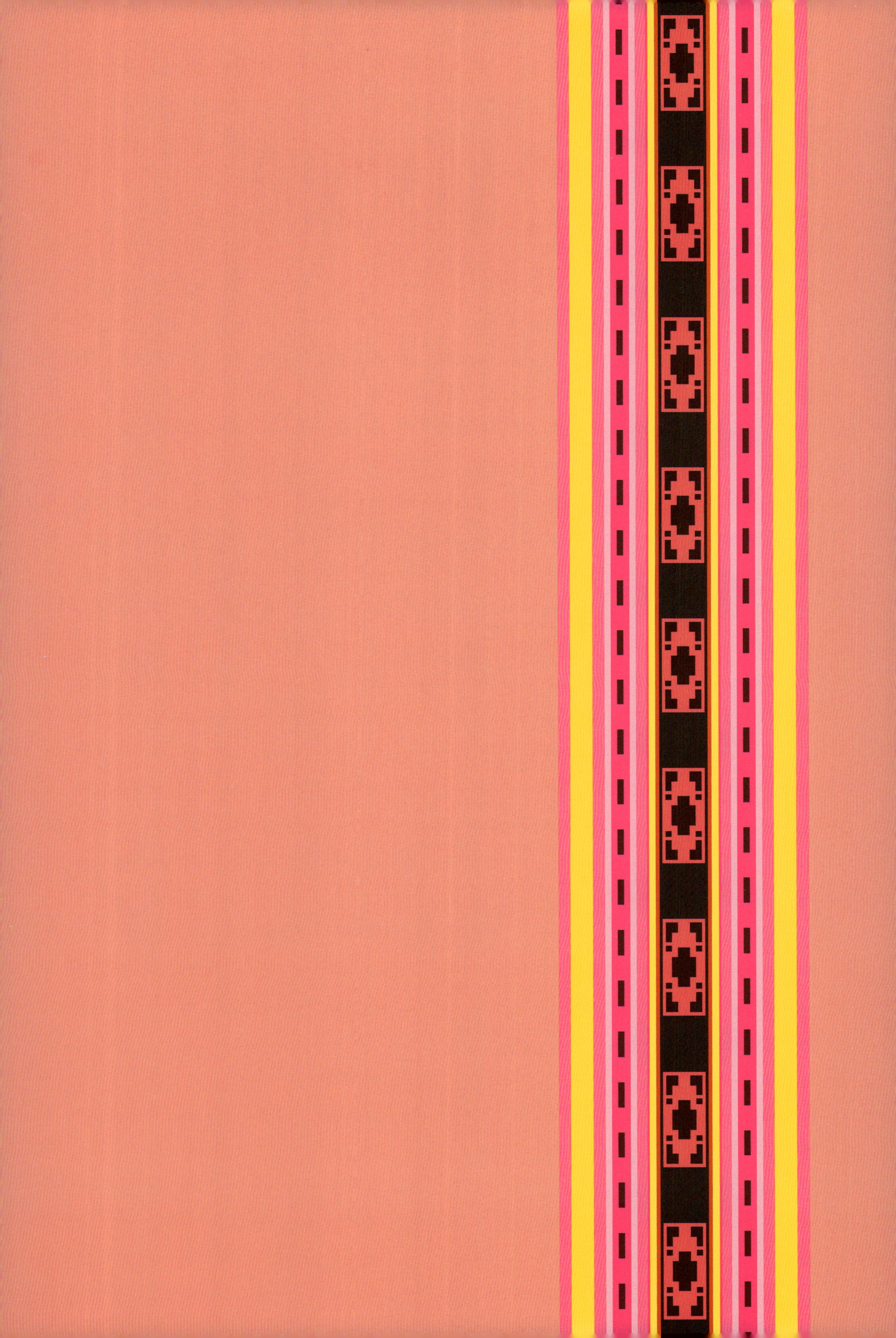

PAZ NO MUNDO

XANANA GUSMÃO

Violência, morte
Sangue e lágrimas
Inteligência arquitectada para destruir
Arte de mobilizar pessoas para morrer
Serão princípios, direitos,
Mas também poder, ambições

Sofrimento, luto,
Desespero, vingança
O resultado não é a dimensão, ignorada,
Só os números ficarão para a história
Enquanto muitos morrem
Alguns semeiam o ódio

E prega-se a paz
Enquanto há guerra
Oprimem-se os inocentes, os indefesos
Os interesses e as políticas, protegidos
Justificam-se os princípios
E os direitos não existem

E agita-se a guerra
Quando existe paz
Consciência humana alienada
Dignidade pervertida, sem moral
P'la verdade que se advoga,
Suavizam-se as violações

Agita-se a violência
E o diálogo morre
As causas não existem, são esquecidas,
E motivam-se os ânimos e a força
E´ um mundo de medo
Na informática da trauma

Clama –se p´la justiça
P´ra exigir a punição
As pessoas seguem a onda das emoções
E distorcem o lado humano da vida
Onde não há coragem
E o perdão não tem lugar!

WORLD PEACE

XANANA GUSMÃO

Violence, death
Blood and tears
Intelligence in the service of destruction
The art of mobilising human beings to die
For principles, rights?
or power, ambition?

Suffering, grief
Despair, revenge
The result eclipsing their dimension
The numbers alone recorded by history
While many die
Others sow a hatred

Speaking of Peace
When a war rages
Innocents, the defenceless oppressed
Interests, politics at the fore.
Principles to justify
And rights do not exist

Speaking of war
When peace prevails
Human conscience in alienation
Dignity debased in the absence of morals
A truth is preached
Then violations downplayed

The violence screams
Dialogue the loser
There are no causes, forgotten
Spirits aroused, force is the answer
A world of fear
In the media of trauma

Justice, the claim
Punishment, a demand
Dragged into the tide of emotions
The human side of life, twisted
Where there is no courage
And no place for forgiveness!

Commissioned by Melbourne Festival, August 2001,
performed by Xanana Gusmão on 11 October 2001.

O LEADER DIPLOMATICO:

A Paz é Possível o Diálago é o Caminho Para a Paz

Pisaste um dia a terra descalça
do bua e do malus
Paraste um dia à sombra dos coqueiros
estranhando o tuaka
e reparaste no seu dono
cobrindo com a nudez do seu langotim
a campa dos seus antepassados.

Miraste o seu suor tórrido
que caia em bátegas do seu rosto sujo
e o mistério dos seus hamulaks
envolvido em tais dos seus luliks
e conheceste, na pobreza da sua pele
um longo olhar altivo
rudemente profundo
infinitamente intimo...

E o dono da terra
guardou o seu ai-suak
e matou o seu karau
levantou o odan
agarrou no tali
e saíu em busca do seu kuda
esgrimindo sua espado contra o naokten.

E de longe, de mui longe
de cá dos oceanos, arremessou o seu diman
que rude e profundamente
te atravessou a carne
e íntima e infinitamente
abraçou a tua alma...
e tu, amaste-o!

Daqui, das montanhas de Timor-Leste,
um abraço.

XANANA GUSMÃO
MARÇO DE 1989

THE DIPLOMATIC LEADER:

Peace is possible, dialogue is the way to peace

Once, barefoot you trod the earth
that belonged to the betel palm nut and leaf
Once, you stood under the shade of the coconut
palms unaccustomed to sugar cane rum
and you noticed its owner
covering his ancestor's grave
with the simplicity of his loincloth.

You gazed upon his searing sweat
that fell from his dusty face
and you heard the mystery of his prayers
enveloped by sacred cloths
and you met in the poverty of his skin
a proud gaze
crudely profound
infinitely intimate...

And the owner of the land
put down his pickaxe
killed his buffaloes
raised his fence
seized the reins
and went in search of his pony
brandishing his sword against the intruder.

And from far away, from far far away
from this side of the oceans
he hurled his spear
which roughly and deeply
pierced your flesh
and intimately and infinitely
embraced your soul
and you, loved him!

Here, in the mountains of East Timor, a hug.

XANANA GUSMÃO
MARCH 1989

Sara Niner, *Xanana: leader of the struggle for independent Timor-Leste*, Australian Scholarly
Publishing, Melbourne, 2009, pp. 121–22.

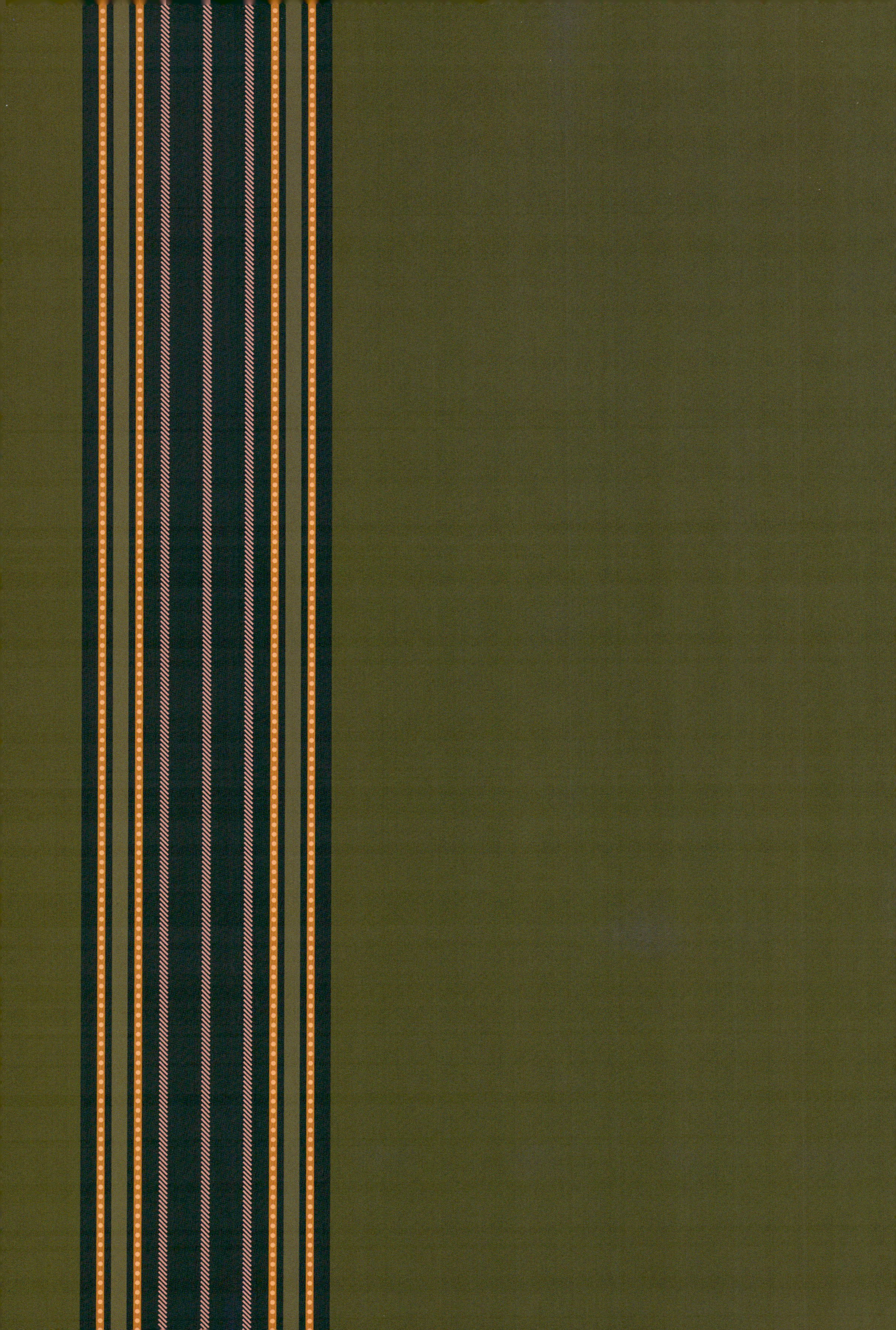

NO MORE LIPSTICK

NATALIE KING

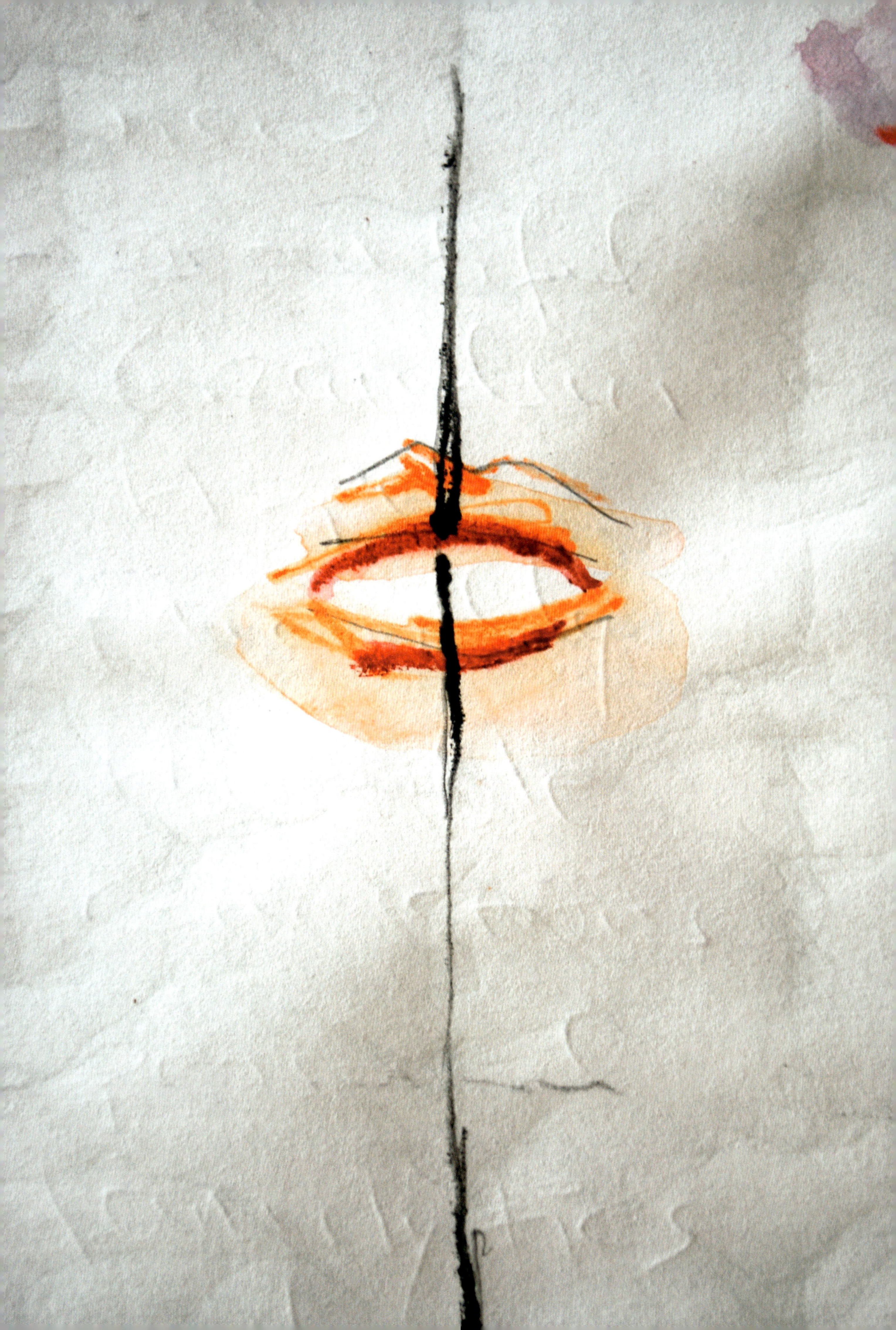

NO MORE LIPSTICK

Natalie King

MARIA MADEIRA,
QUIETLY SPEAKING, 2010

Returning to her homeland after the Timorese voted for independence from Indonesia in 1999, artist Maria Madeira slept in a bedroom with coloured markings along the walls at knee height. After gaining trust from surrounding neighbours, Madeira learned that the marks were the remains of lipstick. During the Indonesian occupation (1975-1999) Timorese women were forced to wear lipstick, kneel down and kiss the walls. Madeira slept surrounded by clear visible impressions of hundreds of lipstick marks, imprinted stains of torment. This silent residue of anguish compelled Madeira to tell the hidden and overlooked story of Timorese women. For Madeira, these unacknowledged heroines are silent martyrs who deflected harm from their men by being subjugated. Notably, there is no burial place for the heroines of Timor-Leste's resistance in the cemetery of martyrs or Santa Cruz cemetery in Dili, yet Madeira is determined to tell this harrowing story through *Kiss and Don't Tell*.

Madeira honours these anonymous women who suffered in her site-specific, large-scale installation *Kiss and Don't Tell*. By drenching the walls in drips of paint and betel nut that resemble blood, intensified by the deep crimson hue of antiseptic, Madeira alludes to wounds and injuries. Given there are no art supply stores in Dili, Madeira deploys materials sourced locally by diluting the red ochre earth of her village Ermera co-mingled with threads of tais, the traditional Timorese textile. The effect is like a stain, teardrops, or even oozing blood. Pale hues of acrylic paint in blue and peach further add a luminous quality to her epic painting installation with a vibrating and pulsating effect, pleading to be seen. Paint is applied over segments of crochet that are subsequently removed to leave a patterned impression. Madeira, thereby, binds women's work with a painterly composition to link the past with the future, and in doing so, tells her remarkable tale. The fingerprints of her foremothers are embedded in the work.

Shush … Labele Koalia (Shush … Do Not Tell), 2009

Madeira's ensemble exhibition *Kiss and Don't Tell* for
the inaugural Timor-Leste pavilion at the 60th Venice
Biennale is proud, political and poetic. *Kiss and Don't
Tell* comprises four components: a large-scale painting
installation, a performance video, an intervention
of lipstick marks onto the gallery window and a live
performance during the opening days. The central
installation comprises 25 conjoined, panelled paintings
that are draped from floor to ceiling with red earth at the
base, connecting earth and sky. Redolent with pain and
anguish, Madeira smears red earth from her birthplace
in Timor-Leste onto tais, canvas and floor, imbuing the
performative installation with sorrow and memories.

'Everything is about the ground for me, it keeps us
embedded into being Timorese. In sacred ceremonies
and folklore, we talk about Mother Earth and our
umbilical cord is buried next to the most prominent tree
as our oldest eternal connection to Mother Earth. Ermera
is such a beautiful red colour that I just can't ignore it.'[1]

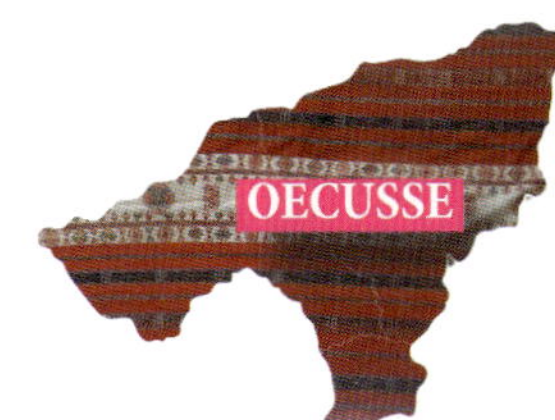

During the opening days of the 60th Venice Biennale,
Madeira kisses the walls with lipstick markings while
singing tradition songs from her village in the Indigenous
language Tetun. In particular, she sings a haunting
Timorese song *Ina Lou*, literally meaning 'Dear Mother
Earth'. It is a spiritual mourning song known from the
youngest generation to the oldest members of society
with lyrics that refer to the cycle of birth and the journey
of life and death. Singing was a form of salvation for
Madeira. It allowed her to retain her cultural heritage
while displaced in a refugee camp in Portugal as an
adolescent. She joined Coro Loro Sa'e, a traditional
Timorese dance and choir, travelling and performing
around Portugal, England and Wales.

Imbued with sorrow, hope and healing, Madeira insists
on being heard while making visible the women of
Timor-Leste. Murmuring or speaking in whispers can
be a powerful tactic and feminist methodology of
revolution whereby demands are generated quietly.
With fervour, sincerity and force, Madeira lures us into
a visceral symbology of scorch marks and stains, kisses
and tales, stitches and spit. Some sections of the canvas
are burned, recalling Madeira's memory of the lingering
stench pervading the city of Dili after the invasion.
Madeira singes the edges of the canvas panels as if the
painting is searing in pain. Lipstick stains are imprinted
across the lower part of the painting installation as
Madeira re-enacts the humiliation and degradation of
kissing the walls in tacky shades of lipstick. These pink
and red smudges and stains are interspersed with sewn
and stitched cut-outs of lips in tais.

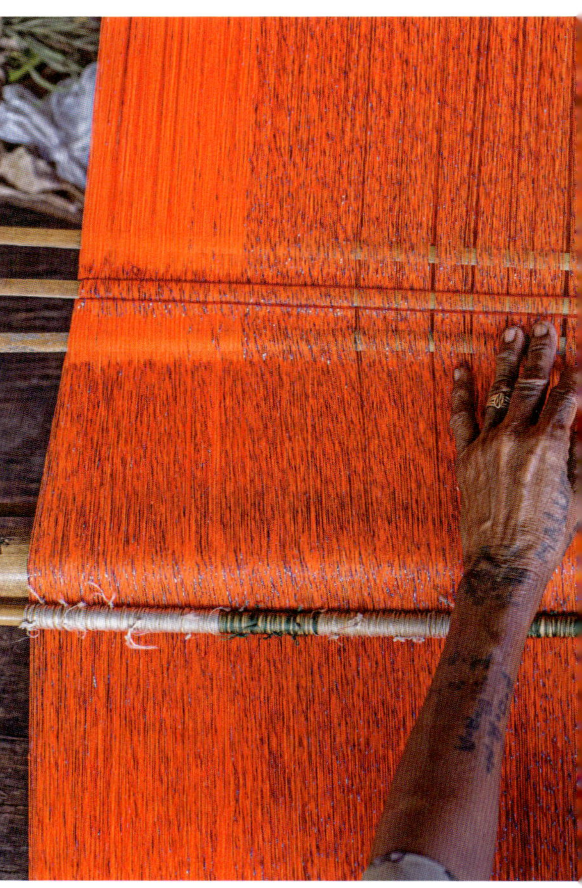
Tais weaving, *Tais: Traditional Textile*, 2023

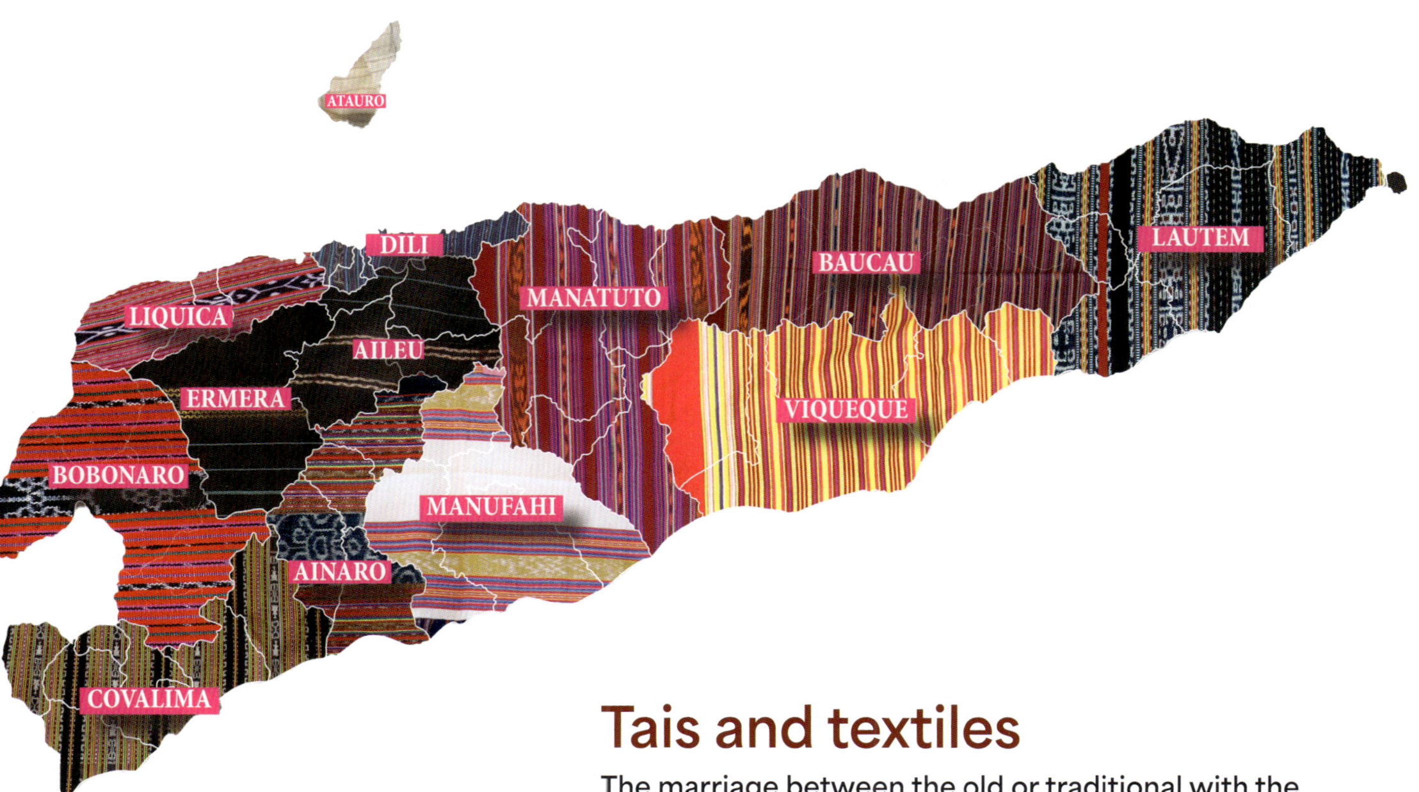

Map of tais styles in Timor-Leste, *Tais: Traditional Textile*, 2023

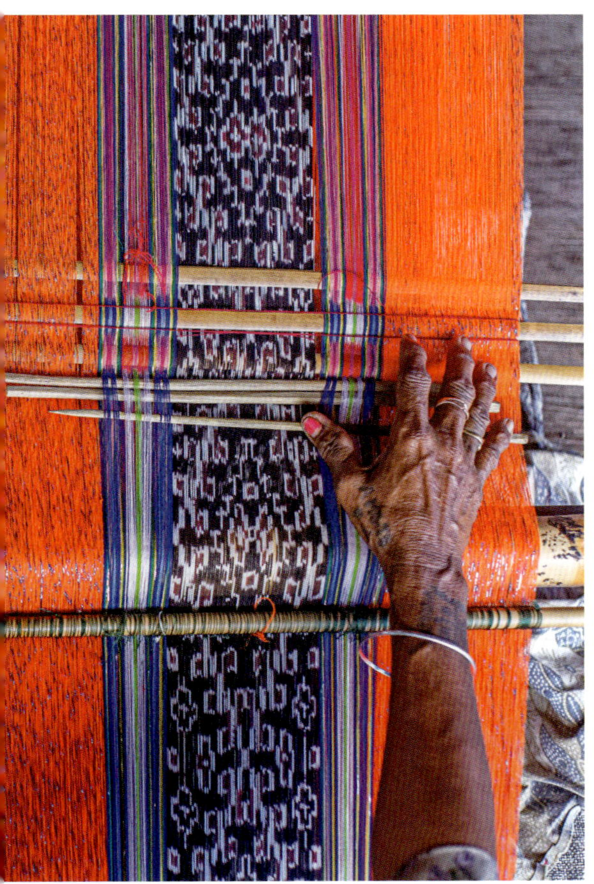

Tais and textiles

The marriage between the old or traditional with the new and contemporary will bring wonders.[2]

An integral part of Timor-Leste's cultural heritage, tais is considered of such importance that it was added to the UNESCO *List of Intangible Cultural Heritage in Need of Urgent Safeguarding* in 2021. Tais are often gifted as a symbolic gesture of friendship and placed around the neck of the recipient to bind them together. Relationships are maintained by the exchange of textiles that preserve clan affinities and alliances during life-cycle rituals such as harvest festivals, weddings, funerals, and celebratory dances.[3] Tais afford women small-scale commerce and an income source while binding makers to ancestral traditions.

There are 13 districts for tais in Timor-Leste, each with its own palette, pattern and iconography. Imagery often includes animals such as the crocodile, which is central to the Timorese creation story. According to legend a 'crocodile, seeking its destiny, emerged from the depths of the ocean through a crack of light. Tired, it stretched through time, and its scales transformed into chains of mountains where people were born and people died.'[4] Weaving techniques are passed down from generation to generation in an oral tradition and as an activity of communal gathering and self-expression. For example, tais from Ermera, Madeira's birthplace, is composed of inky blacks and vivid indigo as the dyeing technique utilises mud. Ermera means 'red water' and Madeira recalls the rivers, lakes and red water of her hometown. By contrast, other regions use dyes derived from mango skin, potato leaf, cactus flower and turmeric. Tais is woven by women with a back-strap loom which allows tension on the cloth while the warp is manipulated. Typically loom-woven textiles are made from locally grown cotton that is harvested, prepared and spun with a spindle.

Madeira places embroidered lips in tais across the textured painting, highlighting both tenderness and trauma further reflected in her poetic title, *Kiss and Don't Tell*. Here the intimacy of a kiss is contrasted with secrets, silencing, and hidden stories. Madeira adeptly melds ancestral influences and traditional crafts with contemporary concerns for the plight of the voiceless. Working with the traditional textile tais, Madeira sources offcuts, unpicks the threads, and reconfigures the strands into slender lines or bands that resemble surgical sutures. She acknowledges the labour of women by incorporating tais collaged and overlayed with sewn mosquito net to add both texture and an emotive quality to the canvas.

The associative range of these fine bands of tais also recall soundwaves, as if the women's lipstick imprints are giving voice to pain and suffering. Other sections of this epic painting cycle contain additional markings formed when Madeira has placed segments of crochet onto the canvas to leave a filigree residue. Madeira recalls that her mother made two crochets in the refugee camp on the outskirts of Lisbon. Her mother gave one to her, which Madeira uses as a memento of their difficult history of multiple displacements in the large work *Coro Loro Sa'e*, 2023. Madeira spread the crochet over her painted surface and left it for several months exposed to the hot sun of Perth. When she removed the crochet, its pattern remained as the exposed paint had faded, letting the sun do her painting.

The subversive stitch

Madeira invokes a tapestry of memory, remembering and remorse. Sami scholar Liisa-Rávná Finbog writes about the material manifestation of existence that is both silent and visible: '...a multi-layered and dynamic creation of imaginations and ancestral knowledge'.[5] The British psychotherapist, art historian, writer and feminist Rozsika Parker in her key publication *The Subversive Stitch* declares: 'To know the history of embroidery is to know the history of women.'[6]

MARIA MADEIRA,
QUIETLY SPEAKING, 2010

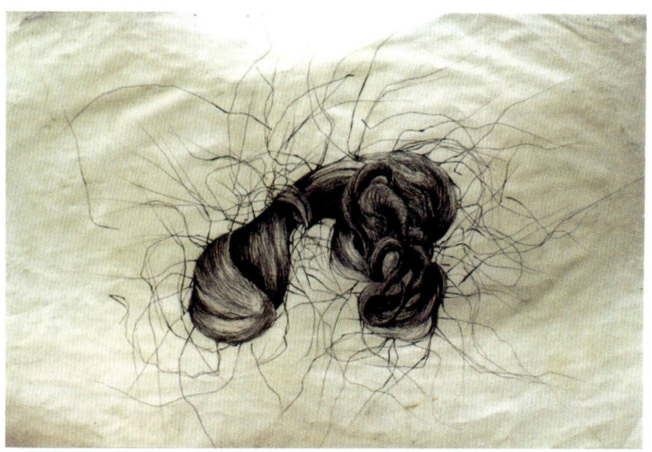

LEFT
Abut- Ama nia Fuk (Raizes-Cabelos Da Mãe; Roots-Mum's Hair), 1990

OPPOSITE ABOVE
Coro Loro Sa'e, 2023

OPPOSITE BELOW
Coro Loro Sa'e (detail), 2023

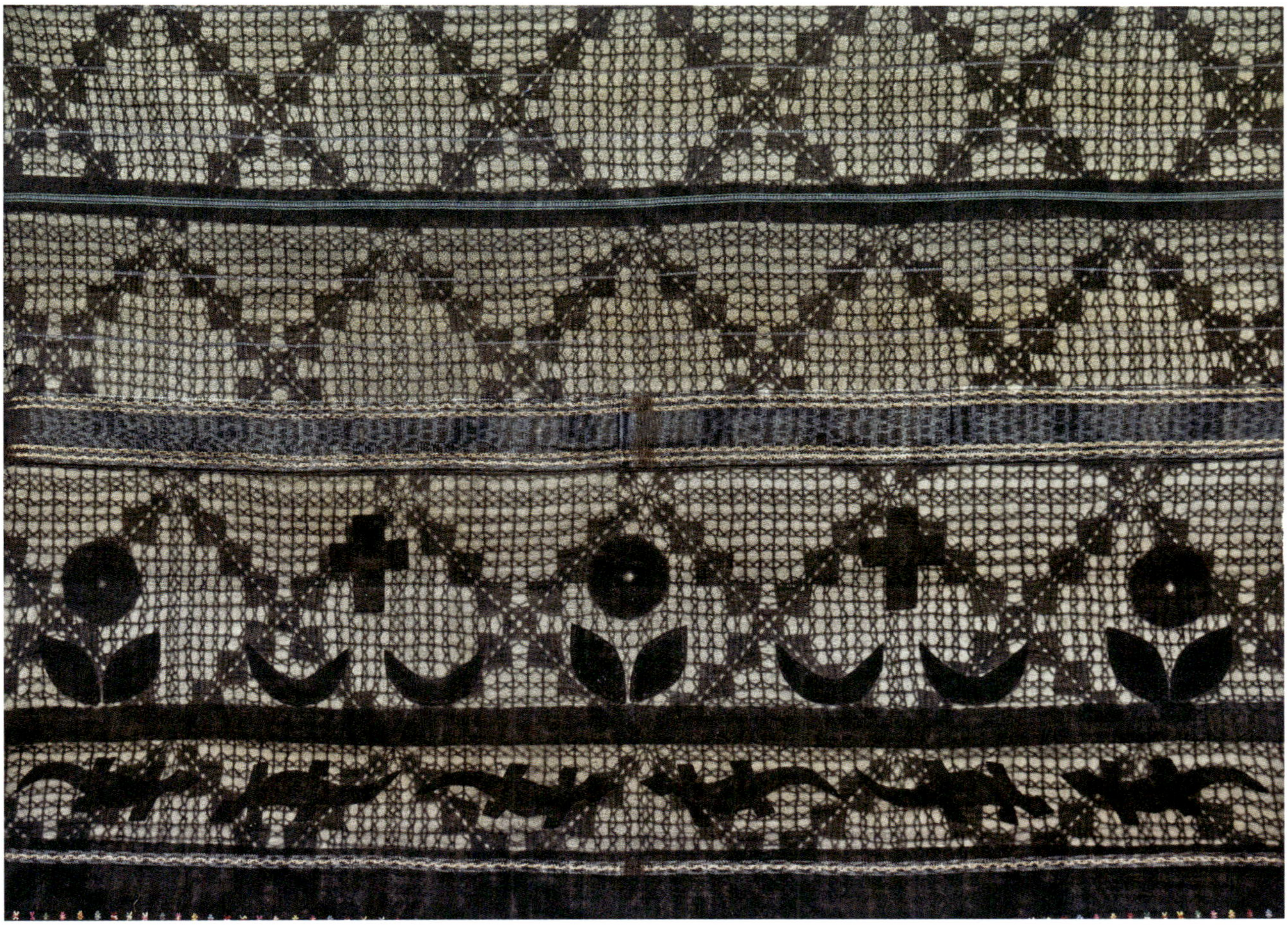

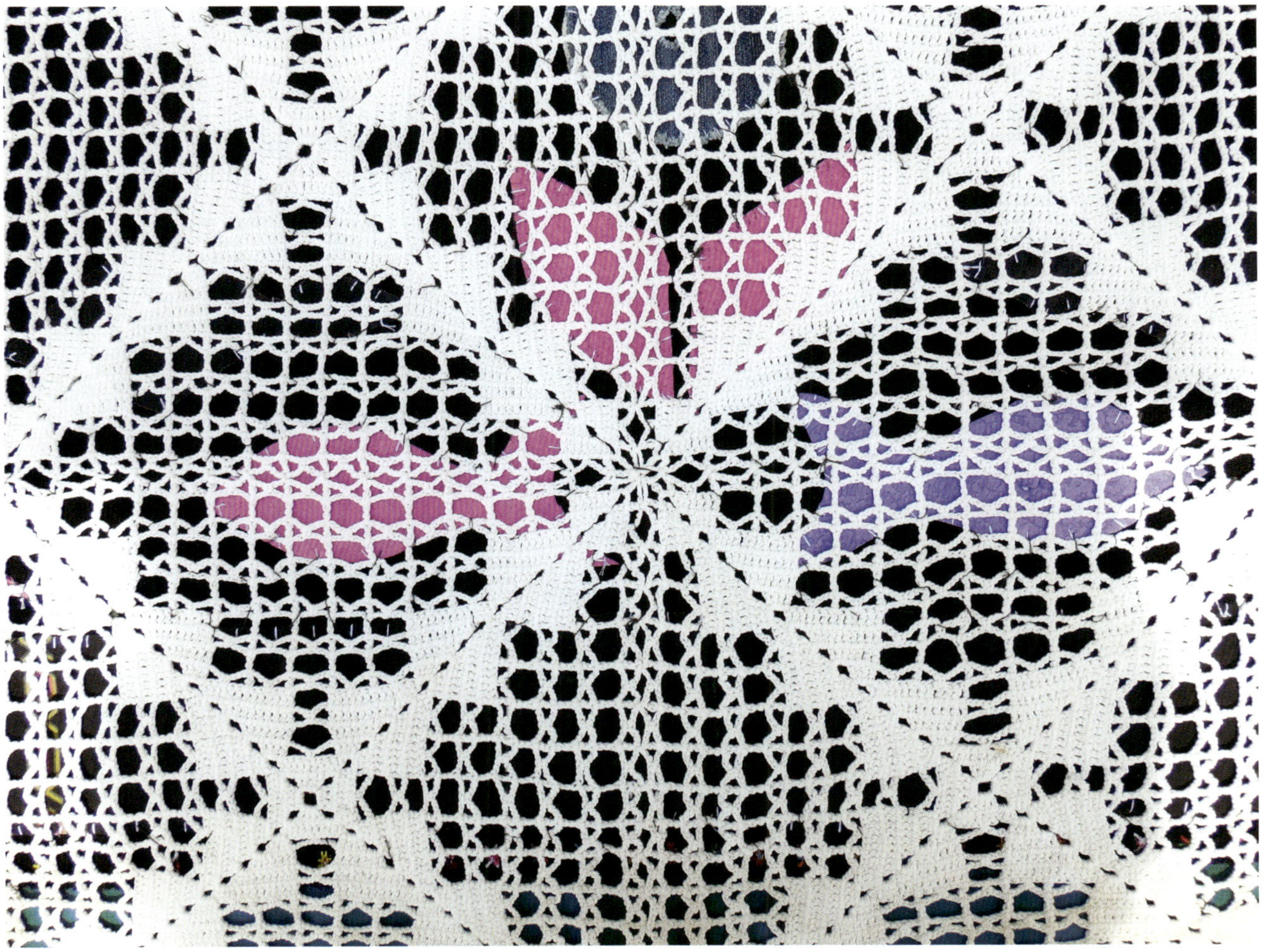

The Subversive Stitch threads together textile practices that have addressed the histories of domesticity, labour and femininity bound to embroidery and stitching, yarn and the narrative qualities of textiles. The pliable qualities of yarn and strands allow Madeira to unravel histories and weave new patterns of awareness for the plight of Timorese women under occupation. Part of a major breakthrough in art history, the use of textiles and embroidery and the stitched art of Louise Bourgeois, Tracey Emin and Rosemarie Trockel, inculcated female subservience with a defiant co-opting of materials and making.[7] So, too, does Madeira invoke the tactility of fibre art while unpicking strands of cloth from her female community ensuring that 'your work is in my work'.[8]

—

Spitting in silence

Female voice

A conversation between sisters

A conversation between mother and daughter

A conversation between friends

A dialogue between local communities

A flowery connection

Maria Madeira, *Flowery Talk*, 2024

During her performance of *Kiss and Don't Tell*, Madeira chews betel nut and spits it on to the canvas leaving brown markings. Betel nut is traditionally used in informal casual gatherings and during sacred ceremonies. Offering betel nut to each other is deeply embedded in a way of life:

When I returned to my birth place in Gleno, my family greeted me by inviting me to chew betel nut all together. I could see that chewing was something beautiful, bringing a community together, a village, and gathering for all Timorese people. So chewing betel nut together I came up with the idea of spitting the betel nut onto the canvas. Because I am an artist.[9]

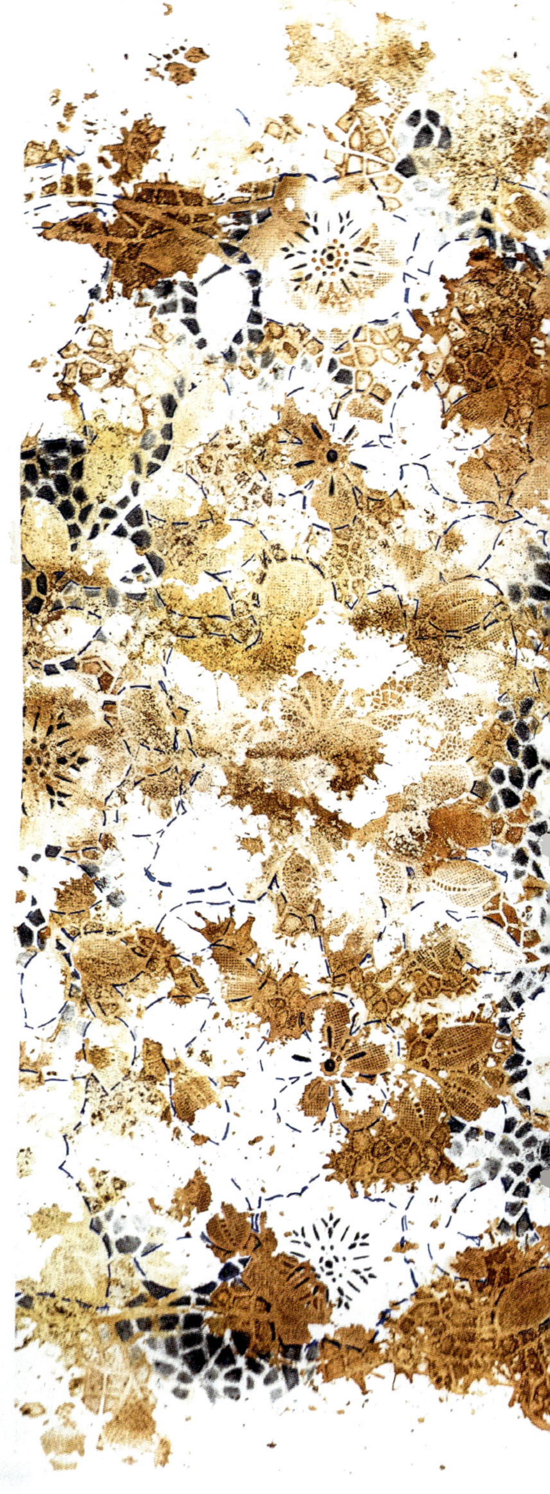

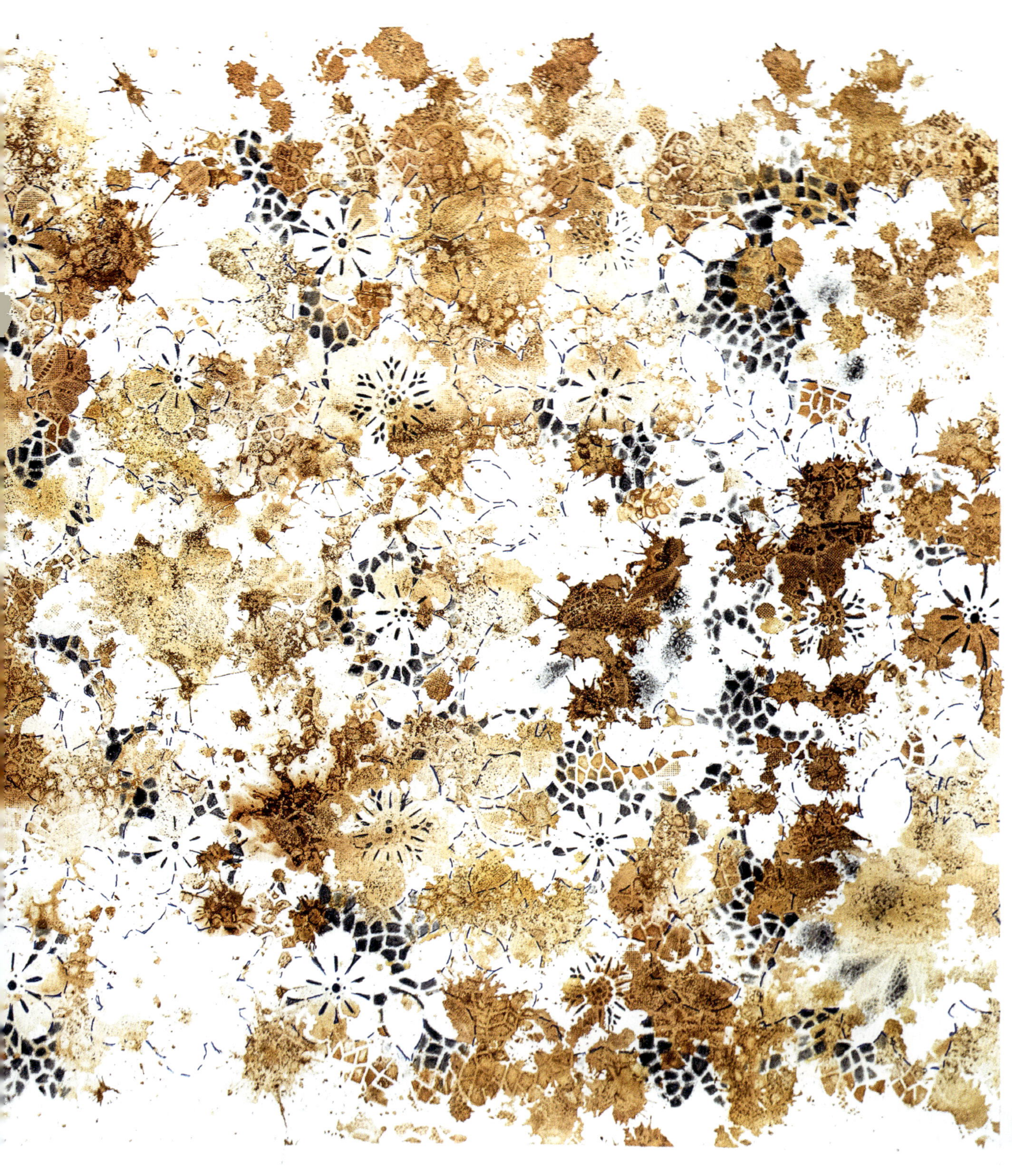

Ko'alia Funan-Funan I/Conversa Floreada I/Flowery Talk I, 2023

Resembling a gunshot wound, Madeira spits and sings, telling her story of truth telling with emotional intensity and honesty. A film of Madeira's performance, directed by Robert Connolly, is presented alongside her vast painting, completing the cycle of *Kiss and Don't Tell*. An act of resistance, survival and resilience, Madeira's cultural activism pays homage to the women of Timor-Leste and the suffering of women globally. She offers solace and a murmur of hope and healing.

As an artist, arts educator, cultural advisor, researcher and mentor, Madeira skilfully draws on traditions from a contemporary perspective. Looking backwards to go forwards, Madeira adeptly fuses the complexities of harsh histories and deploys customs, methods, imagery and symbology that are deeply embedded in Timor-Leste's culture.

"We can create an environment, able to provide room for the traditional/ contemporary: the old/ new, as well as the past/ present. Adding to this notion is the belief that such marriage and combination will create a new language and bring wonders, as this will reach not only the more traditionalists but also the younger generation."[10]

MARIA MADEIRA

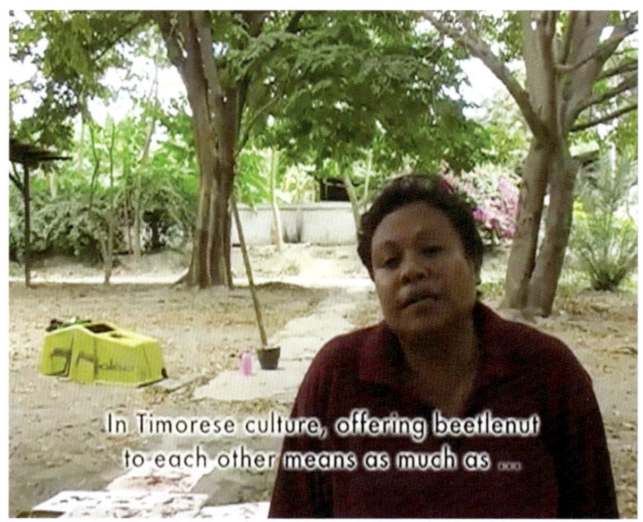

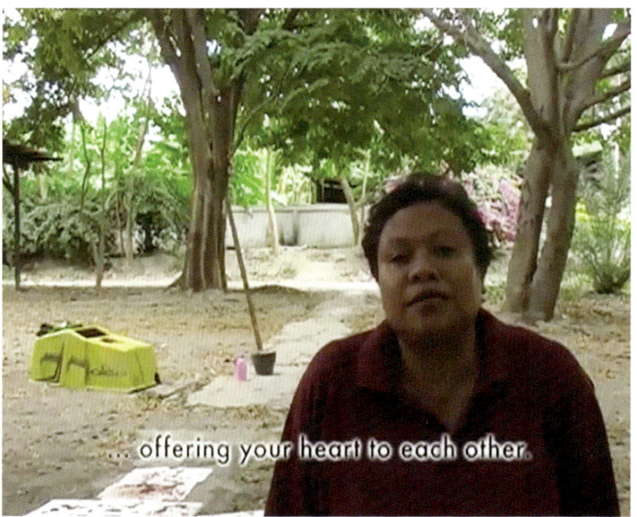

Stills from *Halo Pintura ho Bua Malus* (*Painting with Betel nut*), 2008

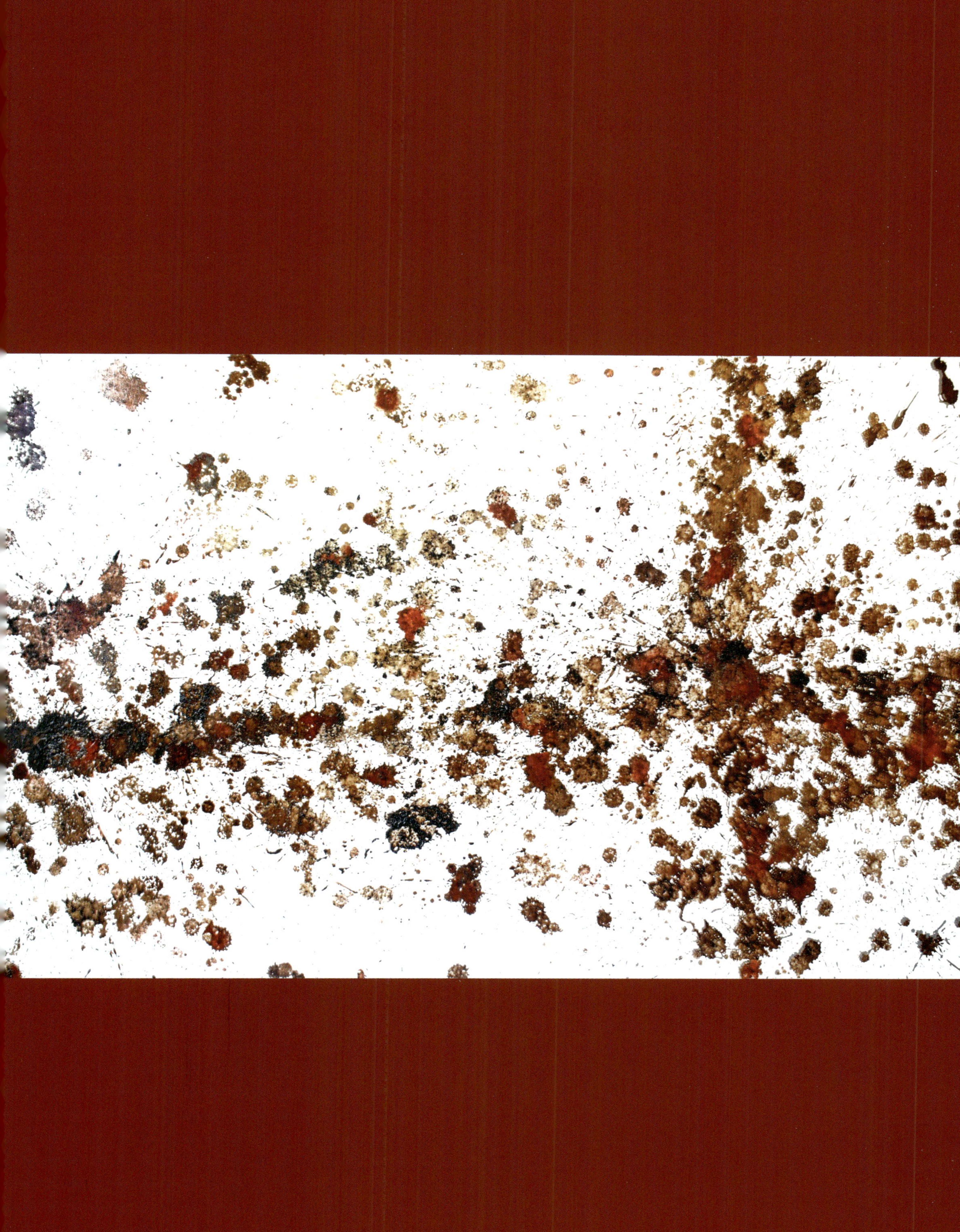

Hamutuk/Juntos/Together, 2009

Lao Rai – walking endlessly yet *koalia neneik deit /* quietly speaking

Madeira's life and art practice are intertwined with the tides of Timorese challenges. Her personal history of place and displacement, witnessing and remembering, journeys and departures, is a peripatetic existence that returns us to the beautiful boat that she carved with her father and placed outside their home on the streets of Dili. Despite being stationary, the boat amplifies the multiple migrations of Madeira (and her family). Her transit to the 60th Venice Biennale with *Kiss and Don't Tell* is a powerful reminder that storytelling and intimacy propel us to care for each other and our community.

In her softly spoken clarion call and final words of her performance, Madeira demands 'no more lipstick': a refrain she repeats, reminding us to pause, listen and hear each other amidst the cacophony of distractions and within a world of tumult.

"Even though at times I only quietly speak, often my quiet and lonely voice, is loudly and eternally heard."

MARIA MADEIRA,
QUIETLY SPEAKING, 2010

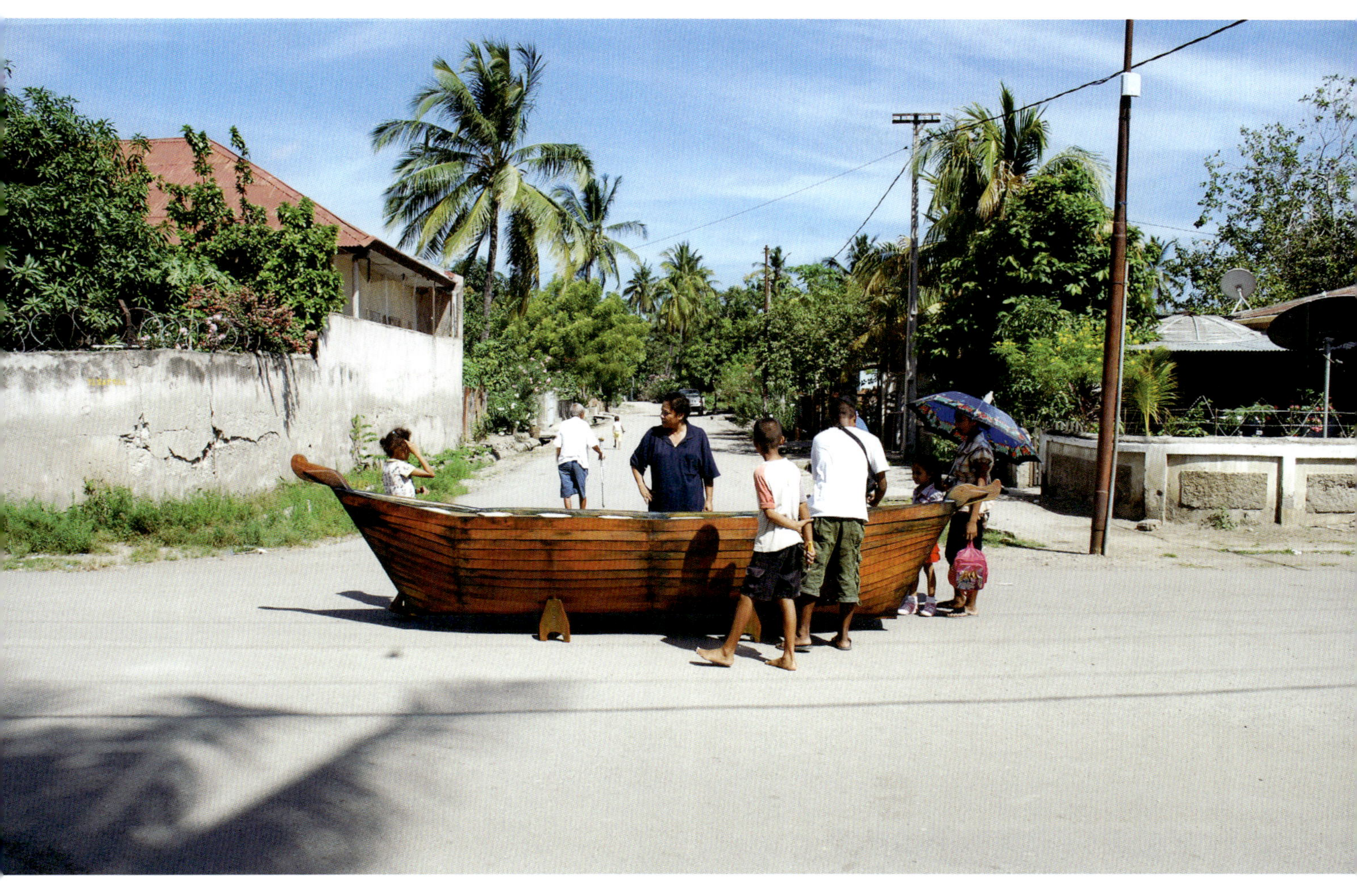

> *"It has taken us far too long to realise that we must not continue to swim against the tide of challenges that have constantly confronted us, to realise that we must unite to be able to face up to these challenges, to achieve more tangible and worthwhile results."*[11]

XANANA GUSMÃO

NOTES

1. Conversation between the author and artist, January 2024.
2. Maria Madeira, 'On Elastic/Borracha/Elástico Mobile Residency' in *Elastic/Borracha/Elástico: Timor-Leste/Australia Mobile Contemporary Artists' Residency*, (ed) Jo Holder, Northern Centre for Contemporary Art, Darwin and The Cross Art Projects, Sydney, 2016, p. 54.
3. Joanna Barrkman, 'Binding Identities' in *From the Hands of Our Ancestors*, Museum and Art Gallery, Northern Territory, with the Direcção Nacional da Cultura, Timor-Leste, 2008, p. 67.
4. Xanana Gusmão, *My Sea, My Timor, Ha'i nia Tasi, Ha'i nia Timor*, Timor-Leste Land and Maritime Boundary Office, Timor-Leste, 2024.
5. Writing about the cloth of her ancestors, Sami Liisa-Rávná Finbog, 'Stitches of Memory: living the past and remembering the future', NGV Magazine, 2024.
6. Roszika Parker, *The Subversive Stitch: Embroidery and the Making of the Feminine*, Women's Press, University of California, United States of America, 1984.
7. *Vitamin T: Threads & Textiles in Contemporary Art*, Phaidon, London and New York, 2019.
8. Conversation between the author and artist, January 2024.
9. Maria Madeira, *Halo Pintura ho Bua Malus (Painting with Betel nut)*, film by Victor de Sousa, teaching Arte Moris students to use betel nut in painting, Dili, Timor-Leste, 2008, <https://vimeo.com/90615869>.
10. Maria Madeira, 'Traditionally Contemporary' in *Timor Runguranga: A photographic journey through Timor-Leste*, by David Palazón, United States of America, 2016, p. 185.
11. Xanana Gusmão, *To resist is to win!: The autobiography of Xanana Gusmão with selected letters & speeches*, Aurora Books with David Lovell Publishing, Victoria, Australia, 2008, pp. 213-14.

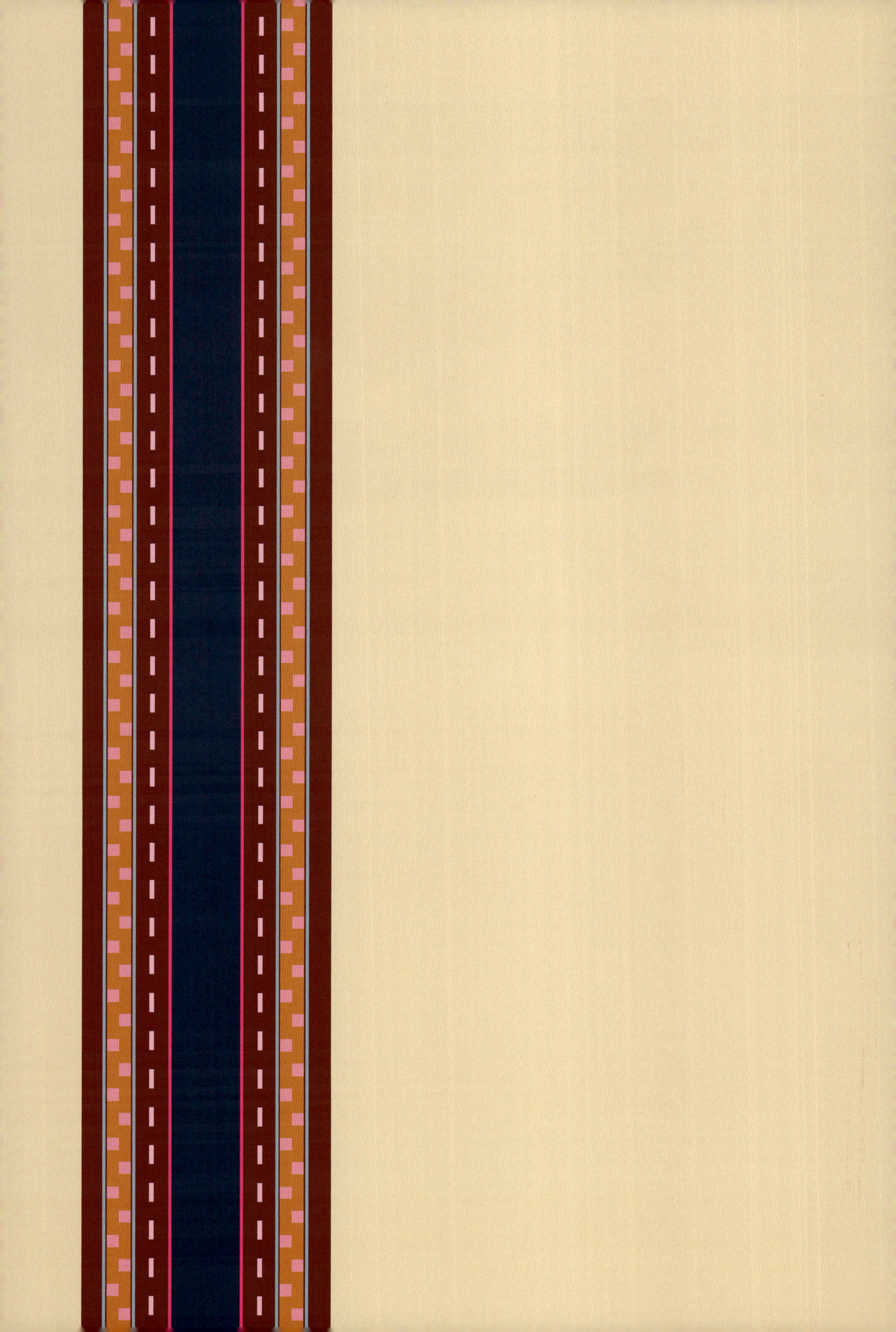

KISS AND DON'T TELL

MARIA MADEIRA

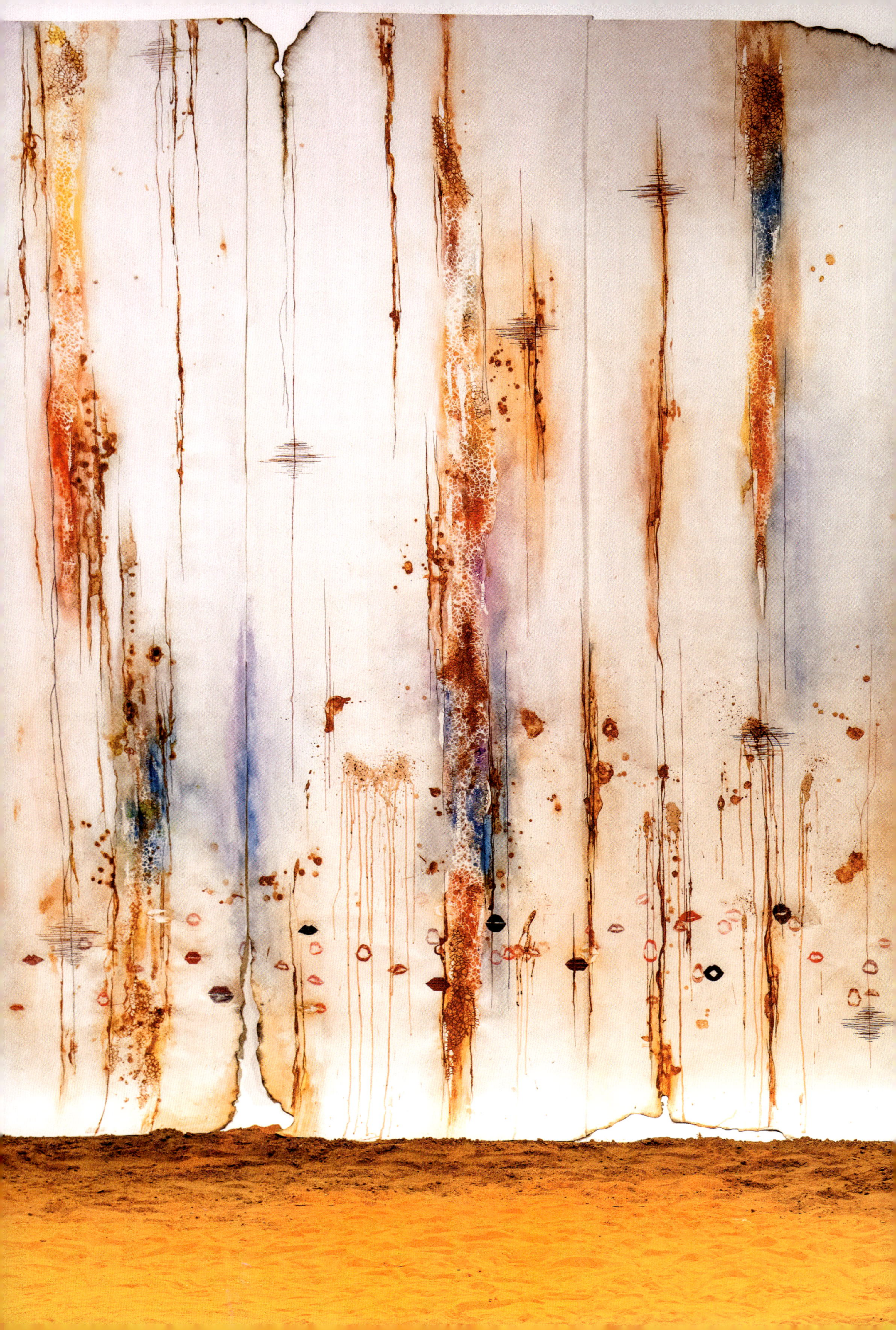

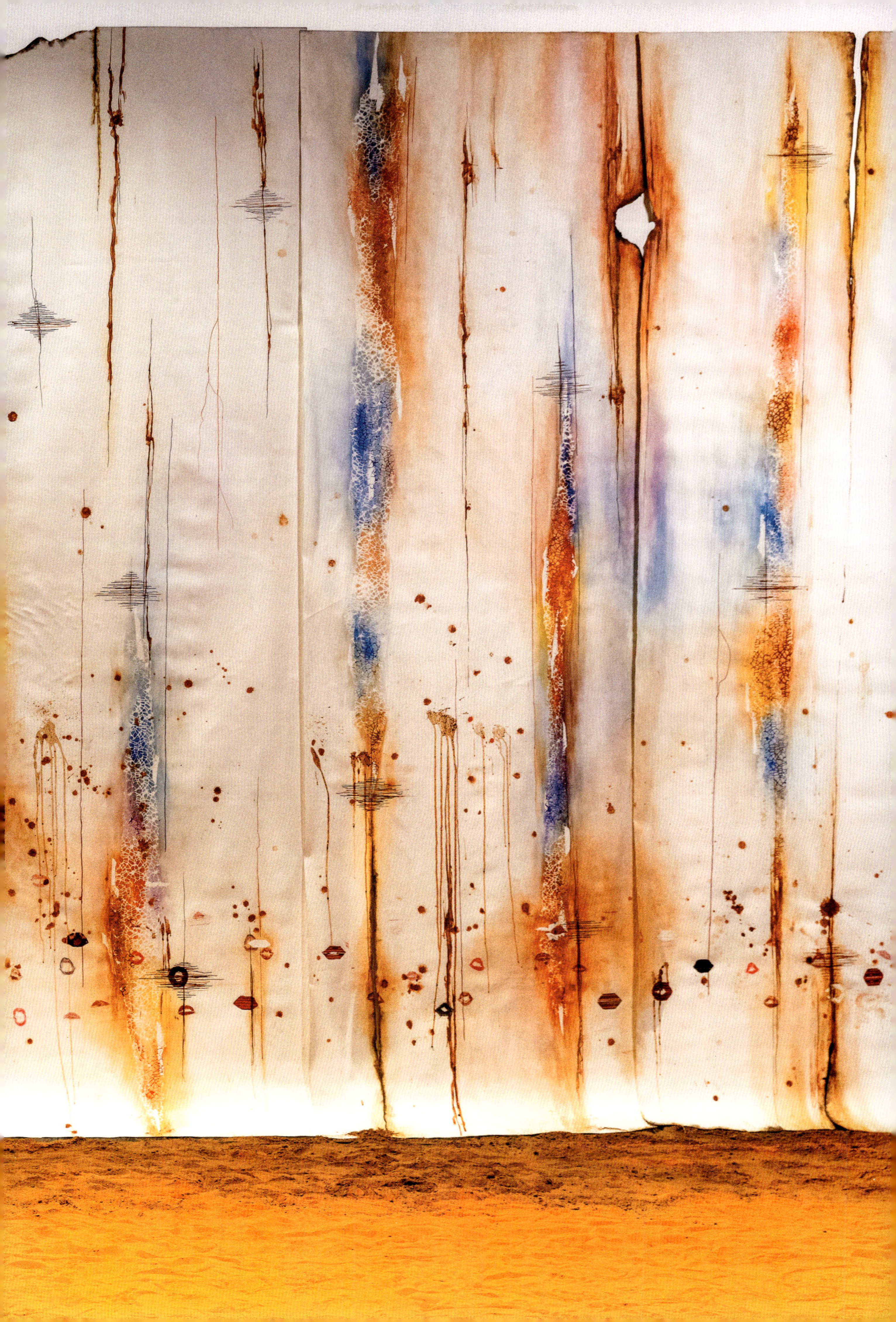

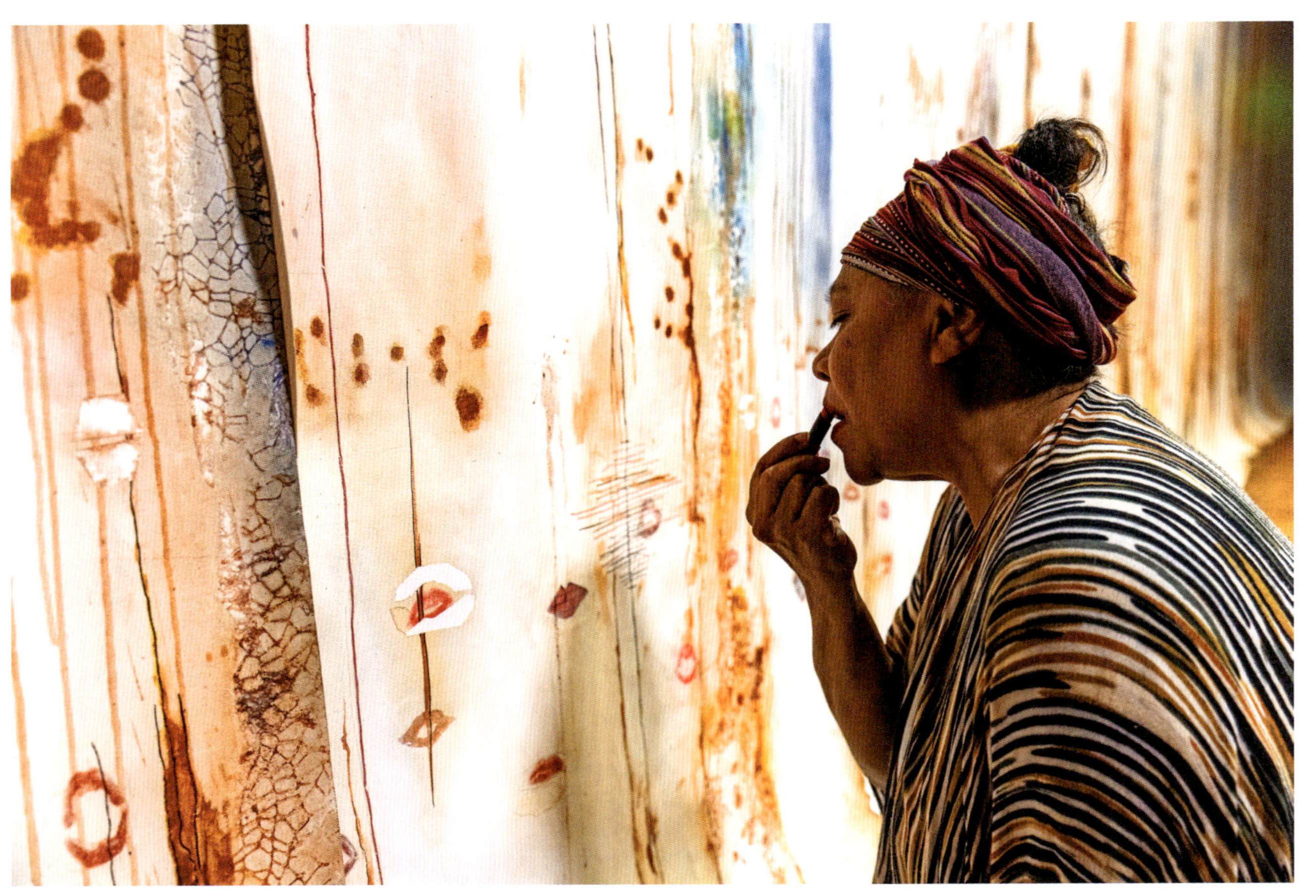

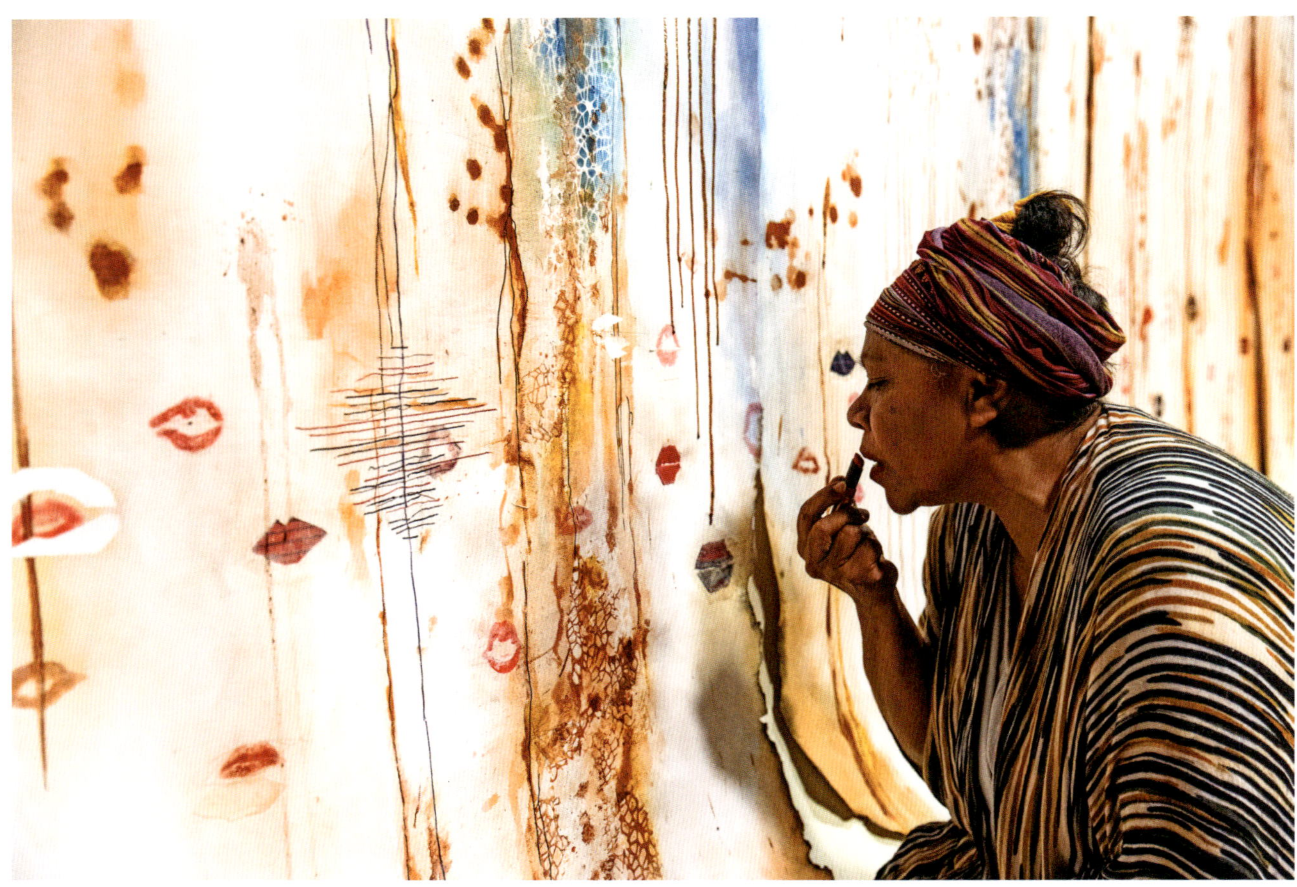

Kiss and Don't Tell, 2024

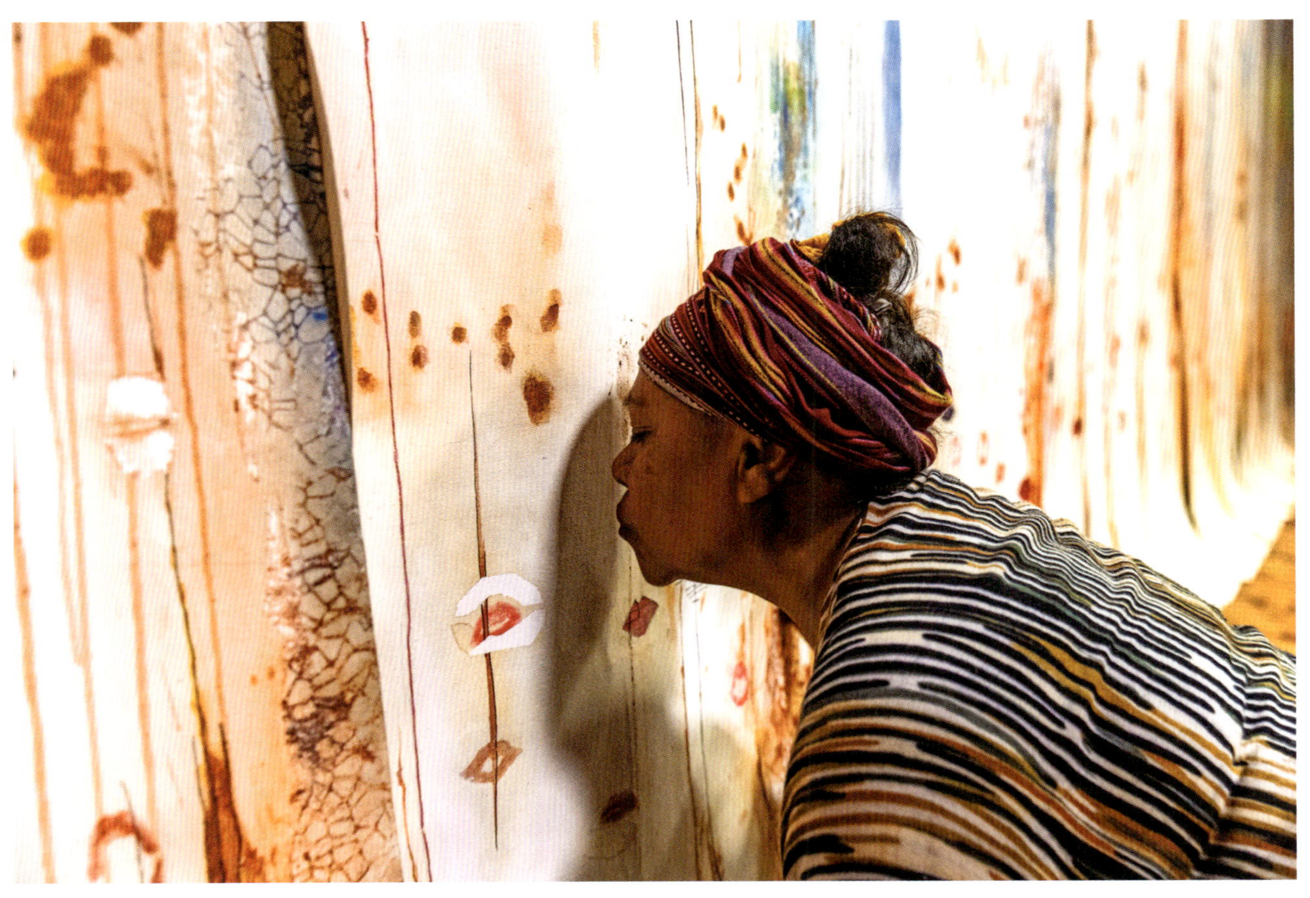

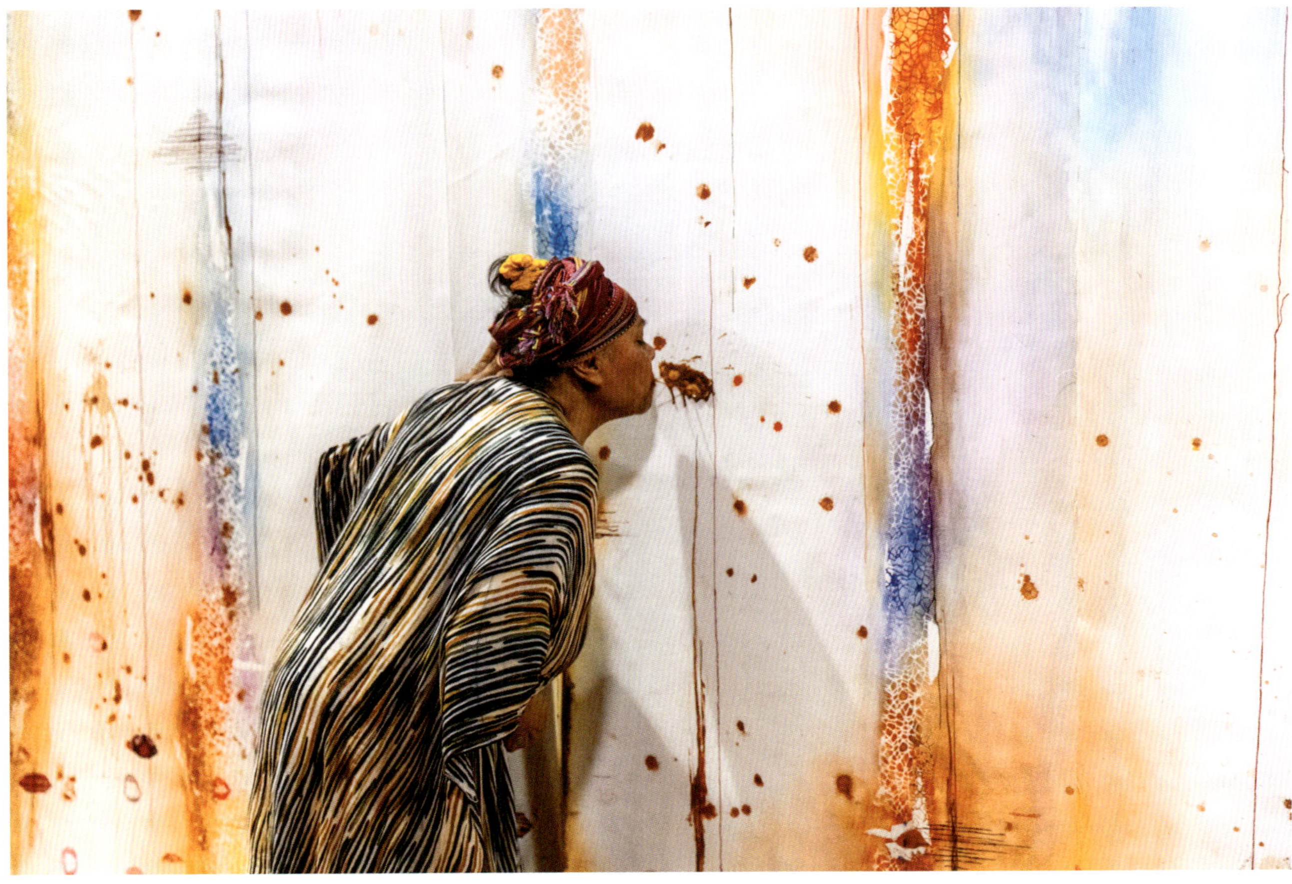

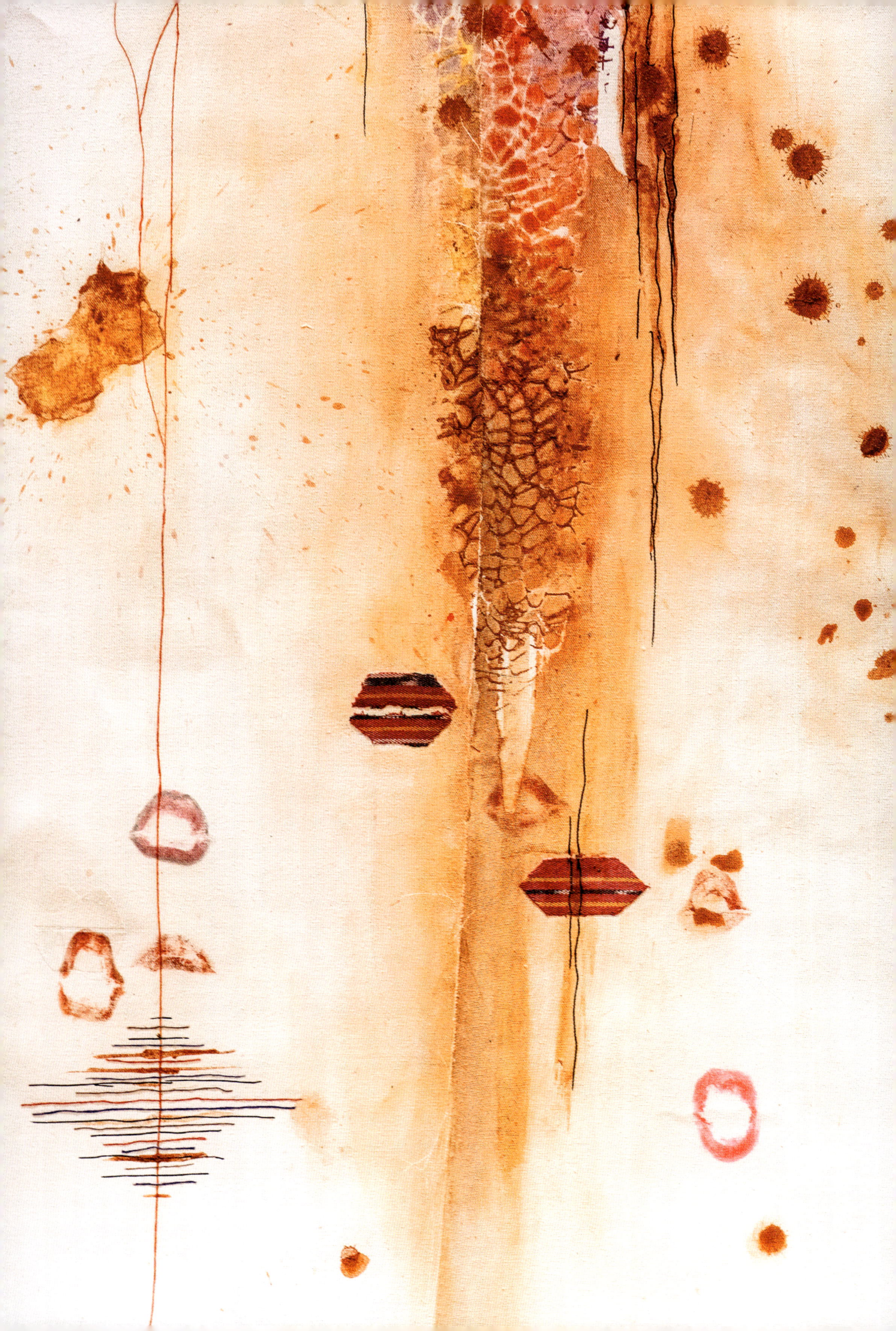

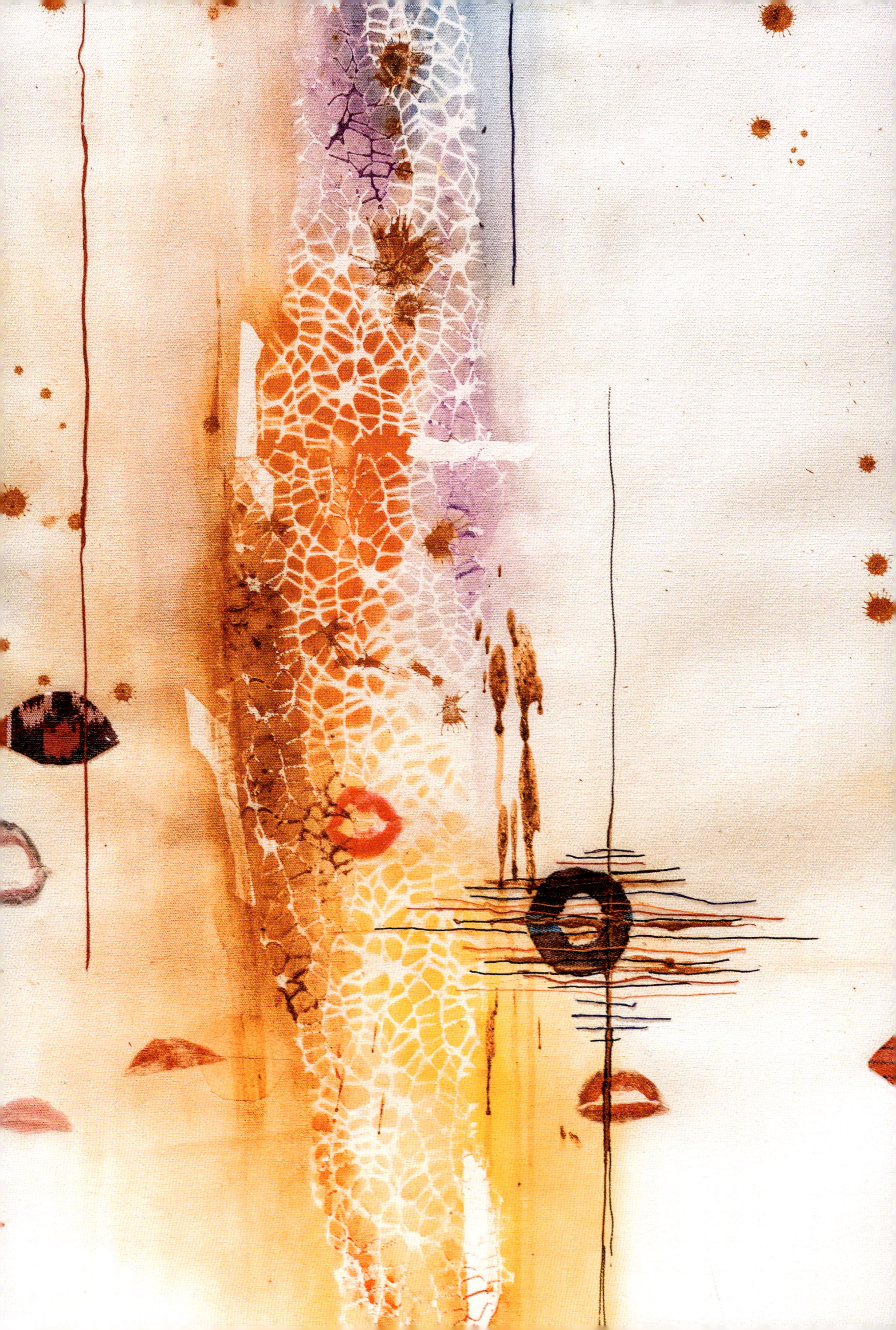

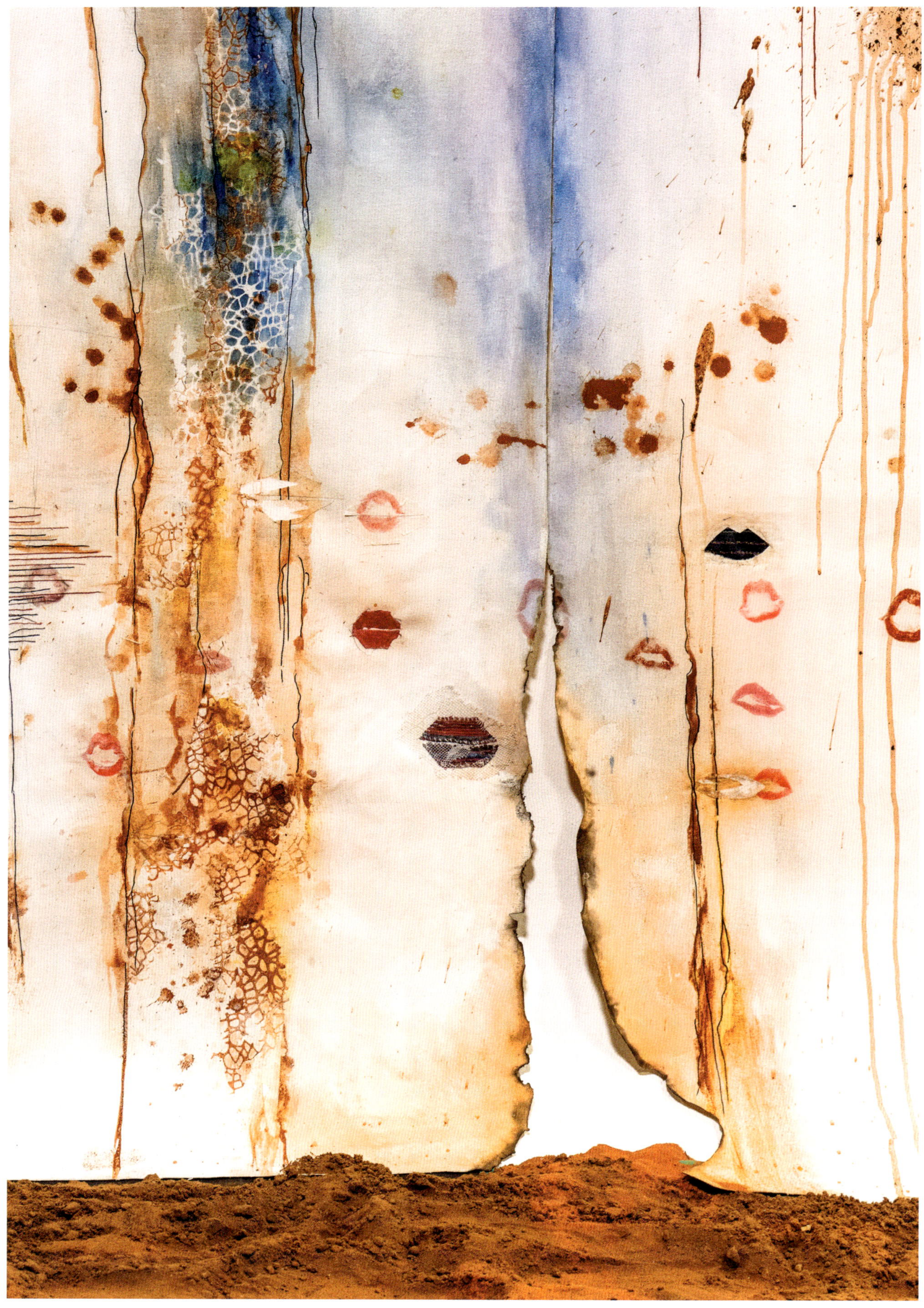

Kiss and Don't Tell, 2024

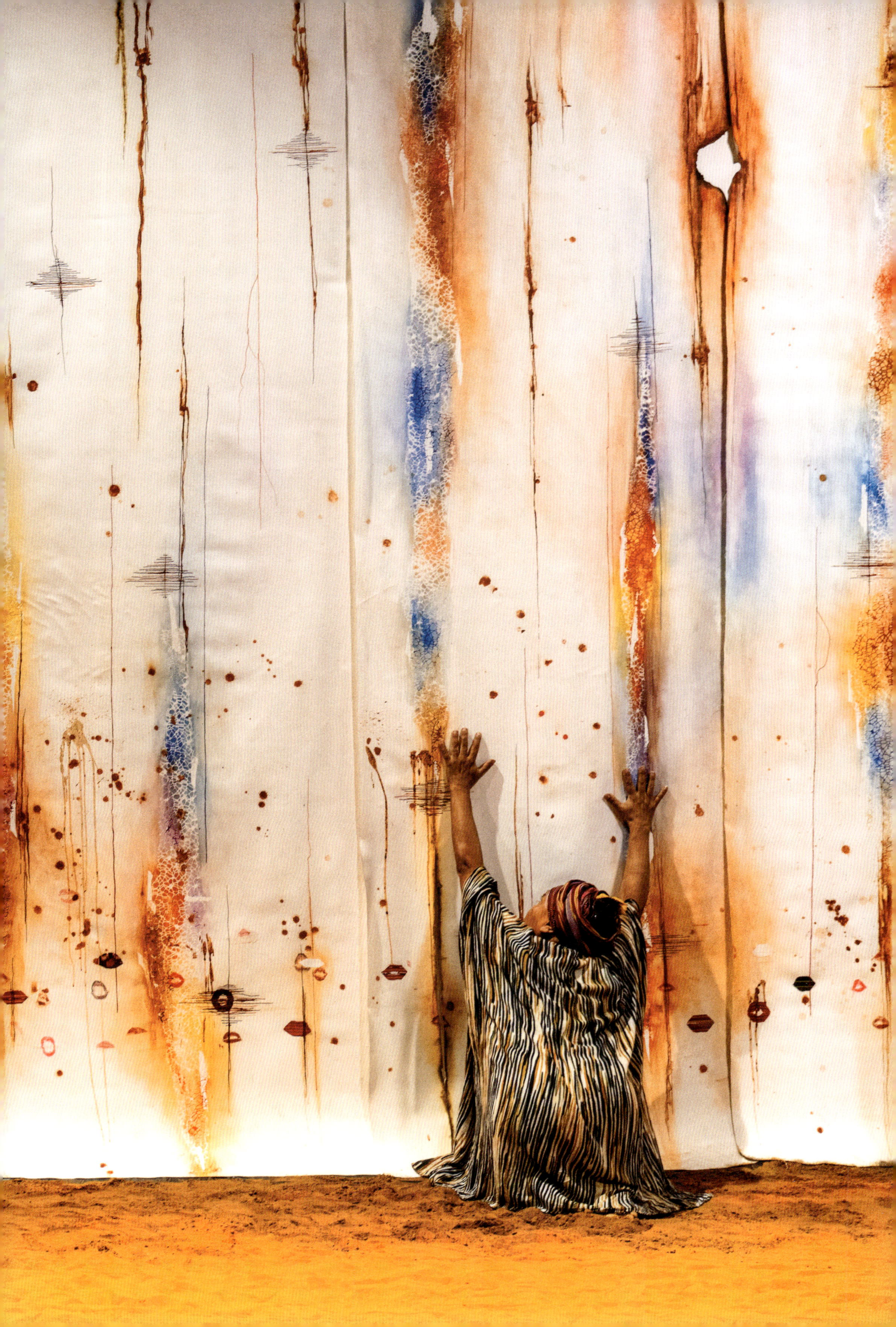

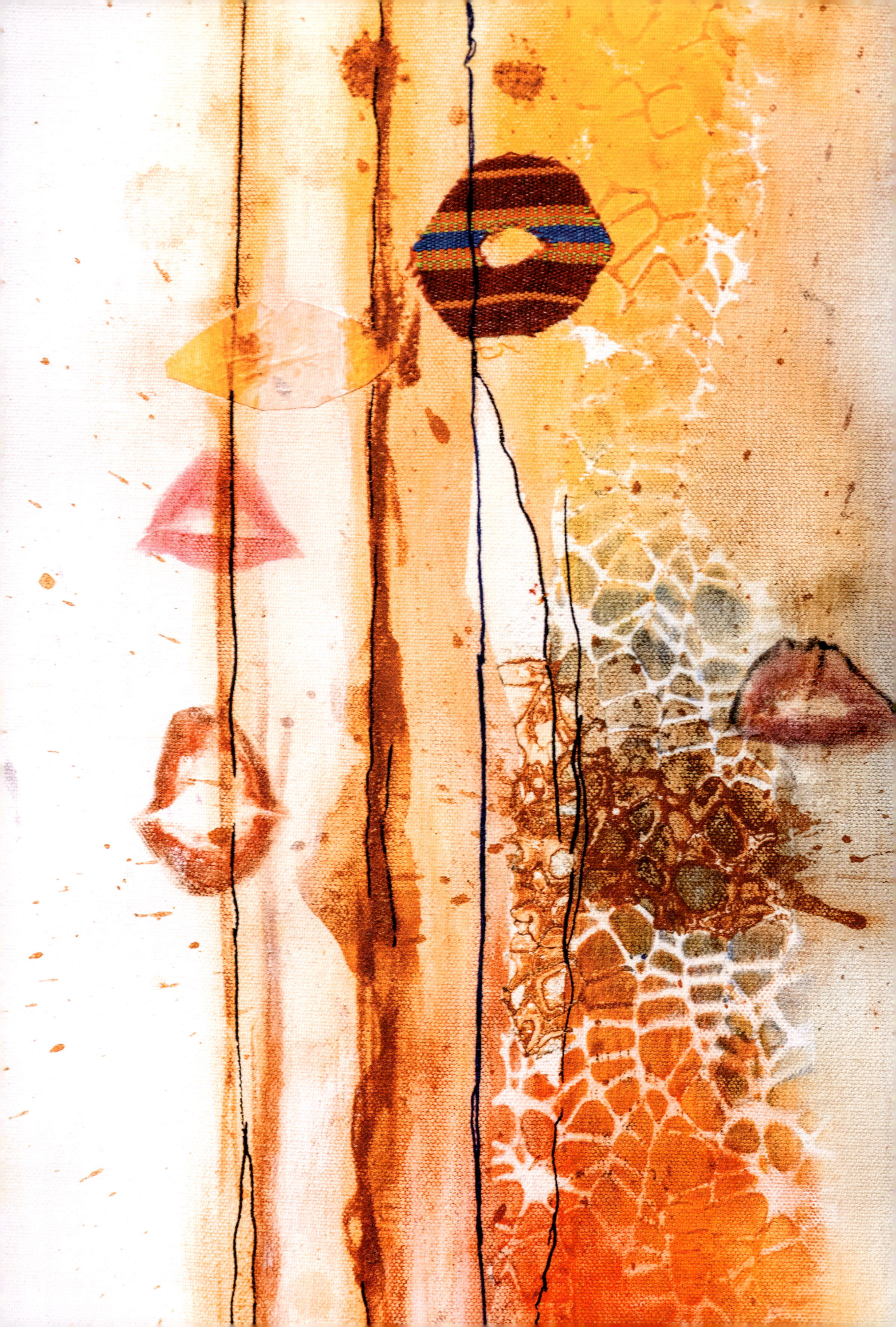

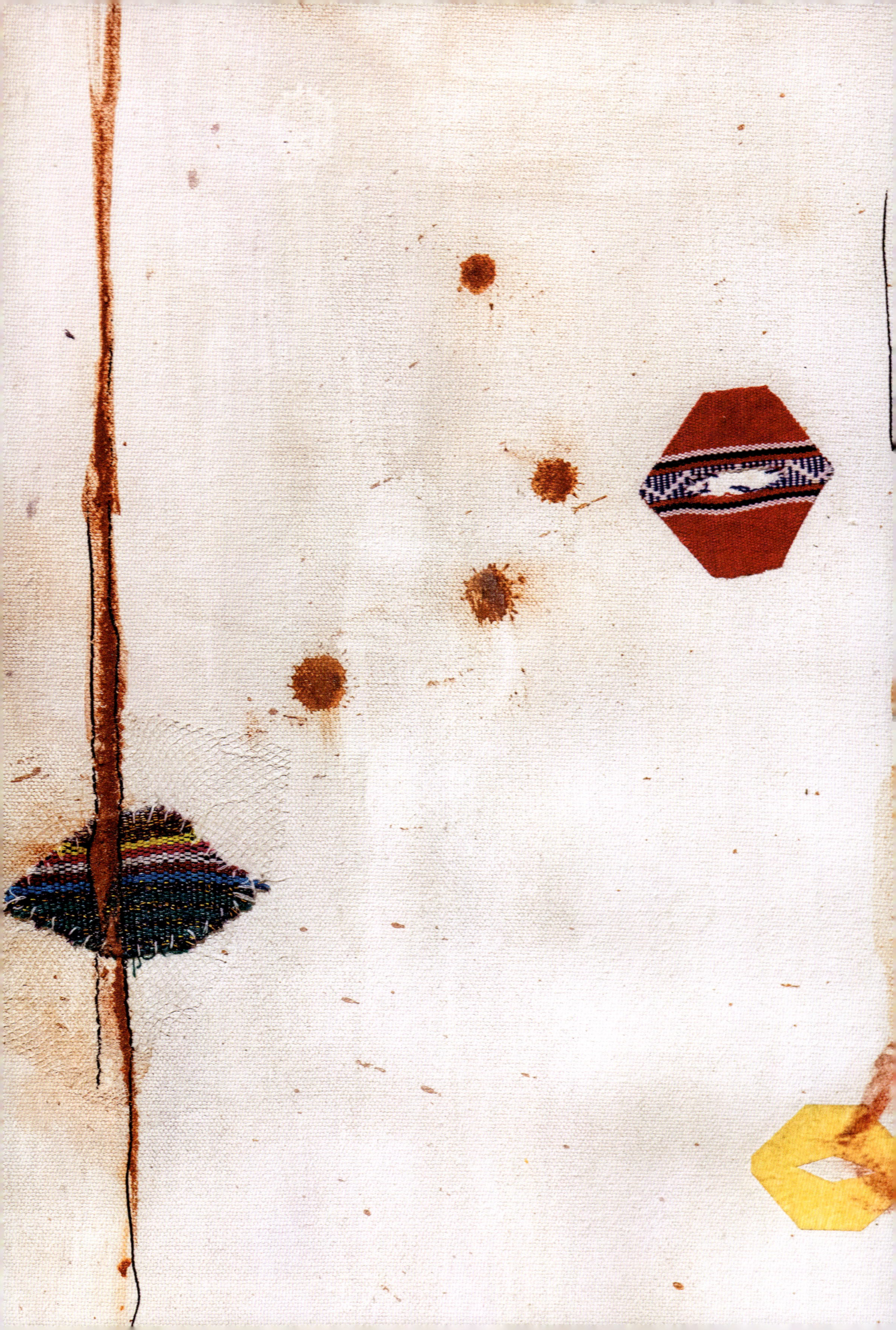

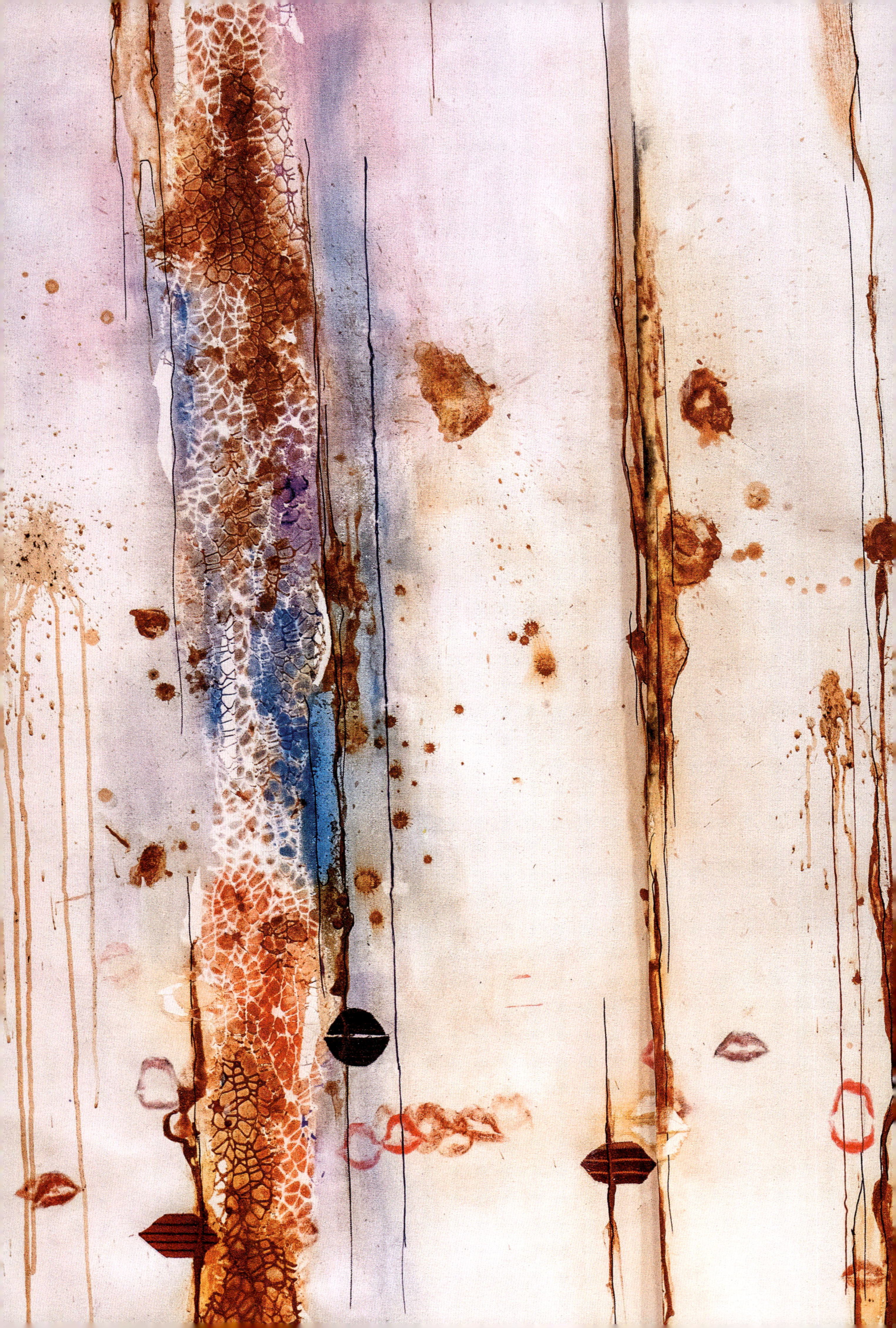

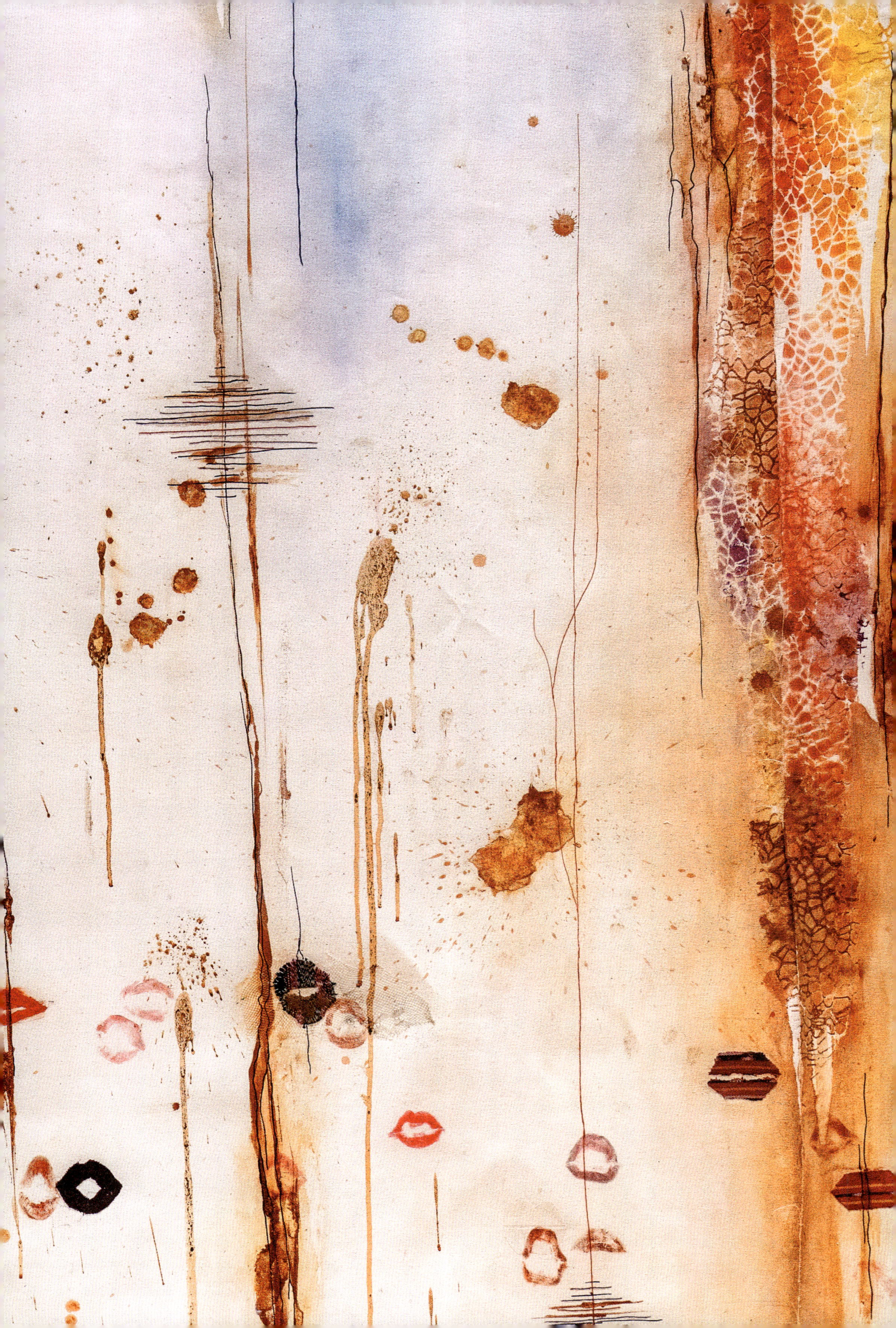

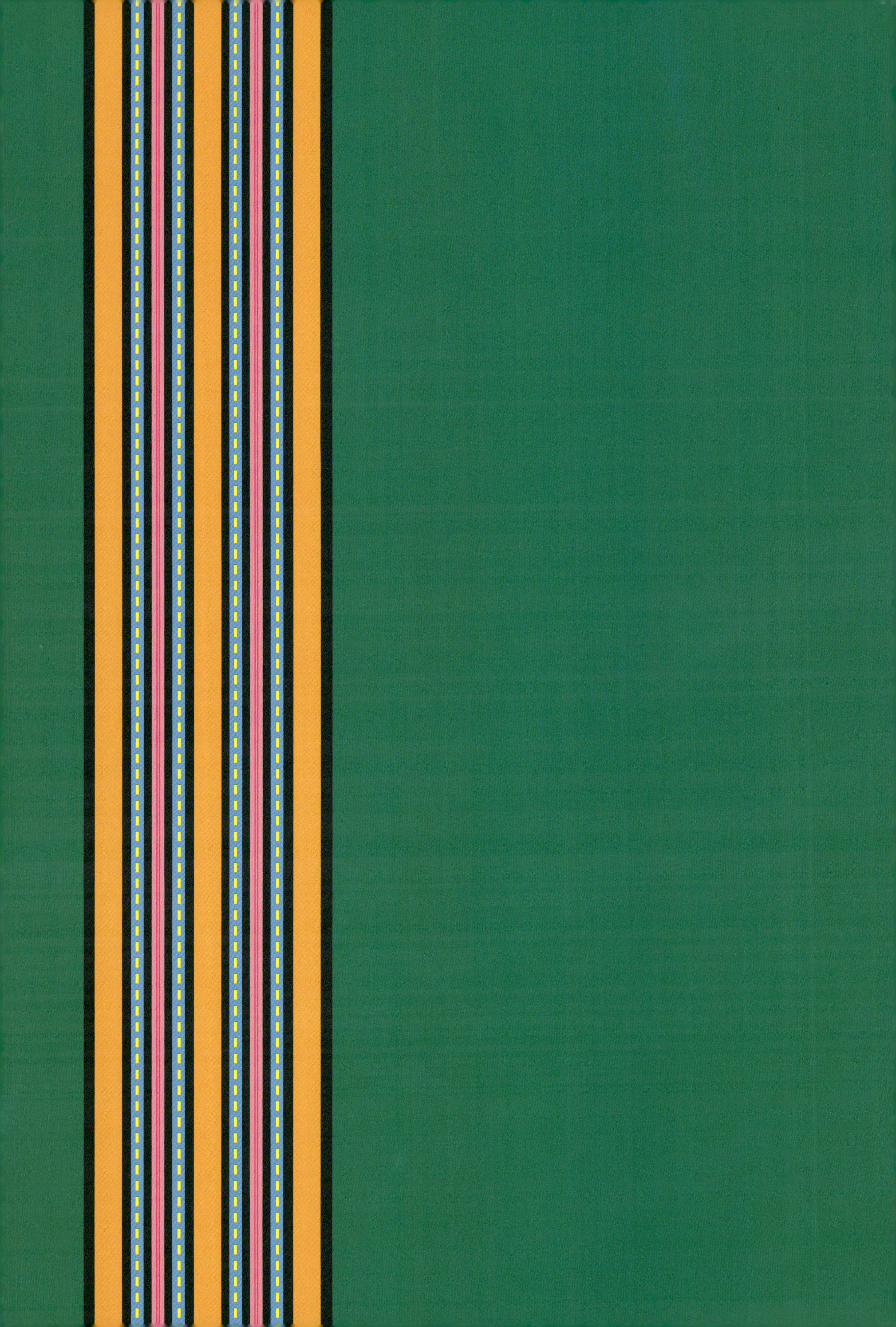

FROM FOREIGNNESS TO FRATERNITY

KIM McGRATH

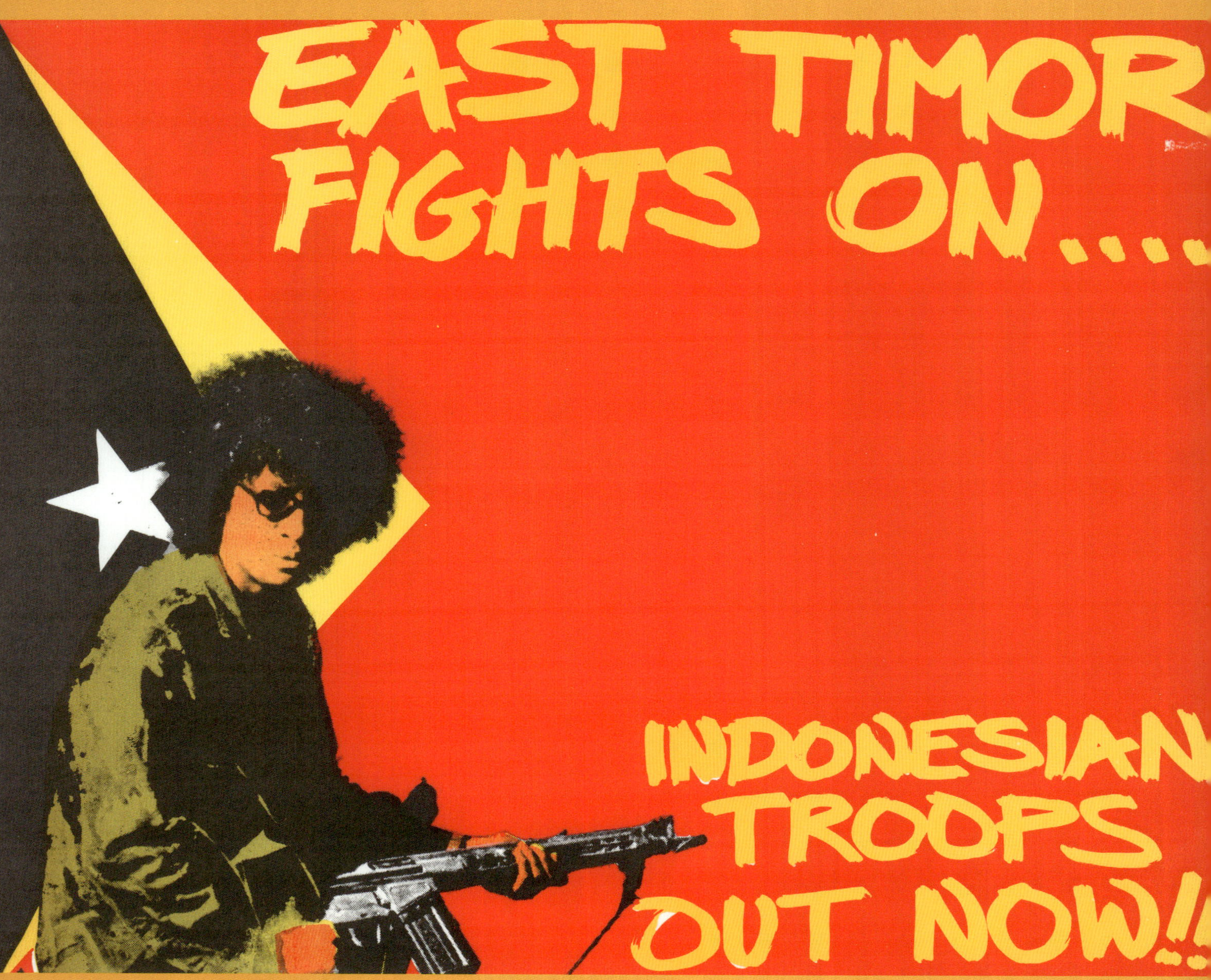

EAST TIMOR
FIGHTS ON.....
INDONESIAN
TROOPS
OUT NOW!!

FROM FOREIGNNESS TO FRATERNITY

Kim McGrath

"Madeira's work reveals the spirit and soul of Timor-Leste to be vibrant, strong, resilient and forgiving."

Stranierie Ovunque – Foreigners Everywhere, the title of the 60th International Art Exhibition, challenges us with the notion 'we are all foreigners'. Timorese artist Maria Madeira was a refugee in Indonesia and Portugal, an immigrant in Australia, and an outsider from the diaspora when she returned to her homeland Timor-Leste. Madeira fled, she escaped, she was displaced. She was a refugee in the global south and the global north. She lived foreignness.

Her art sustained her and fuelled her activism for Timorese independence. Madeira believes 'art and culture are the spirit and soul of a nation'. Her work reveals the spirit and soul of Timor-Leste to be vibrant, strong, resilient and forgiving.

On 20 May 2002, the Democratic Republic of Timor-Leste became the 191st member of the United Nations. The ceremony was attended by former US president Bill Clinton, Portugal's president Jorge Sampaio and Australian prime minister John Howard. The most surprising and anticipated guest was Indonesian President Megawati Sukarnoputri. Just before midnight Xanana Gusmão warmly welcomed Megawati. The two leaders held hands and raised them aloft as the crowd cheered and clapped. At that moment, and in the decades since, Indonesia and Timor-Leste have demonstrated to the world that the reconciliation of bitter enemies is possible, that foreignness to fraternity is possible.

The Democratic Republic of Timor-Leste comprises the eastern half of the island of Timor, Atauro and Jaco islands, and the enclave of Oecussi in West Timor. For over 400 years it was part of the Portuguese colonial empire and known as Portuguese Timor. The other half of the island was part of the Dutch East Indies until Indonesia won a war of independence against the Dutch in 1949.

When Maria Madeira was born in October 1966 in the mountain village of Gleno in Portuguese Timor, she was baptised Catholic and grew up speaking her mother tongue Tetun and Portuguese. Across the border in neighbouring Indonesia the authoritarian 'New Order' regime of President Suharto came to power a year earlier. It was the height of the Cold War between the United States and the Soviet Union. The United States and its western allies watched on as half a million suspected communists were killed.[1]

Portugal was also ruled by an authoritarian militarist regime. António Salazar had governed since the 1930s and while other European colonial powers relinquished their African colonies in the 1950s and 1960s, Portugal went to war. From 1961 to 1974, the Portuguese army brutally sought to suppress independence movements in Angola, Mozambique and Portuguese Guinea.

Salazar's regime was overthrown in a peaceful rebellion on 25 April 1974. The coup was instigated by young Portuguese soldiers, no longer willing to fight pointless wars on the African continent. The broadcast of Portugal's entry in the 1974 Eurovision Song Contest signalled the start of the rebellion. The song came last at Eurovision, but it created, and changed, history.[2] Ignoring warnings to stay home, the people of Lisbon gathered near the Lisbon flower market. Carnations were in season, and some of the rebels put red flowers in their rifle butts – inspiring the name 'carnation revolution'. The new leadership immediately announced Portugal would grant independence to all its colonies – raising the prospect of independence for Portuguese Timor.

Newly formed political associations in Dili advocated independence, a continuing relationship with Portugal, or integration with Indonesia. The Cold War had shifted south, to Asia, focused on United States/China rivalry. Indonesia was the prize. Nations in the Western alliance supported Portuguese Timor's integration with Indonesia, believing it was inevitable and in their national interests.

Another prize was sovereignty over oil-rich areas of the Timor Sea off the south coast of Portuguese Timor. Portugal contested Australia's claim to areas north of the median line. One reason for Australia's fulsome support for Portuguese Timor to become part of Indonesia was the expectation that Indonesia would agree to a maritime boundary that gave Australia the lion's share of oil and gas in disputed areas of the Timor Sea.[3]

In August 1975, clandestinely encouraged by Indonesia and the West, civil war broke out between fledgling political groups in Dili. More than 1,500 people were killed.[4] In September, nine-year old Maria Madeira and her family fled the violence, escaping to a refugee camp at Atambua in West Timor, Indonesia. By the end of the month Fretilin, the Revolutionary Front for an Independent East Timor, controlled Portuguese Timor.

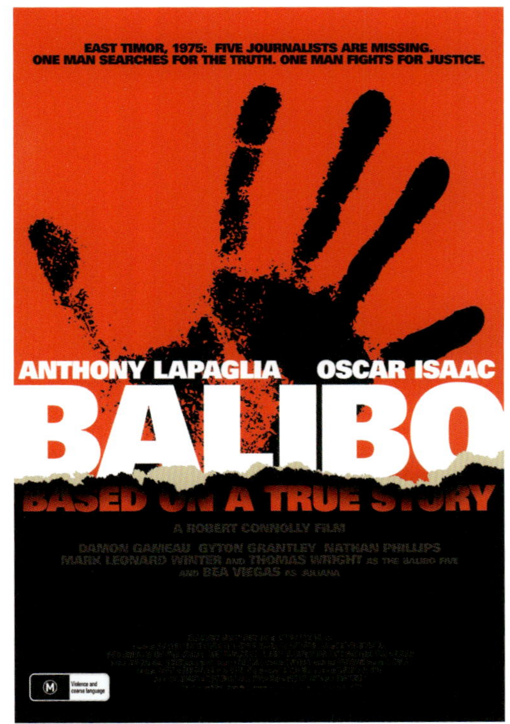
Balibo, 2009

In October, Indonesian forces attacked the border town of Balibo and murdered five international journalists; two Australians, two Britons and one New Zealander.[5] None of the three governments protested. Robert Connolly's 2009 film Balibo is a fictionalised account of their deaths through the eyes of Roger East, the only international journalist left in the country when Indonesia invaded on 7 December 1975.[6]

Nine days before the invasion, on 28 November, the Timorese leadership read a proclamation declaring independence. The flag-raising ceremony was photographed by journalist, poet and editor of a new newspaper *Jornal Do Povo Maubere*, Kay Rala Gusmão.[7] Crowds joyously sang *Patria Patria*, the new national anthem, and celebratory grenades were thrown into the sea.[8]

Over 2,000 people were killed in the first days of the invasion. The Indonesian military and its Western confidantes believed Timorese resistance would be quickly overwhelmed. They were wrong. The Indonesian presence was resisted for twenty-four dark, painful years.

Gusmão, known by all as Xanana, assumed leadership of the resistance in the early 1980s. He lived in the mountains, surviving napalm attacks, malaria and hunger for 17 years. Western governments turned a blind eye to reports of massacres, rape and deliberate mass starvation.

On 12 November 1991, Indonesian forces murdered 271 young people at the Santa Cruz cemetery in Dili. Journalist Max Stahl was there. His footage of the carnage was a turning point in the campaign. It made international headlines and focused world attention on the Timorese struggle for independence. Maria Madeira's first solo exhibition *East Timor – Land of Crosses* paid homage to those who died at Santa Cruz.

Gusmão was captured in Dili in November 1992. He continued to lead the resistance from prison in Jakarta. His poem *Mountain,* written in 'six minutes, thinking of you all', was smuggled out and shared with resistance supporters in the diaspora.[9]

Another turning point was the awarding of the 1996 Nobel Peace prize to José Ramos-Horta, who led the international diplomatic campaign for independence. Gusmão's 1997 poem *The Diplomatic Leader: Peace is Possible,* dedicated to a Portuguese activist, reflects his growing belief that Portugal could broker a diplomatic solution to the conflict.[10]

The fall of Indonesian President Suharto in 1998 saw the awakening of democracy in Indonesia and the prospect of self-determination for the Timorese. Gusmão was permitted visitors, including Nelson Mandela. On 27 January 1999, new Indonesian President Bacharuddin Jusuf Habibie announced the East Timorese would be allowed to exercise their right to self-determination.

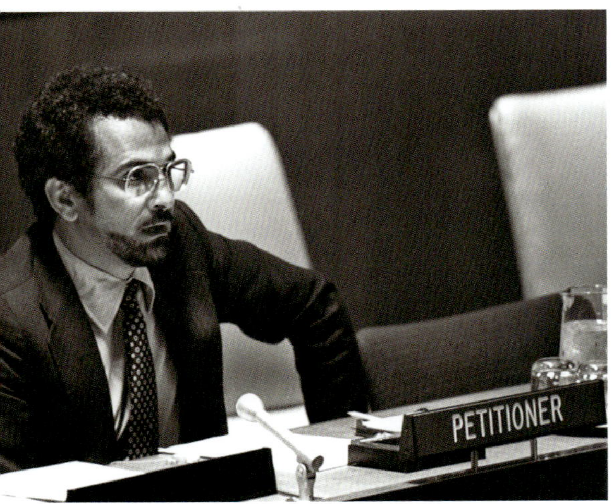
José Ramos-Horta speaking at the United Nations on the 'Question of East Timor,' 20 August 1982

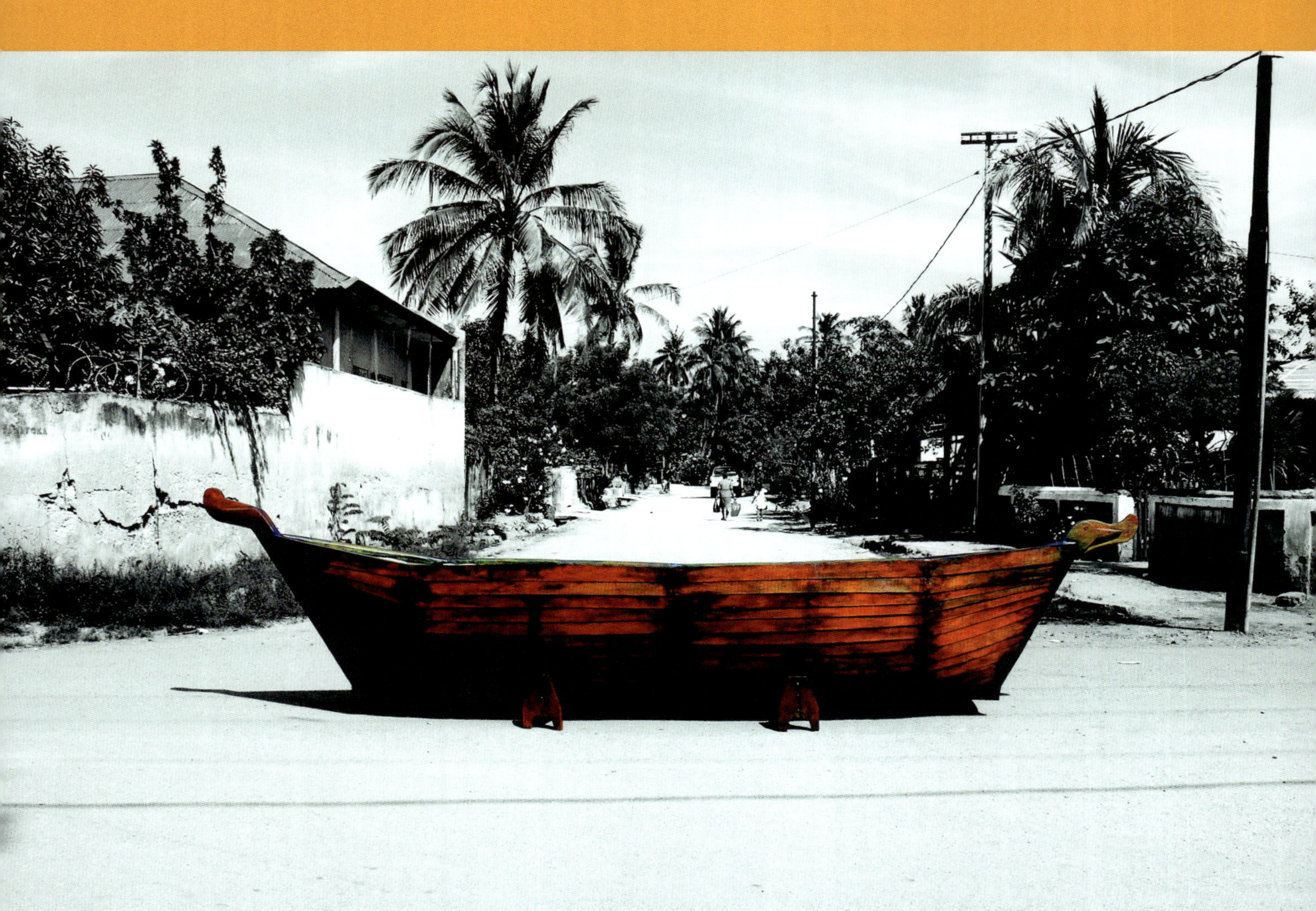

Lao Rai (Traveller), 2010

Maria Madeira was in exile in Australia when the people of her homeland voted in favour of independence on 30 August 1999. Anarchy reigned for three weeks after the result was announced. Militia killed independence sympathisers, burnt homes and destroyed schools, hospitals and bridges. On 20 September, a United Nations-led force landed in Dili to restore peace. In October, the United Nations Transitional Administration in East Timor was established under the leadership of Brazilian diplomat Sérgio Vieira de Mello. It was responsible for working with the Timorese to feed and heal a devastated population, draft a constitution for a new nation, decide on a currency and official language, establish a judicial system and civil service administration.

Madeira packed her bags and returned home to help rebuild a shattered nation. The population was traumatised. Everyone grieved – for a parent; a child; a sibling; a friend. Dili was in ruins. Madeira worked as a translator, she volunteered at the newly formed Arte Moris collective, and she listened to women's stories about the occupation. She learned the story behind the lipstick marks on her bedroom walls that led to *Kiss and Don't Tell*.

It was during this period that Xanana Gusmão visited Australia as a guest of the Melbourne Festival. He was commissioned to write a poem for opening night. *World Peace* is a raw condemnation of war – 'onde não há coragem, ee o perdão não tem lugar! – 'where there is no courage, and no place for forgiveness'.[11]

Gusmão became the new nation's first elected president and served as Prime Minister from 2007 to 2015. In April 2010, Timor-Leste jointly initiated the g7+, a unique international group that collectively advocates for peace and state-building efforts in countries affected by conflict and fragility.[12]

Gusmão commenced a third term as Prime Minister in May 2023. One of his greatest achievements post-independence was Timor-Leste's success in the David v Goliath battle with Australia over sovereignty in the Timor Sea.[13] Timor-Leste was accepted as a member of the World Trade Organisation in February 2024, and with Indonesia's strong backing, will become a member of ASEAN (the Association of South-East Asian Nations) in 2025.

Nobel Laureate José Ramos-Horta held a series of leadership roles and is now President. Ramos-Horta and Gusmão together have consistently called on the Timorese to look forward, not back. To seek reconciliation, not revenge.

When Xanana Gusmão returned to Dili in October 1999 the city appeared deserted. Word spread and a crowd gathered outside the Palacio do Governo. Gusmão delivered an emotional speech. He concluded saying 'we must put in the past the evil they have done to us. Tomorrow is ours!'[14]

This forgiving, powerful message guided Timor-Leste's restoration of independence and development. It made Timor-Leste a beacon of hope in a fraught world. Looking to tomorrow has led to Timor-Leste's presence at the Venice Biennale. Looking to tomorrow has enabled Maria Madeira's dream journey from the mountains of Timor-Leste to the Grand Canal in Venice. A courageous journey from foreignness to fraternity.

"Tomorrow is ours!"

XANANA GUSMÃO

NOTES

1. Vannessa Hearman, *Unmarked Graves: Death and Survival in the Anti-Communist Violence in East Java, Indonesia*, NIAS Press, 2018, pp. 1–4.

2. *E depois do adeus* by Paulo de Carvalho.

3. Kim McGrath, *Crossing the Line, Australia's Secret History in the Timor-Sea*, Black Inc, Melbourne, 2017.

4. Sara Niner, *Xanana: Leader of the Struggle for Independent Timor-Leste*, Australian Scholarly Publishing, North Melbourne, 2009, p. 27.

5. Australians, Greg Shackleton & Tony Stewart; Britons, Malcolm Rennie & Brian Peters; and New Zealander, Gary Cunningham. The Balibo Fort today is an idyllic hillside retreat established as a social enterprise by the Balibo House Trust, founded by the families' of the murdered journalists, <https://balibohouse.com>.

6. *Balibo*, Director Robert Connolly, Producers Rebecca Williamson, John Maynard, Timor-Leste, Australia, 2009

7. Niner, 2009, p. 28.

8. Constancio Pinto & Mathew Jardine, *East Timor's Unfinished Struggle: Inside the Timorese Resistance*, South End Press, Boston, MA, 1997, p. 39.

9. Xanana Gusmão, *Mountains*, quoted in Gusmão, *To Resist is to Win! The Autobiography of Xanana Gusmão, selected letters and speeches edited by Sara Niner*, Aurora Books, Richmond, Victoria, 2000, p. 183.

10. Xanana Gusmão, *The Diplomatic Leader: Peace is Possible*, quoted in Niner, 2009, p. 122.

11. Xanana Gusmão, *Poem for Peace*, commissioned by the Melbourne Festival, October 2001.

12. Simon Fenby, 'The g7+ Group of Fragile States: Towards Better International Engagement and Accountability in Aid Delivery to Fragile Nations' in (ed) Damien Kingsbury, Critical Reflections on Development, Palgrave Macmillan, London, 2013, pp. 33–49.

13. Land and Maritime Boundary Office, Democratic Republic of Timor-Leste, < https://www.gftm.gov.tl>.

14. Niner, 2009, p. 210.

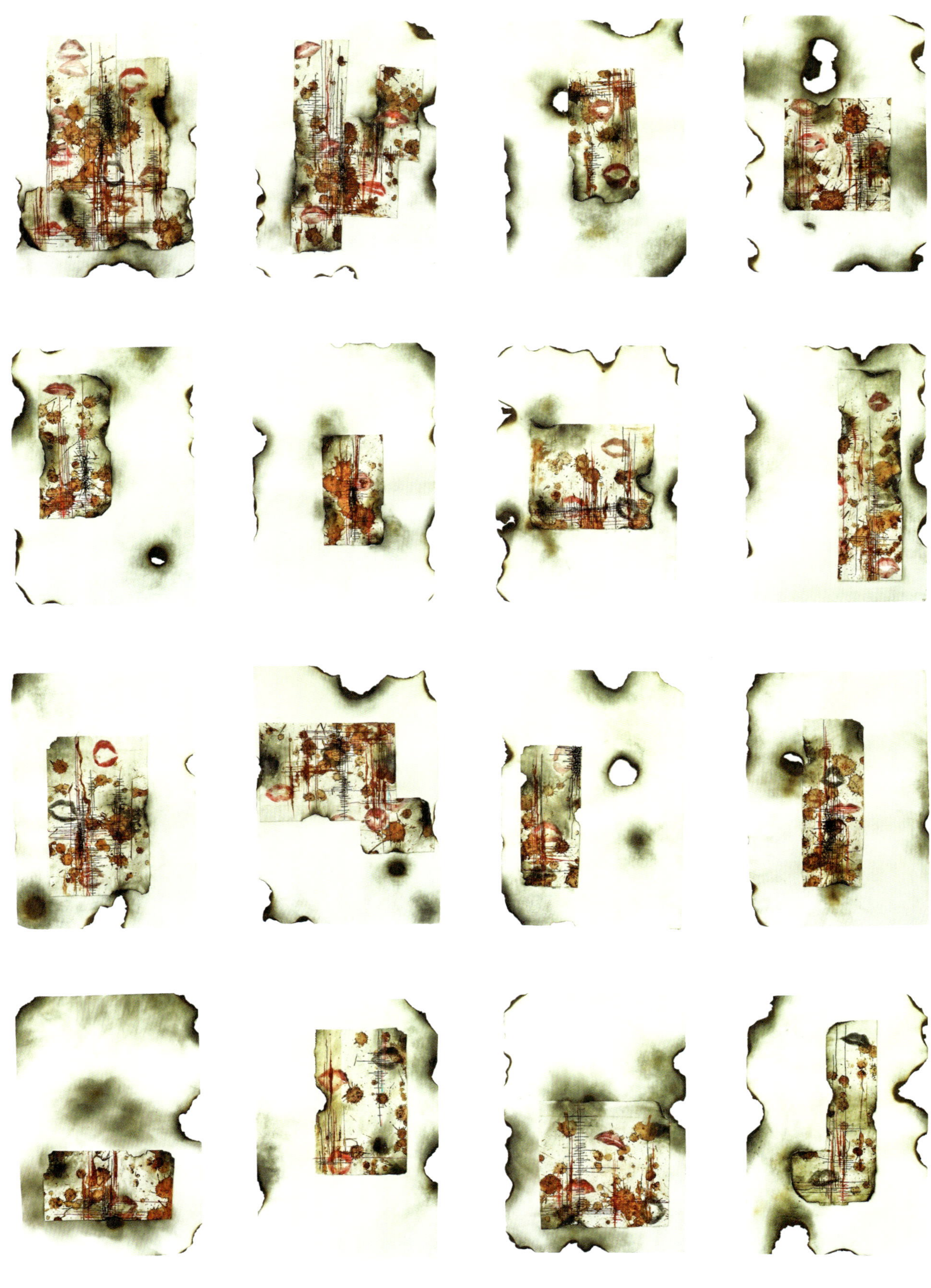

Asuntus Kontemporáneus/Contemporary Issues/Masalah
Comtemporary, 2014

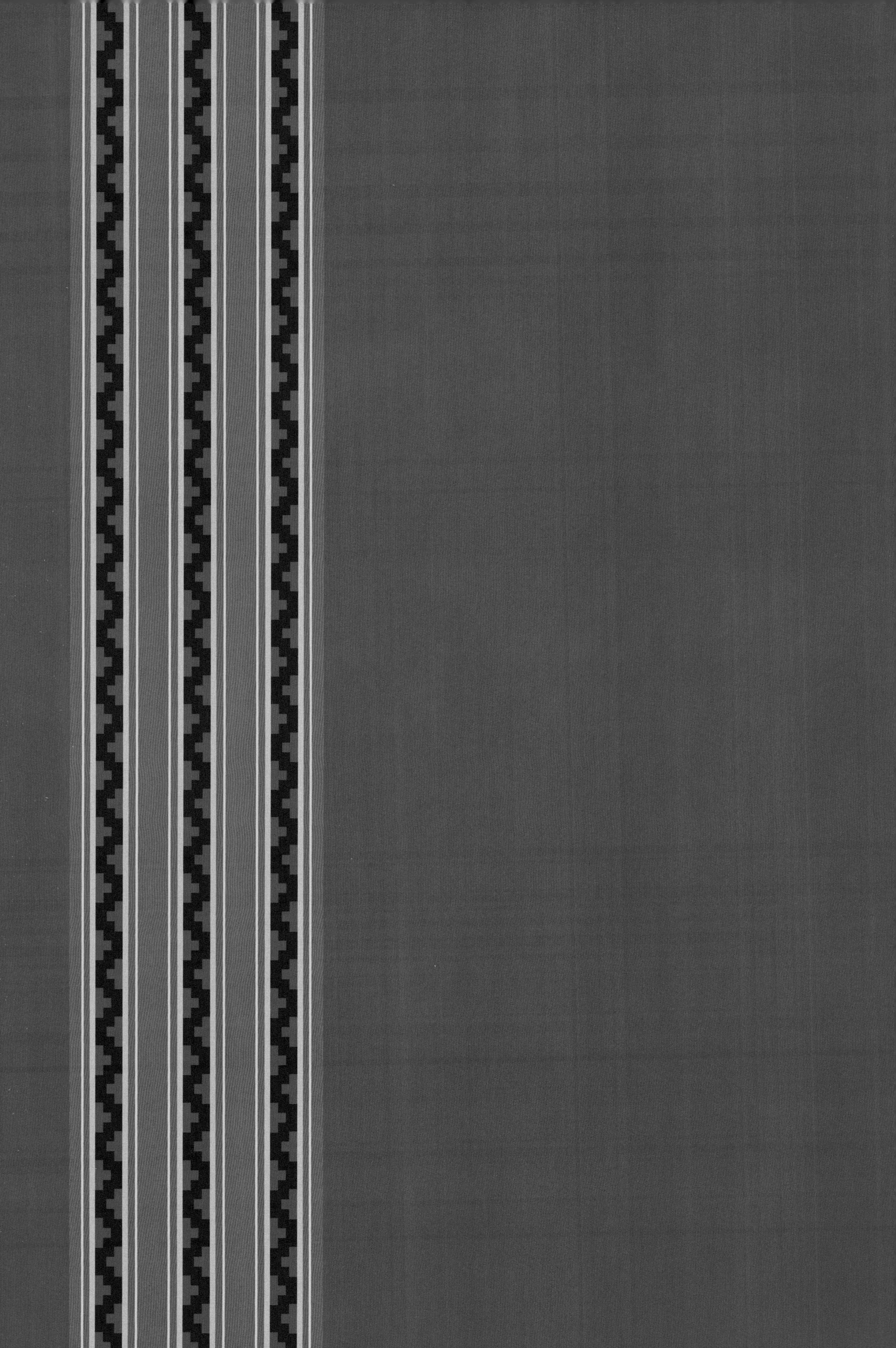

THE DAY AFTER TOMORROW

ANTONIO SAMPAIO

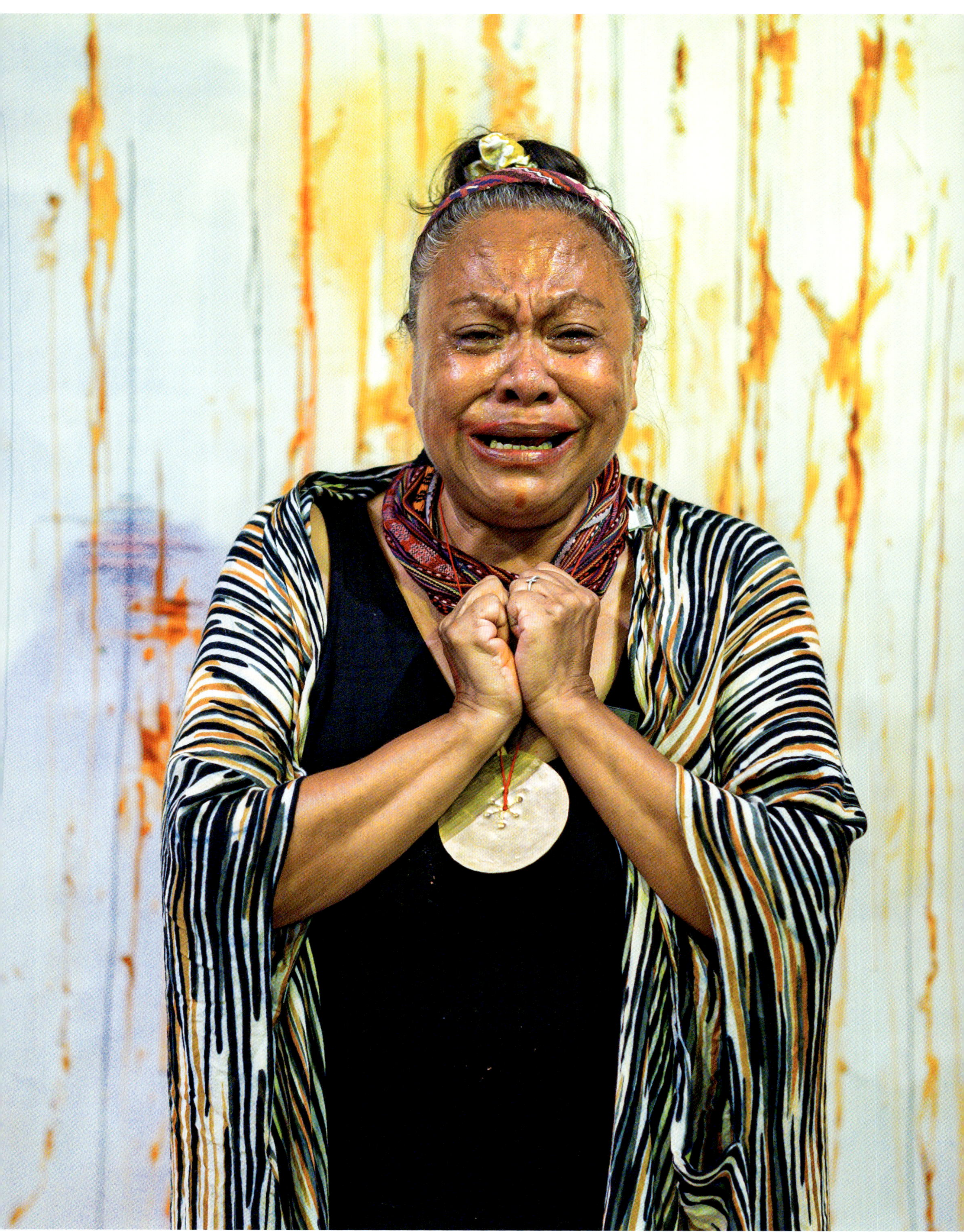

THE DAY AFTER TOMORROW

Antonio Sampaio

Kiss and Don't Tell is more than art, it is a cry of silent pain, on behalf of many women who suffered in East Timor as comfort women, as protectors and as heroes of the resistance.

I share this story from October 1999, set in the village of Balibo. Because memory is important.

—

Timor-Leste: Balibo, a ghost town with marks of violence in every house and red lipstick walls

BALIBO, TIMOR-LESTE, 2 OCTOBER 1999[1]

Australian soldiers today patrolled the ruins of the village of Balibo, now a ghost town, a few kilometres from the border with West Timor. They found bloody walls that testify to the wave of violence that swept through the region. The village is destroyed and abandoned, without life, with houses empty, traces of violence everywhere.

In one of the houses, almost every wall has marks that the soldiers identify as blood, and which they repeatedly photograph. In another room, two walls have even more heinous marks: red lipsticks. As if someone had been kissing the walls.

This won't be the only house with these stains in Timor-Leste. In other places, like this one, women also suffered.

The bloodstains are especially strong on the once white tiles in one of the house's divisions. Almost shamefully, some of the spots are covered up by a poster of Jesus Christ, placed to hide what happened there, to cover the violence.

The windows show gunshot marks, and on the walls, there are bullet holes. Just like in all of the other houses that I visited in Balibo, there is nothing left of the interior …

In one of the neighbouring homes, the only thing left is an electricity bill, dated July 1999, in the name of Clotilde Tavares. The bill hangs from a rusted nail, on the wall of the living room, where a strong wind bangs, rhythmically, a semi-destroyed door that has partially jumped off its hinges.

In Balibo, there is another mandatory space to visit, the house where five Australian journalists were killed by Indonesian troops, on 16 October 1975. For a few minutes confusion reigns, with journalists and soldiers trying to figure out exactly in which house they were killed?

For many, it was in the house immediately at the bottom of the ramp that connects the main road to the Portuguese fort, as the latest images sent in by the group shows one of the journalists, Greg Shackelton, painting the Australian flag, and the word 'Australia' on the outer wall.

This tragically famous house, now roofless and with visible marks of destruction, still stands, with the walls marked by other inscriptions, mostly in favour of Timor-Leste's independence, with poorly drawn portraits of Xanana Gusmão on all walls.

The only sign of life is a bouquet of fresh flowers placed in a vase made from half a plastic water bottle, a symbol that is traditionally used in Timor-Leste to mark places where someone has passed away.

Others say, however, that the journalists were in a house on the other side of the roundabout, marked by a statue honouring a pro-Indonesia integrationist, and that they only wrote the word Australia in the first house, because it was to that side that the Indonesian soldiers came.

Australian soldiers are betting on the house where blood on the walls was found, which will now be 'properly investigated' by a team of forensic experts.

From Integration Avenue, the part of the road leading to the coast, there is not a single house left. Traces of destruction and the rush with which the inhabitants left are visible in the street, dominated by garbage and zinc and wood remains removed from buildings.

Next door, an equally destroyed elementary school, with dozens of stones, used to break almost all glass, scattered throughout the classrooms. What appears to have been the library, cupboards lying on the floor with hundreds of schoolbooks, all in Indonesian, scattered around.

The town is proof of the destruction that swept across Timor-Leste in the days after the 30 August referendum results were announced.

But perhaps the clearest sign of violence is the total absence of inhabitants.

Besides the soldiers, the only movement that was seen today in Balibo was that of a dog, limping with one leg, running between houses. Perhaps trying to escape the ghost town of destroyed houses and violent kiss marks on a rough wall.

NOTE

1. First published in *LUSA: Noticias do Dia*, news agency, 1999.

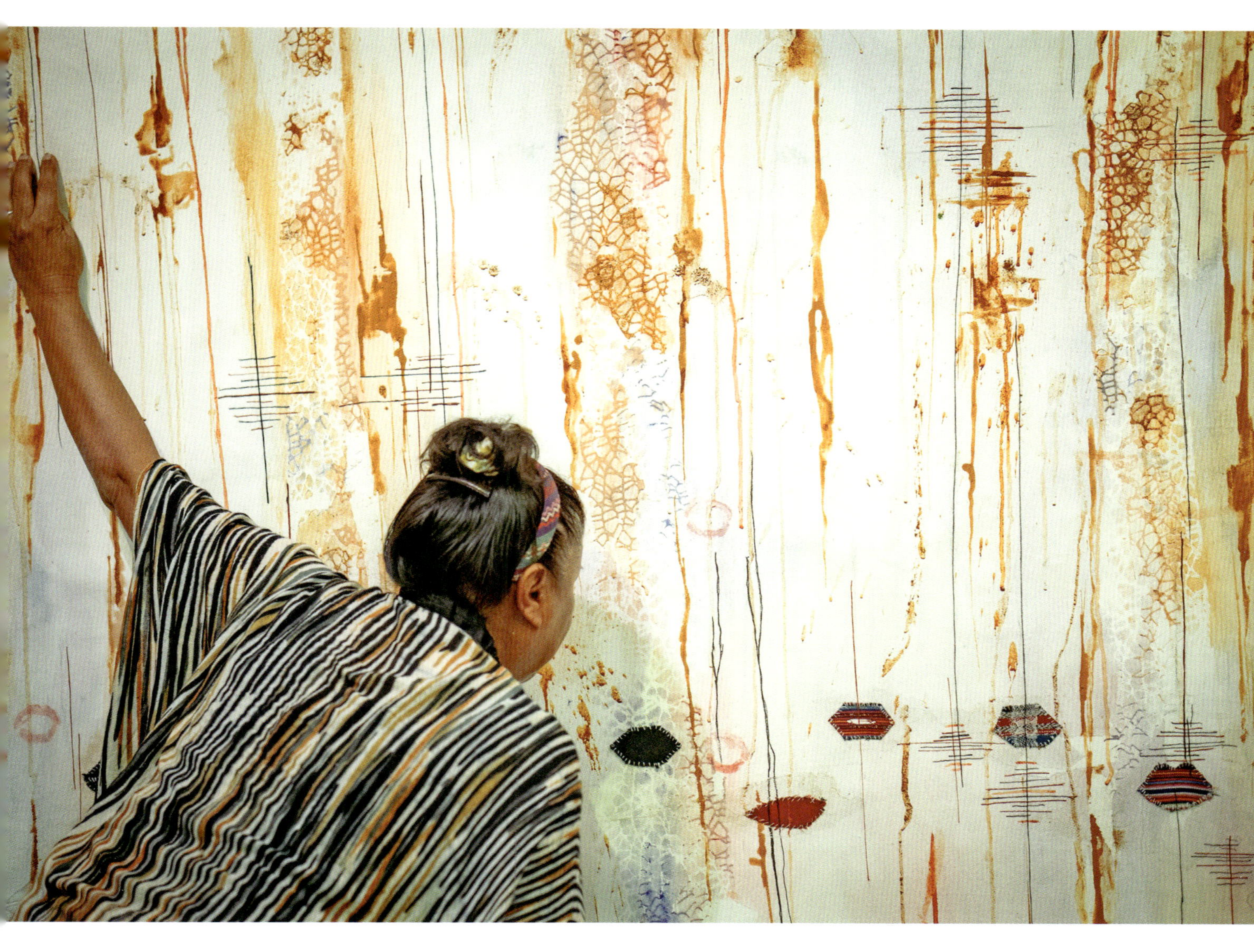

Maria Madeira performing with *Kiss and Don't Tell*, 2024

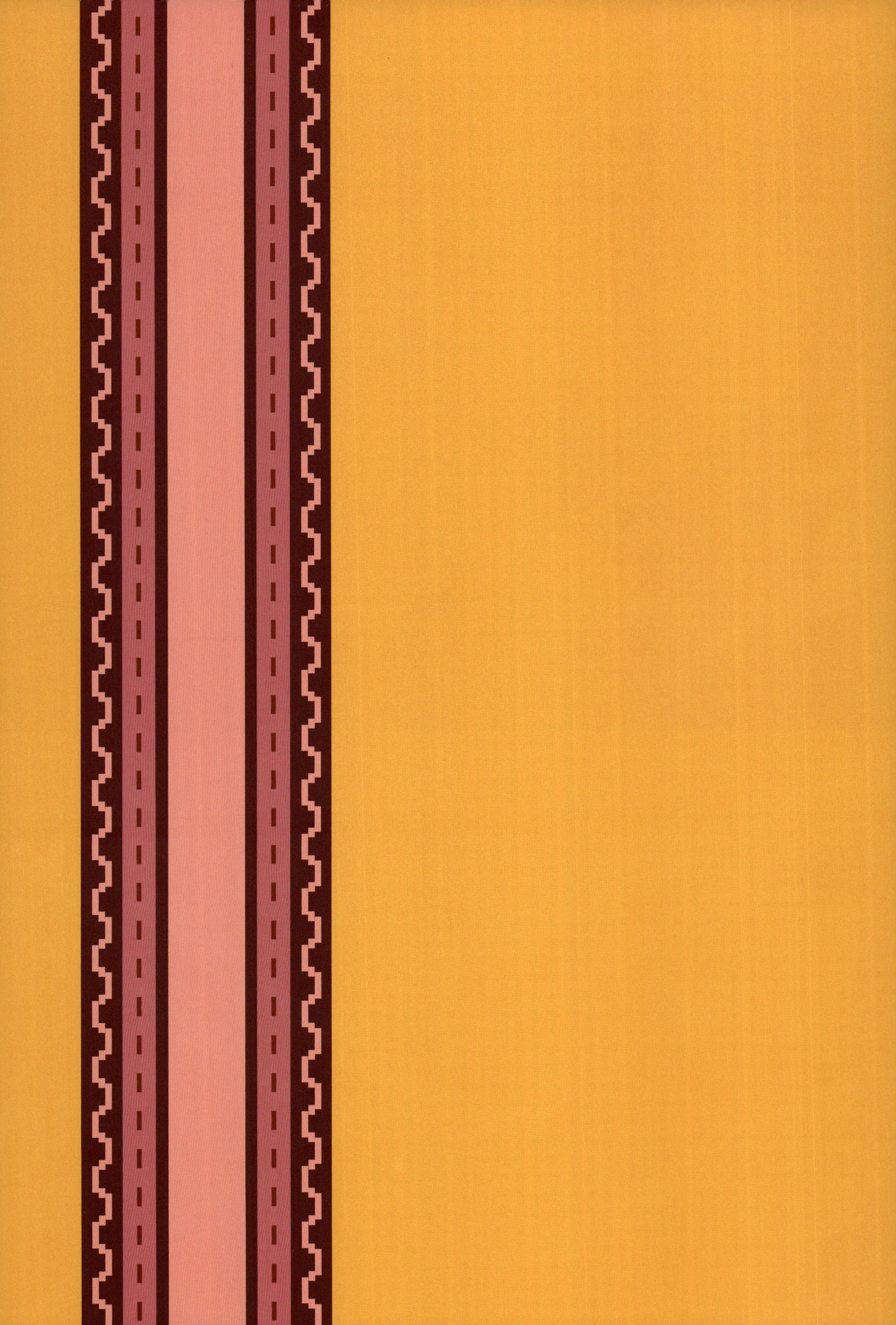

SONGS PERFORMED BY MARIA MADEIRA

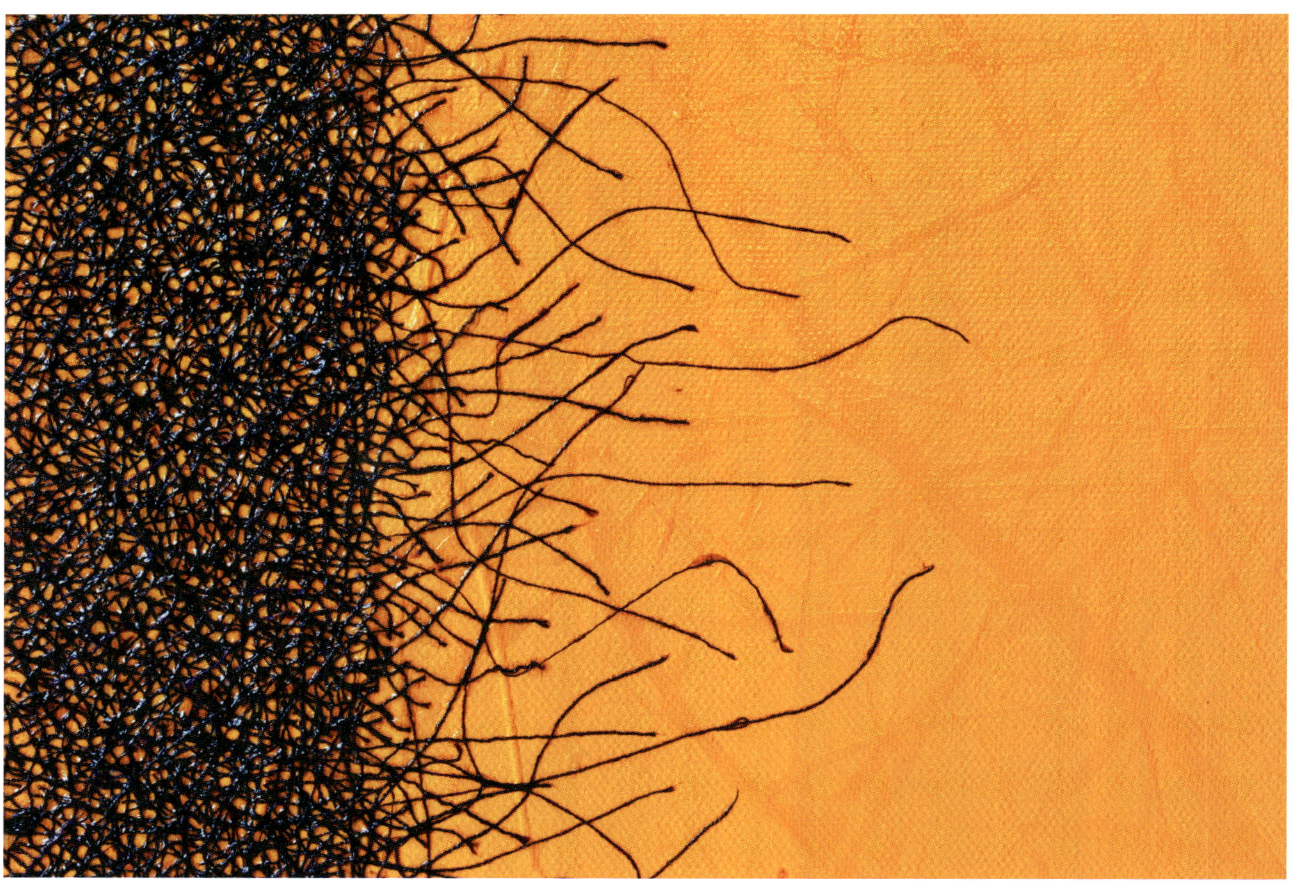

KOLE LELE MAI

Kole lele mai, rade koko dele kole lele mai
Kole lele mai, rade koko dele kole hele la loi
kolele mai

Sa, sa ha'a nalo o batar la fulin
Sa, sa ha'a nalo o hare la burit

Se, se ha'a nalo o kabun la bosu
Se, se ha'a nalo o kosar la maran

Balu dehan o baruk, balu katak o beik
Balu ra'ak o baruk, balu katak o ki'ak

Sa, sa ha'a nalo?
Se, se, se los, se?

KOLE LELE MAI

What, exactly, is preventing your corn
from sprouting?
What, exactly, is preventing your rice
from blooming?

Who eats you out of hunger?
What, who, and what stops your sweat
from running off your body?

Some people call you foolish,
while others call you lazy.
Some people call you impoverished, while
others call you lazy.

How, how do you do it?
Who is it, precisely who?

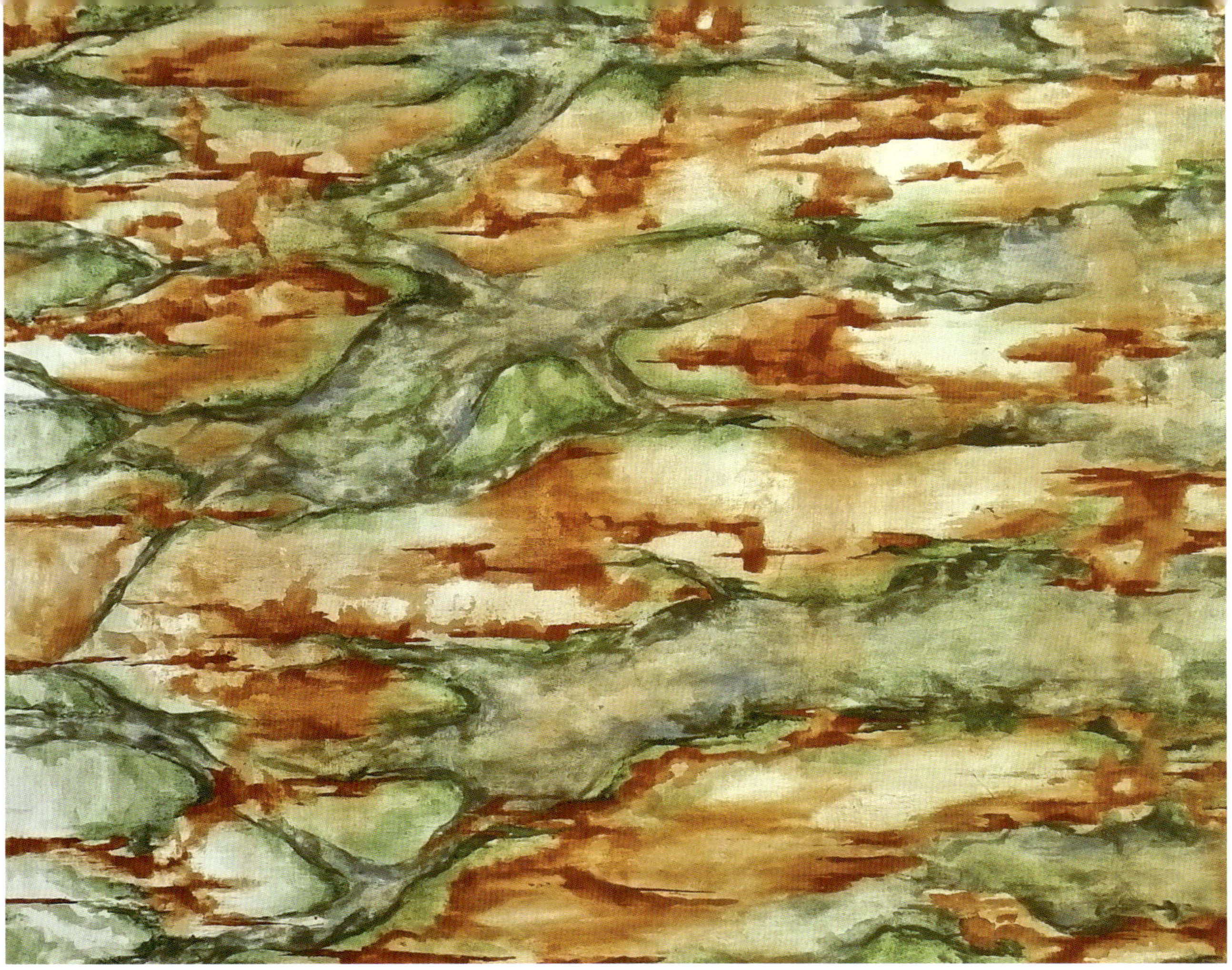

KDADALAK

Oh! hele oh!
Oh! Hele ole
Oh! Hele le oh! Oh, hele oh
Oh! Hele oh hele! oh le le oh!

Kdadalak suli mutuk, fila ué inan
Ué inan tan malu sa be tahan

Nanu'u Timoroan sei hamutuk
Hamutuk atu tahan, anin su'ut tasi

Anin su'ut sut tasi, sut kabala
Sut ita mata laran, ita kotuk laran

Sut ita lun turu, ita kosar turu
Susu ita rai bokur, ita isin bokur

Kdadalak suli mutuk fila ué inan
Timoroan hamutuk tane ita rain

STREAMS

Converging streams transform into
mother streams
As the power opposes them, the
mother streams unite!

Thus, the Timorese people unite
Come together to resist the wind from the sea

Our clothes are whipped by the wind that comes
from the sea
Both the back and the eyes suffer from it

The sweat and tears roll to the ground
It drains the fat from our bodies and the land

Mother streams are created when
streams converge
Together, as Timorese, let us embrace
our homeland

INA LOU

Lai, lai lai lai lai lai ina lou ina lou, la la
Kole la let ona, betena!
Ai lai lai lai, ina lou
Ai kole la let ona, betenah!

Ita ema sei moris
Halo rai nia naran ina lou
Ai lai lai lai ina lou
Ah ita ema sei moris
Halo rai nia naran, betenah

Mate ona rai taka
Tilun labe rona, ina lou
Ai! Lai lai ina lou
Ai! Mate ona rai taka
Tilun labe rona betenah

Inan Aman mota sorin
Oan mota sorin, ina lou
Ai! Lai lai lai, ina lou
Ai inan aman mota sorin
Oan mota sorin, betenah!

Lolo liman la to'o
Matan-uén suli, ina lou
Ai! Lai lai lai, ina lou
Ai! Lolo liman la to'o
Matan-uén suli, betenah

DEAR MOTHER EARTH

Lai, ai lai lai lai lai ina lou ina lou,
(Expression of honouring the queen)
All tiredness is in vain – Ina Lou (Queen)
Ai lai lai lai, Ina Lou (expression of honouring
the queen)
All tiredness is in vain – Betenah
As long as we humans exist – the land has
a meaning – Ina Lou
All tiredness is in vain – Ina Lou
As long as we humans exist – the land has
a meaning – Betenah

In death, the soil covers the ears, don't listen
anymore – Ina Lou
All tiredness is in vain – Ina Lou
In death, the soil covers the ears, don't listen
anymore – Betenah!

Mother and father are across the river
The child is across the river – Ina Lou
All tiredness is in vain – Ina Lou
Mother and father are across the river
The child is across the river – Betenah
Reached out to each other but to no avail – Tears
fell – Ina Lou
All tiredness is in vain – Ina Lou
Tears fell – Ina Lou

Kdadalak, Kole lele mai and *Ina Lou*, translation by Claudio Marques Cabral, 2024

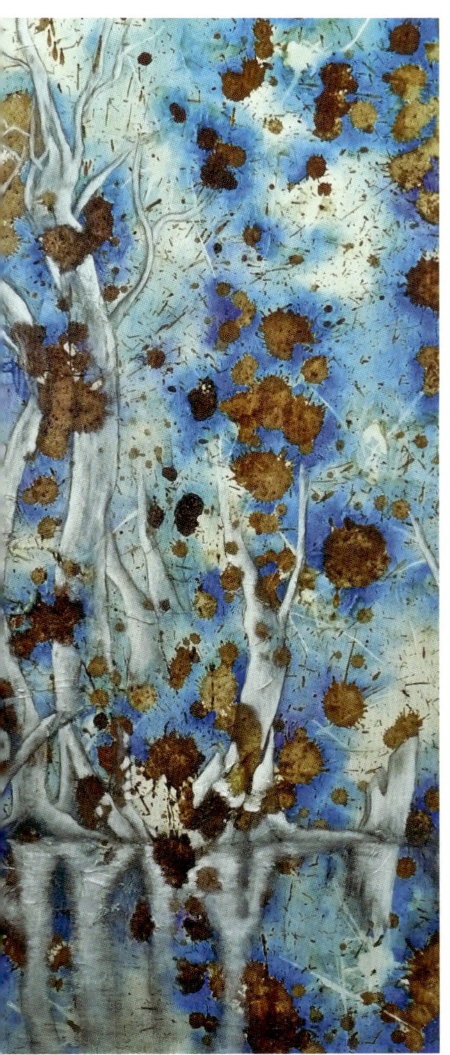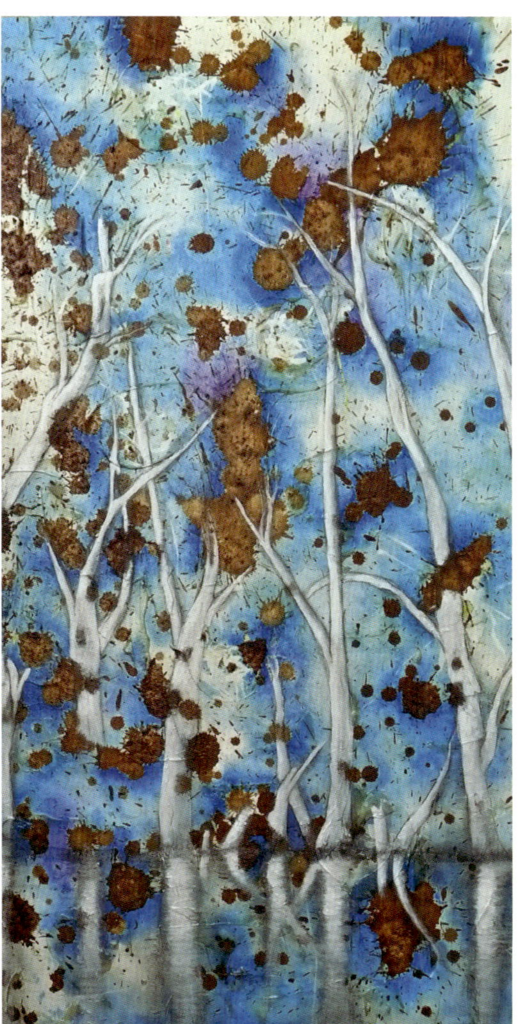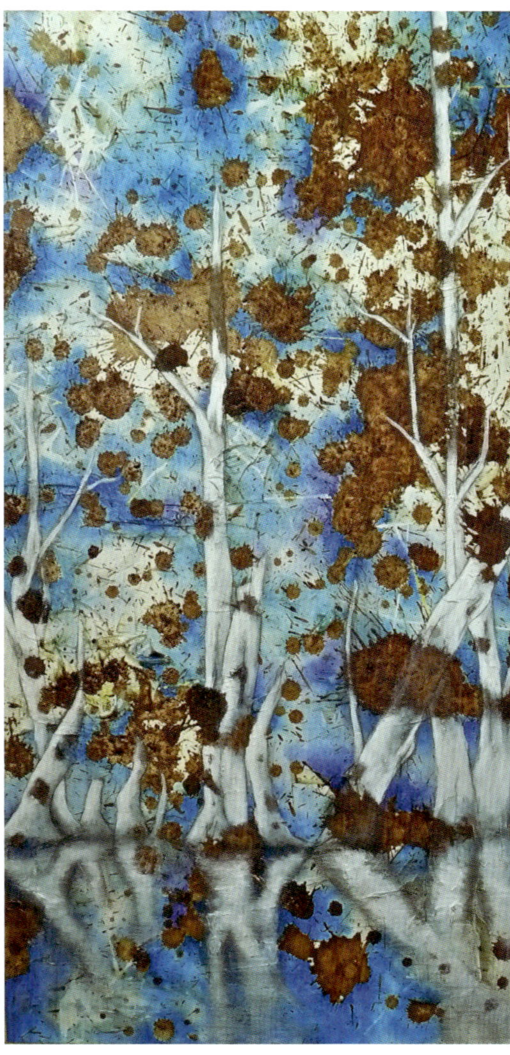

Ina Lou I, II & III (Dear Mother Earth I, II & III/Ibu Pertiwi I, II & III), 2010

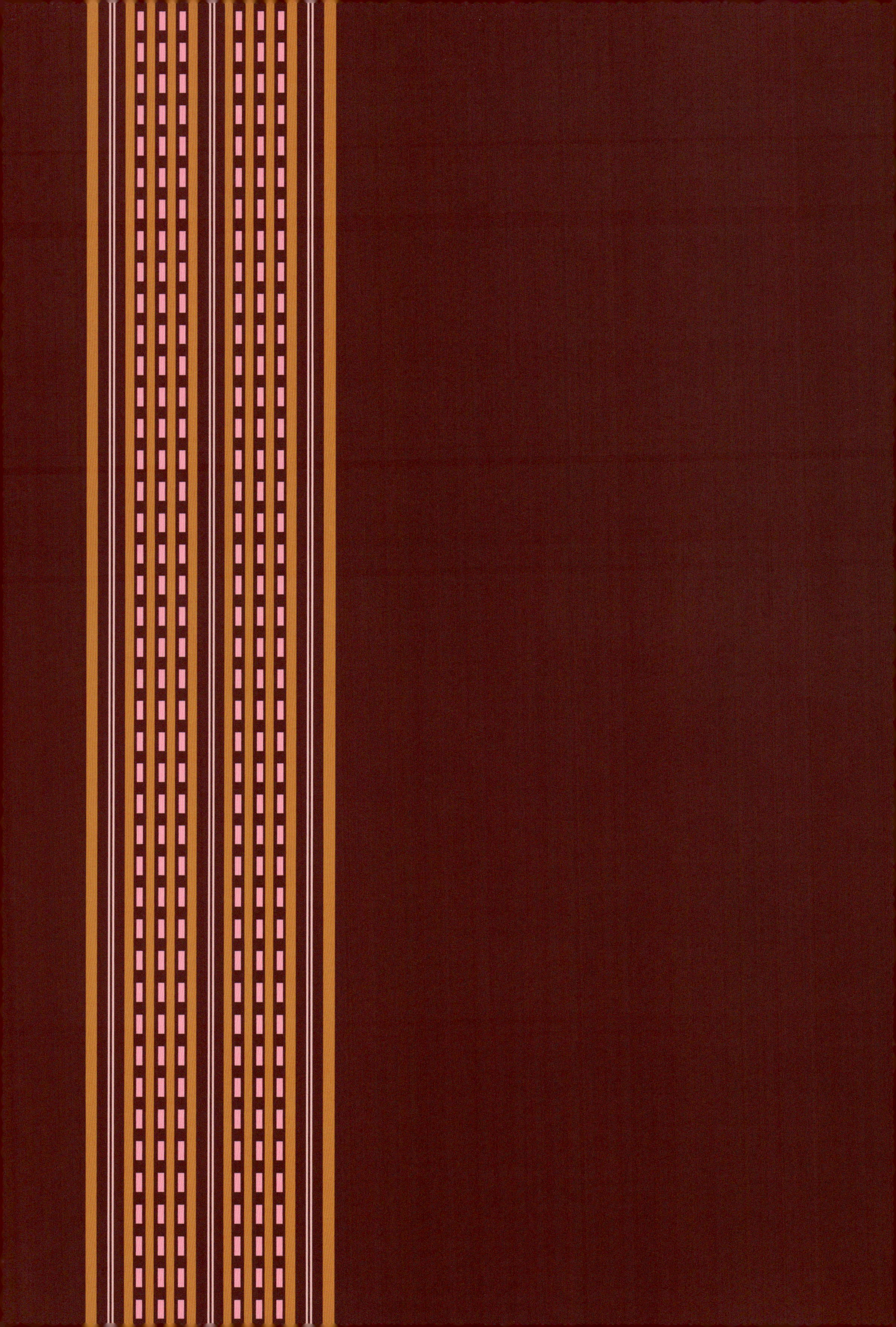

MARIA MADEIRA

IN CONVERSATION WITH

NATALIE KING

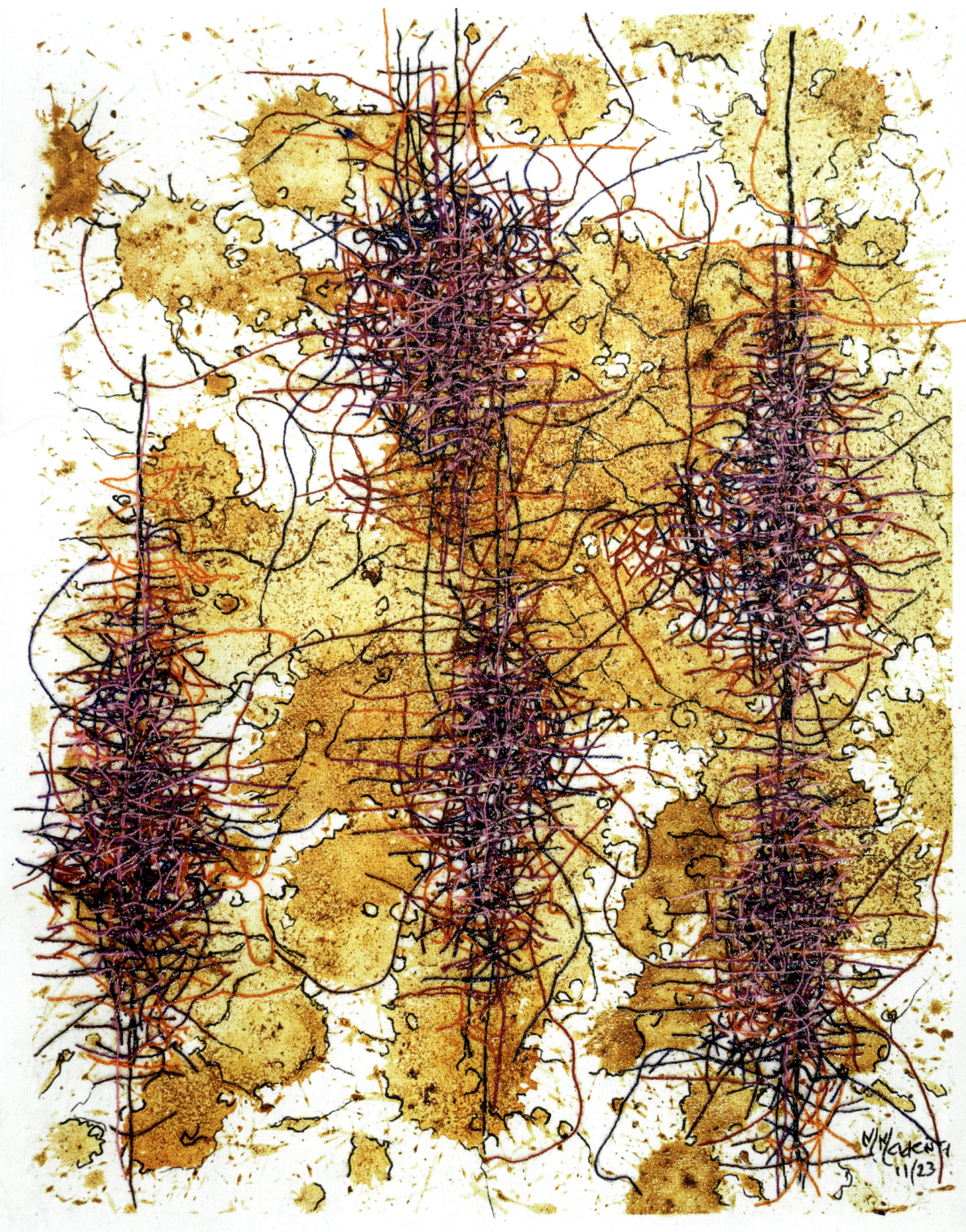

MARIA MADEIRA IN CONVERSATION WITH NATALIE KING

Maria Madeira adeptly melds ancestral influences and traditional crafts with contemporary concerns for the plight of the voiceless. Madeira's dexterous practice deploys material from her village Ermera, including betel nut, tais, red earth and sewing. She conflates the traditional with the contemporary, telling stories of loss, trauma, hope and healing from the women of Timor-Leste. By giving voice to the silenced, her work commemorates atrocities yet it is imbued with hope and beauty.

During the early months of 2024 we embarked on an email and zoom dialogue across Dili, Perth and Melbourne, conversing about her early influences, multiple migrations, displacement and the role of song as salvation. In the midst of preparations for the 60th Venice Biennale – La Biennale di Venezia and during a visit to Dili in January to see her exhibition *Flowery Talk* at Fundação Oriente, she shared her resourceful methodology, adolescence in a refugee camp and connecting with Timorese folklore as well as the role of teaching and talking, education and learning as vehicles for cultural empowerment.

NATALIE KING: You were born in the village of Gleno in the Ermera region of Timor-Leste. Can you describe some of the cultural traditions from your village and how these have influenced your art practice, in particular the use of tais and the ancestral creation story with crocodiles?

MARIA MADEIRA: My childhood in Gleno, Ermera was very memorable and filled with cultural traditions. Some of the earliest memories that I often joyfully share with my siblings are about us being present at traditional ceremonies such as rice harvesting ('Tebe Hare/Sama Hare' in Tetun). Here, the locals used to step on rice husks while singing and dancing throughout the night. I used to love it because of the traditional rhythmic songs (all sung in Tetun or Mambai, the local languages), that helped with the rhythmic physical movements needed to separate

OPPOSITE
Untitled I, 2023

the rice from the husks and stems. Such ceremonies often required people, both male and female, to use traditional Timorese cloth such as tais to perform.

Likewise, storytelling was also a permanent feature in my upbringing. For instance, the legend of the crocodile whereby according to folklore Timor-Leste originated from the time a young boy first helped rescue a crocodile, which later returned the favour by helping the young boy to see the world, by becoming the Island of Timor. This mythology is told and retold to most East Timorese from a young age.

NK: Tell me about your childhood. Was your home creative?

MM: It was pure magic. My dad had a camera and film for recording us playing, jumping and swimming in the river. Then, at night, we would have cinema, home movies. The whole neighbourhood would come to sit and watch these home movies of us just being silly in the water.

I was born near the river and it gets very wet during the wet season. Because there are lots of rivers and lakes in Ermera, it's a good area for coffee plantations. The earth is very rich not only with agriculture but also for my spirit. The earth is so beautiful and that's why I love the red of the Kimberleys in Western Australia.

We always grew up with music. My grandfather and my father are into music. My dad bought some guitars, and then my brothers started playing. They are amazing musicians, guitarists and music writers. My dad is a great artisan producing wood-carvings while my grandfather was a great wood-carver as well. He made a lot of *surik*, the traditional sword, and beautiful drums. My dad and I always had a very strong interest in Indigenous art.

I believe that these early experiences helped me to appreciate and grow with traditions in mind. They instilled in me an understanding, deep love and value towards my cultural identity.

NK: In 1976 the Portuguese Air Force evacuated you from West Timor after the Indonesian invasion. You spent most of the following eight years in a refugee camp run by the Red Cross on the outskirts of Lisbon in Portugal where you joined a choir. Can you discuss how song and collective singing became an outlet for you?

MM: Whilst in the refugee camp, I became a member of a successful young East Timorese choir called *Coro Loro Sa'e* which was composed of up to 30 young girls, daughters of the refugee families residing in Portugal. The choir performed extensively, especially traditional dancing and singing throughout Portugal and neighbouring countries.

It was my understanding that the main objective of the choir was to strengthen Timor-Leste's cultural identity while divulging and sharing it with other societies. During

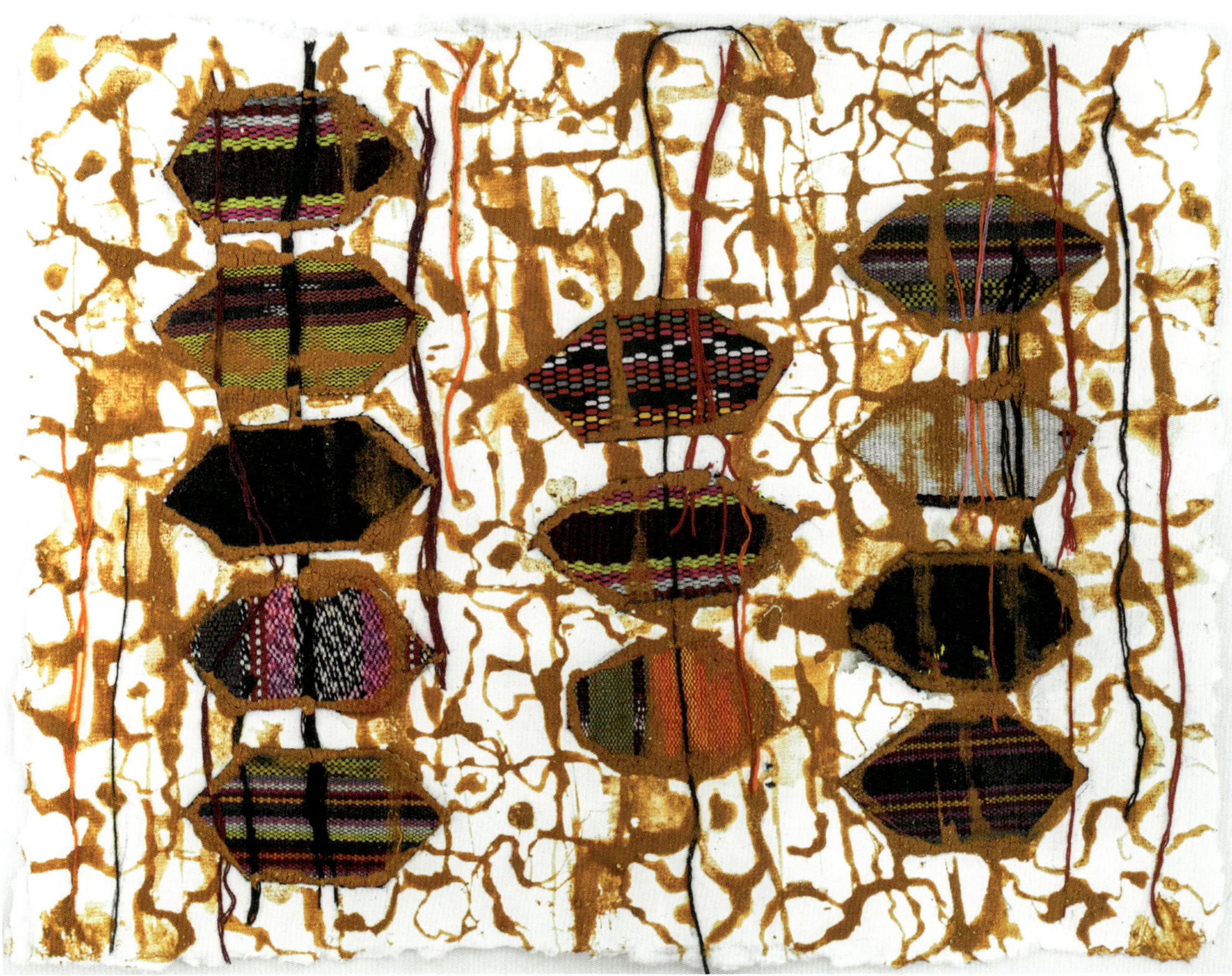

cultural and community events such as fairs, I noticed that when traditional songs and dances were performed, it frequently evoked emotional responses such as sadness and pride from both the East Timorese people and some members of the international community. This kind of reaction made me recognise the value, impact and power of creative language. In this case, traditional East Timorese music and dancing became an effective and efficient way of exposing our troubles and restoring some sense of belonging.

Thus, my experience as a refugee and singer with the East Timorese choir Coro Loro Sa'e was a fundamental factor in learning and growing because it encouraged me to take a closer look at my East Timorese background, to discover who I really am. For me the choir was critical in restoring my sense of worth and belonging. Every time I performed, I experienced happiness. I felt so proud and so free. It was as though I was being healed. Besides, getting away from the refugee camp to perform meant that at least we were going to be fed.

In many ways, the choir was my salvation and I believe that it was one of the main reasons I became a visual artist. It was during these years that I understood and became aware of the power of creative expression.

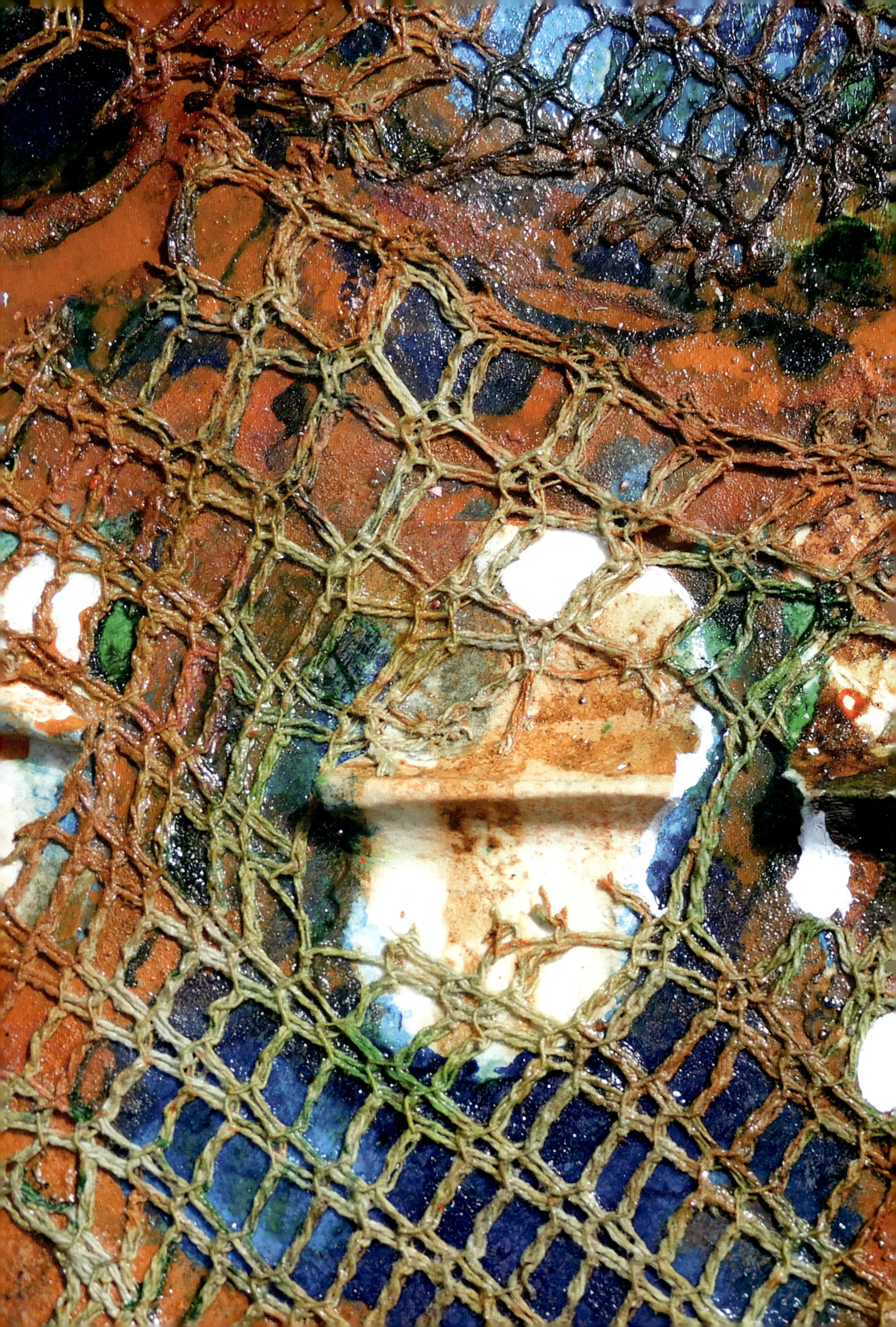

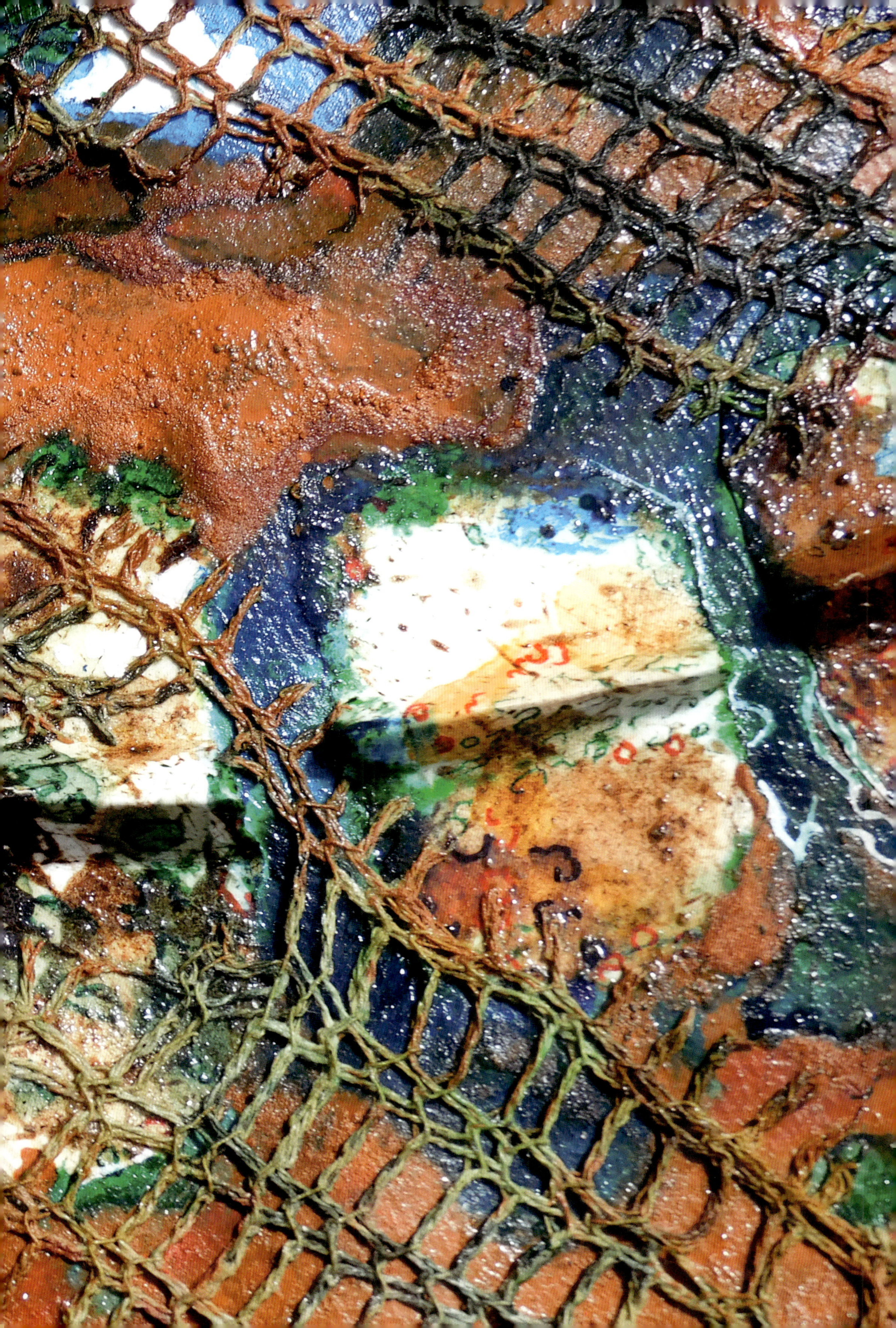

NK: How did you become an artist? Was there an epiphany?

MM: As long as I can remember, creativity was always part of my upbringing like the traditional ceremonies such as rice harvesting and choral work.

In the refugee camp my mother loved magazines and I just happened to turn the page, and there was this beautiful image of mountains and a lake: Lake Louise in Canada. So that was my first colour drawing that I'll never forget, because I did a drawing in my head. I copied the image of Lake Louise to a page, and I was very proud. Where I grew up there's lots of water, so just seeing a vast amount of water in a landscape reminded me of Ermera, which is also mountainous. The image of water and mountain was captivating.

My artistic work grew and developed over the years. It started during my refugee days where I found peace every time I was drawing and sketching.

With the joy and impact of the choir, it made me value art more and I was really captivated by the sense of wellbeing and sense of worth every time I created. Overall, I think it was a passion that evolved and developed progressively.

NK: One of your early works, *270+ The Santa Cruz Massacre*, 1996 is a floor installation that deploys the traditional *kaibauk* silver headdress worn by the Timorese *liurai*, shaped like the horns of a buffalo and configured into a cross formation. Can you discuss this commemorative work?

MM: I try to reach both the western world as well as the East Timorese. I always use materials that I think will be recognised. I use the *kaibauk* for the Santa Cruz massacre installation. I talk to both sides. I'm able to reach out and communicate with both. There has to be an understanding, not only political understanding and religious, but on a cultural level. I use a creative and cultural language that we have used to understand each other since the days of our foremothers and forefathers.

When the Santa Cruz massacre was shown on television, I thought, you are heroes and heroines. At the time, I went to a lot of protests against the military regime. Yet the media coverage was barely for three seconds on the news. I thought it needed more. We needed to talk more. I put the plus on the floor to say that 270 plus people died at the Santa Cruz massacre. They are heroes. They deserve a royal burial, a state funeral. I'm not screaming, my art just speaks and it's such a powerful tool.

NK: For the 60th Venice Biennale you are making an ensemble exhibition called *Kiss and Don't Tell*. What is the inspiration for this installation and the role of cultural activism?

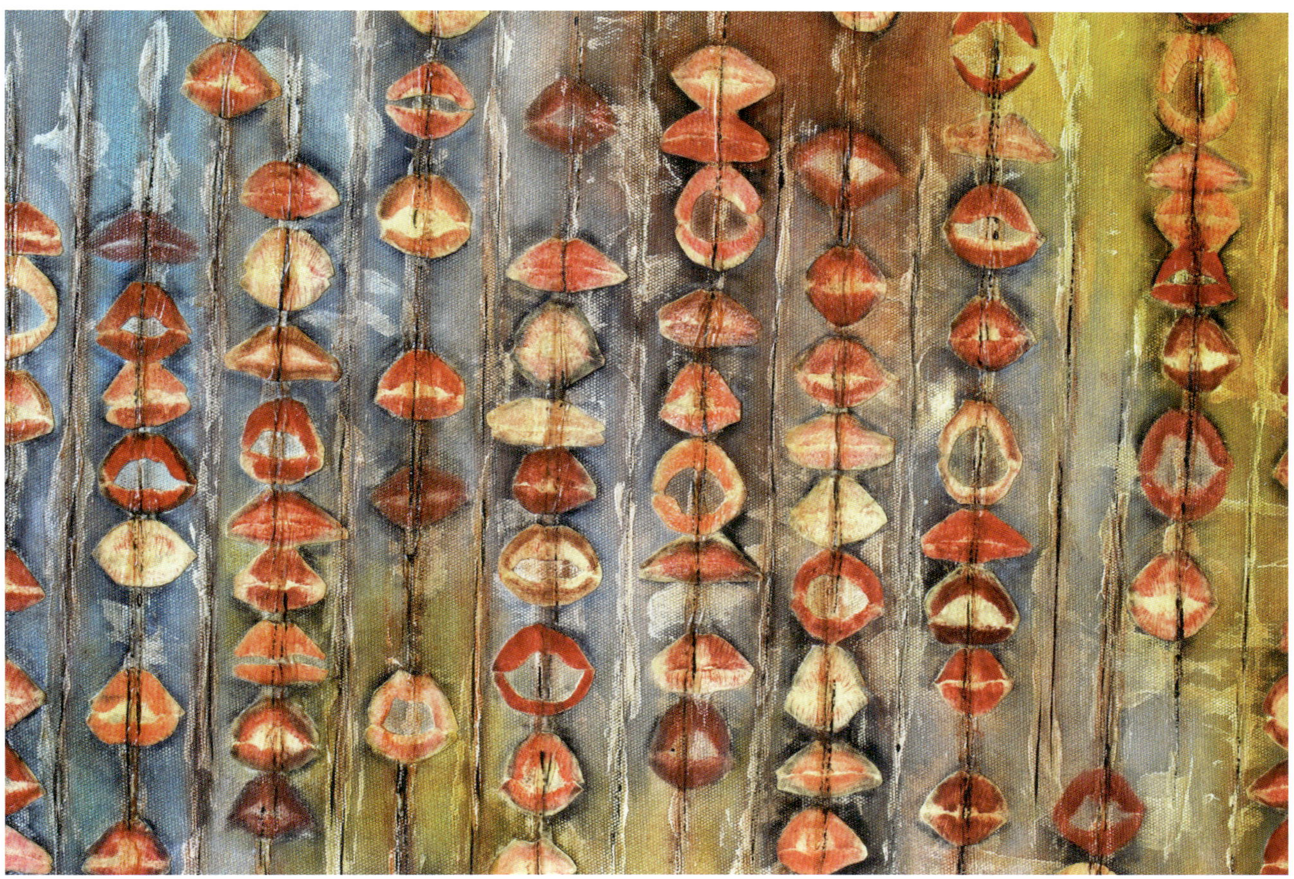

Fan Na'an Fatin/Mercado da Carne/Meat Market, 2010

MM: *Kiss and Don't Tell* was an inspiration that grew out of the need to tell some painful realities about the history of Timor-Leste's fight for independence, particularly the voice of minority groups such as women.

After returning to Timor-Leste, I observed and learned about the atrocities committed against the women of Timor-Leste by the Indonesian military. In their honour, I thought that it was critical to tell these stories, to create awareness for future generations to come. Men fought and we are forever grateful. Lest Not Forget: women also fought. And we are eternally grateful. For men fought with their guns BUT women fought with their bodies.

I was staying with my brother and sister-in-law. At the time, my brother was working for the UN as an interpreter for the serious crimes unit, and I joined him as a translator. Around this time in 2002, I was staying in a bedroom where I found myself staring at lipstick stains, month after month. When I understood, I realised it was trying to tell me something. I decided: I am going to talk, I am going to kiss and I am going to tell.

In short, *Kiss and Don't Tell* talks about the impact and influence of East Timorese women during the occupation. It talks about how strong the women were and how their fight, resilience, survival and triumph led to the freedom of our motherland.

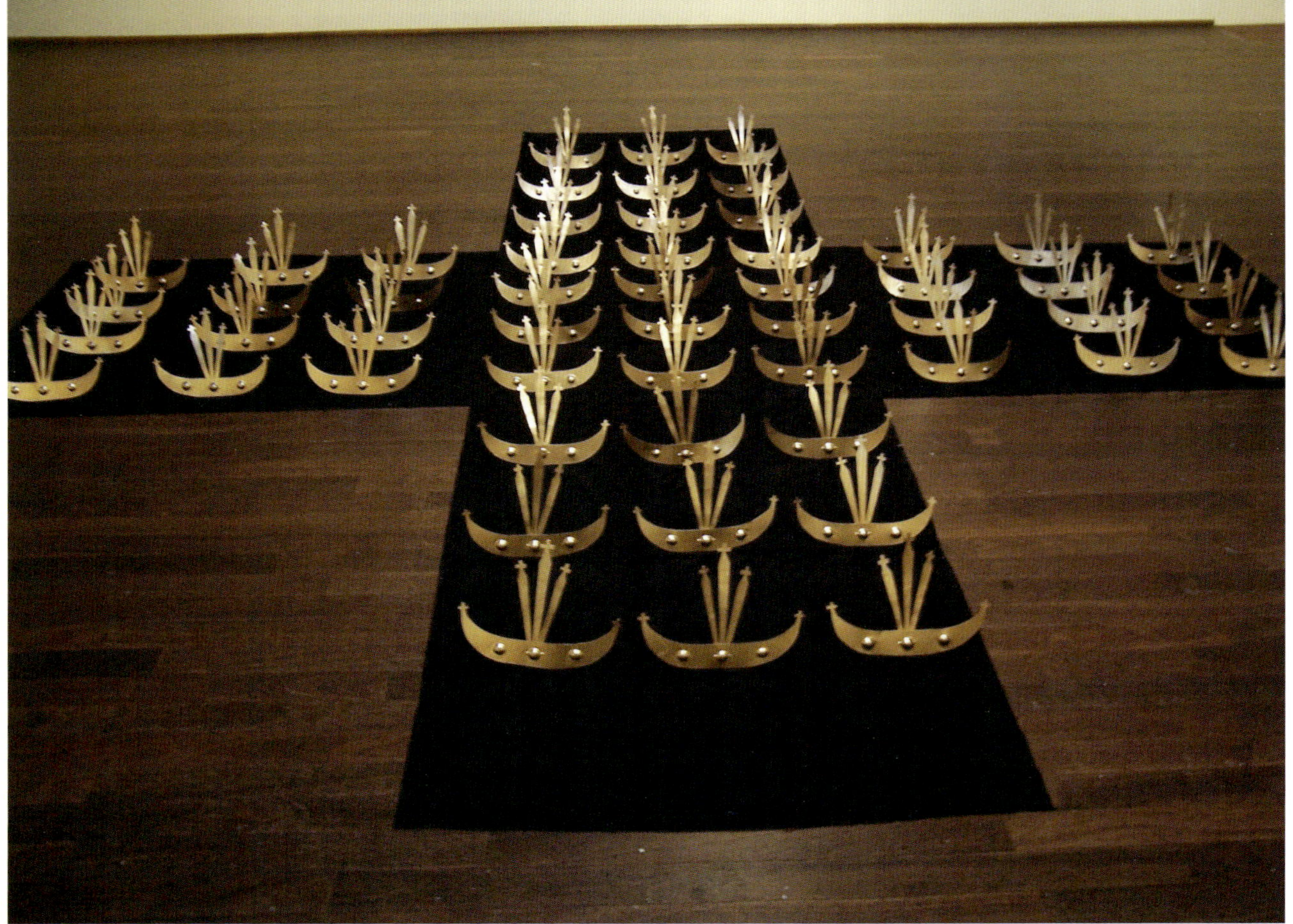

NK: Education, learning and pedagogy have been important to you especially since you have completed a PhD at Curtin University and worked as a teacher. Can you discuss?

MM: Yes, I have always maintained that education was a key factor for personal growth and understanding, especially in relation to Timor-Leste being such a young nation. This country was hidden behind closed doors for decades whilst being occupied by a foreign country. Due to the occupation, many East Timorese were killed and displaced.

For me, it was again the urge to find a sense of belonging and survive the cultural, political, social and religious realms. As a young refugee, this plight became more critical. During those difficult times, I always thought of a better world. 'Life must be better than this,' I often thought to myself.

In regard to my artistic expression, education was a tool to help me grow, better develop and advance my practical perspective. I felt that it was crucial to add a voice to my visual art. And with a formal education and a PhD, I could get more attention. I am asked to participate in all kinds of art and cultural events. I can educate in both practical and theoretical areas in art. I am heard.

More importantly, I believe that education is the best vehicle to create interest and awareness about the current diverse art and culture language. For instance, by teaching the young artistic generation 'up to date' and 'current language' of art, young people will find their own

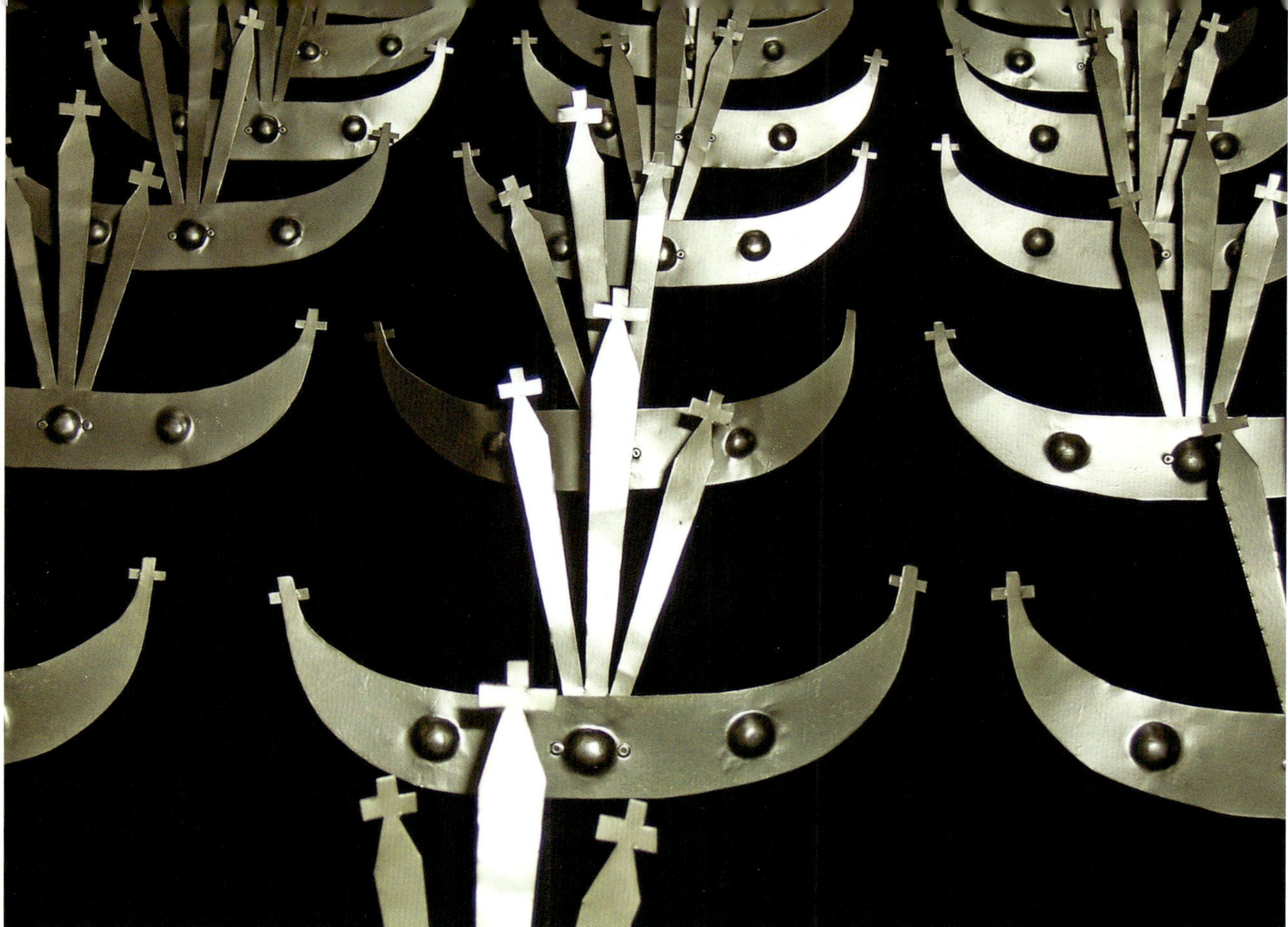

270+ Massakre Santa Cruz Nian (270+ Massacre de Santa Cruz; The Santa Cruz Massacre) (detail), 1996

curiosity to travel to the past in order to find themselves in the present.

NK: There is a unique materiality to your work, sourcing materials that you find such as tais, earth, betel nut. Can you elaborate on how and why you utilise found materials that belong to your homeland?

MM: Since returning to Timor-Leste in the early 2000s I soon came to learn:

- We don't have a proper art material shop in the country.

- We don't have an official Art School.

As a form of survival, I thought, what about the natural resources?

Betel nut?

Natural dyes?

Red earth?

Rock powder? Even traditional items such as the *kaibauk*, and of course our traditional textiles called 'tais'.

I started to use these materials in my work. I believe that it is very effective. Firstly, because I could gather these materials quite easily around the country. Secondly, and most importantly, using East Timorese objects and imagery meant it also spoke to the people of Timor-Leste. Thus, each work can generate interest and curiosity from a national and international level. This made each artwork much more significant.

In terms of using the red earth from Ermera, I have been thinking about the footsteps that you walk on and when

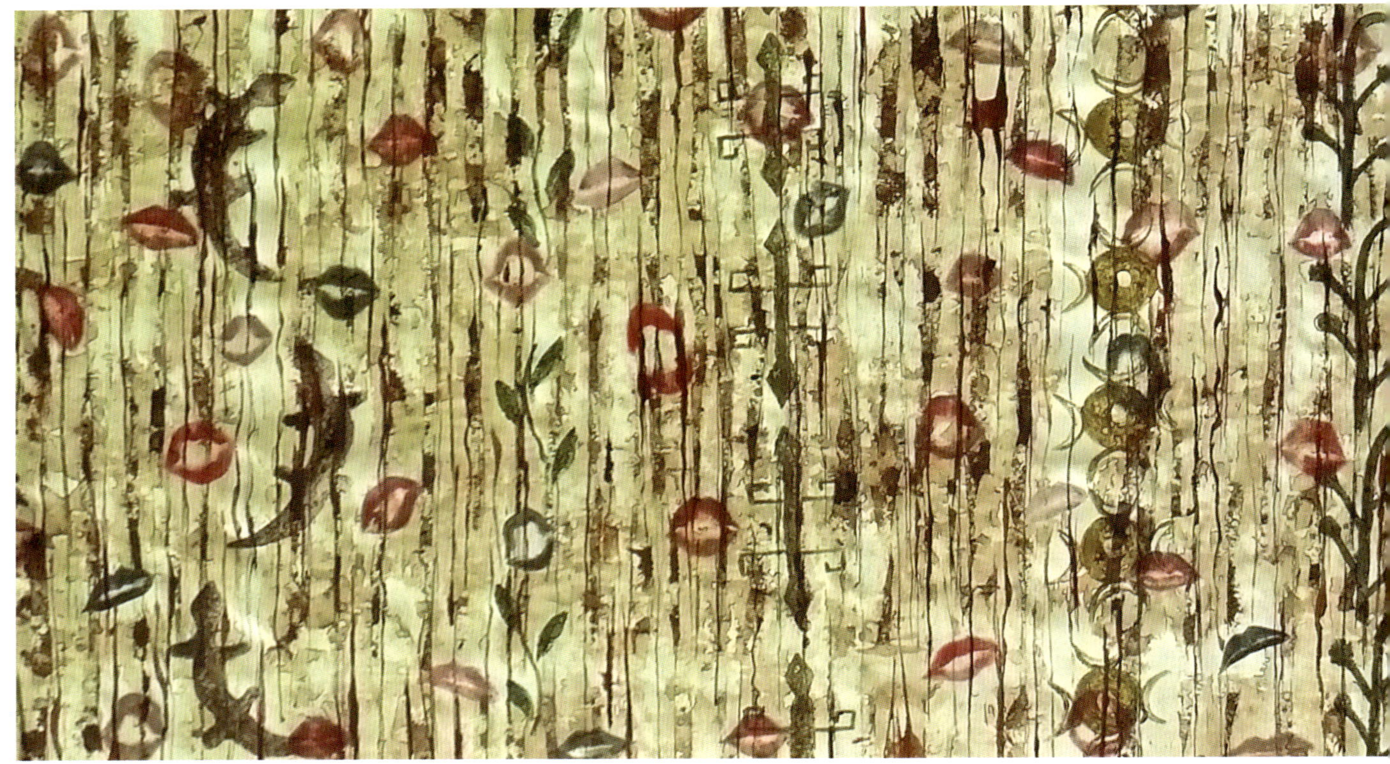

you feel pain, you fall to the ground. Everything is about the ground for me, it keeps us embedded into being Timorese. In sacred ceremonies and folklore, we talk about Mother Earth and our umbilical cord is buried next to the most prominent tree as our oldest eternal connection to Mother Earth. Ermera has such a beautiful red-coloured earth that I just can't ignore it. Everywhere I go I get stained. If it's a very dry, windy day, your face gets all red with mud particles.

I love the red, the blue and the yellow as part of the composition of my work, because for me they bring a lot of beautiful violet purple colours that represent sorrow. You die to grow, to be born again. The women are being sorrowful yet there's hope because we overcame. So the purple really connects very heavily to my work. And then of course, the orange, because it just looks beautiful. I think red earth is red earth. Orange earth is a miracle.

I tend to collect leftover tais, the offcuts from the sewing, like from Timor Aid and from the Alola Foundation. I have a lot of leftover beautiful loose cotton that I can just use as a painting with tweezers while the larger portions, I tend to cut into lips. A cut in a void is a wound. I also burn the edges, and then I stick the tais on the background like burned imagery. It's very effective, like soft pain.

My vision of Dili when I first arrived was the smell of burning, especially all the houses and timber. We had to contend with the stench of burning from the militia rampage. Then, through the smouldering, I saw Dili grow from the ashes. There were a lot of burned houses that were occupied by the UN. We lived under conditions

"In the end, the tears will flow into streams and rivers to create growth."

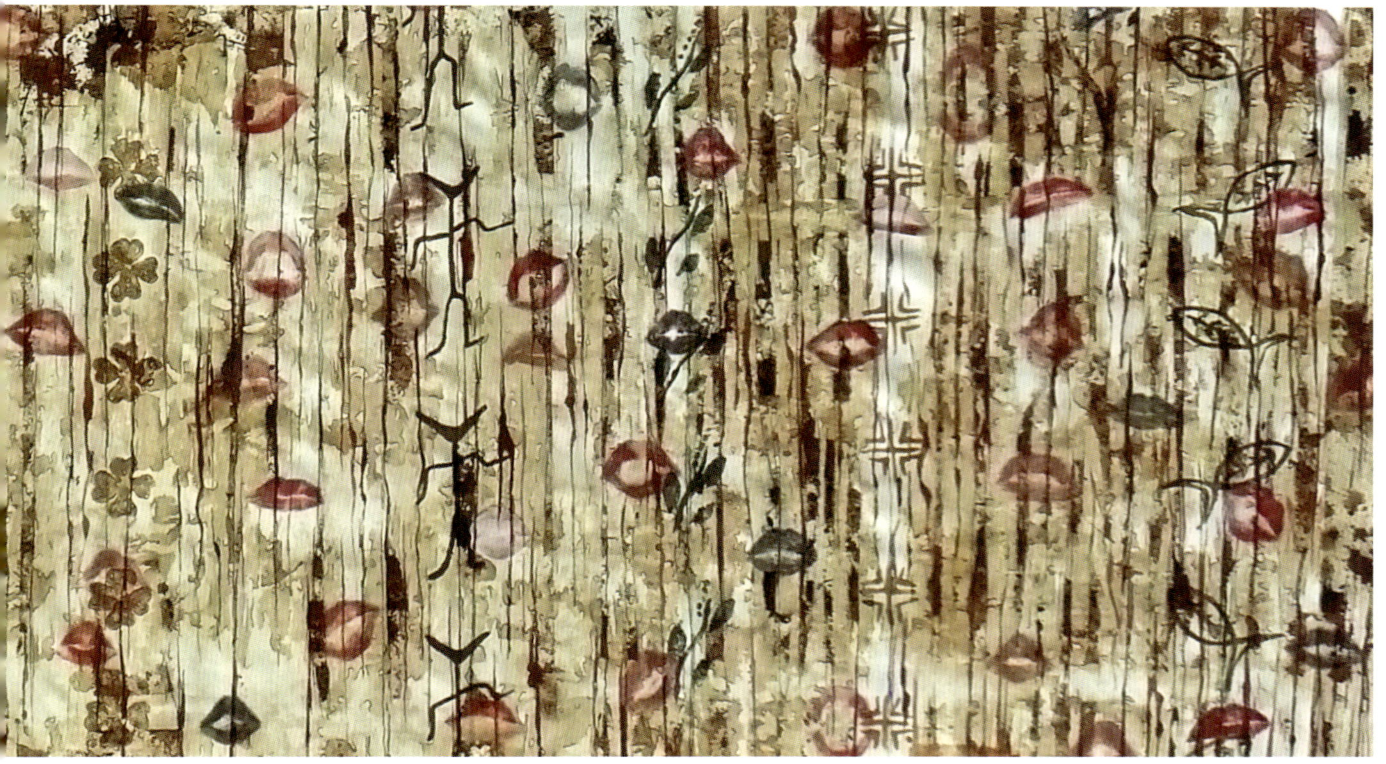

of destruction, predominantly by fire. The next year the flowers grew again, a rebirth from the ashes. I tend to use a lot of those elements that I know will make the story much stronger, so that the work speaks louder if I add the truth. In the end, the tears will flow into streams and rivers to create growth. And that's our strength.

NK: For the Venice Biennale, you will perform during the opening days, singing traditional songs in Tetun as part of your installation with stories of pain, loss and anguish. How is performance a way to complete the exhibition cycle?

MM: Yes, for the Venice Biennale, I will carry out a performance to enhance the story and share the idea and influence behind the installation work *Kiss and Don't Tell*.

This idea relates to my belief in adding voice to the visual. With my artworks, I always want to tell a story. I always want to convey a message. I always hope to evoke some emotional response (whether positive or negative). Because this is my way to communicate more in depth.

I believe the performance will add better understanding to my site-specific installation. It is a story about *Kiss and Don't Tell* that I want to 'kiss' and 'tell'.

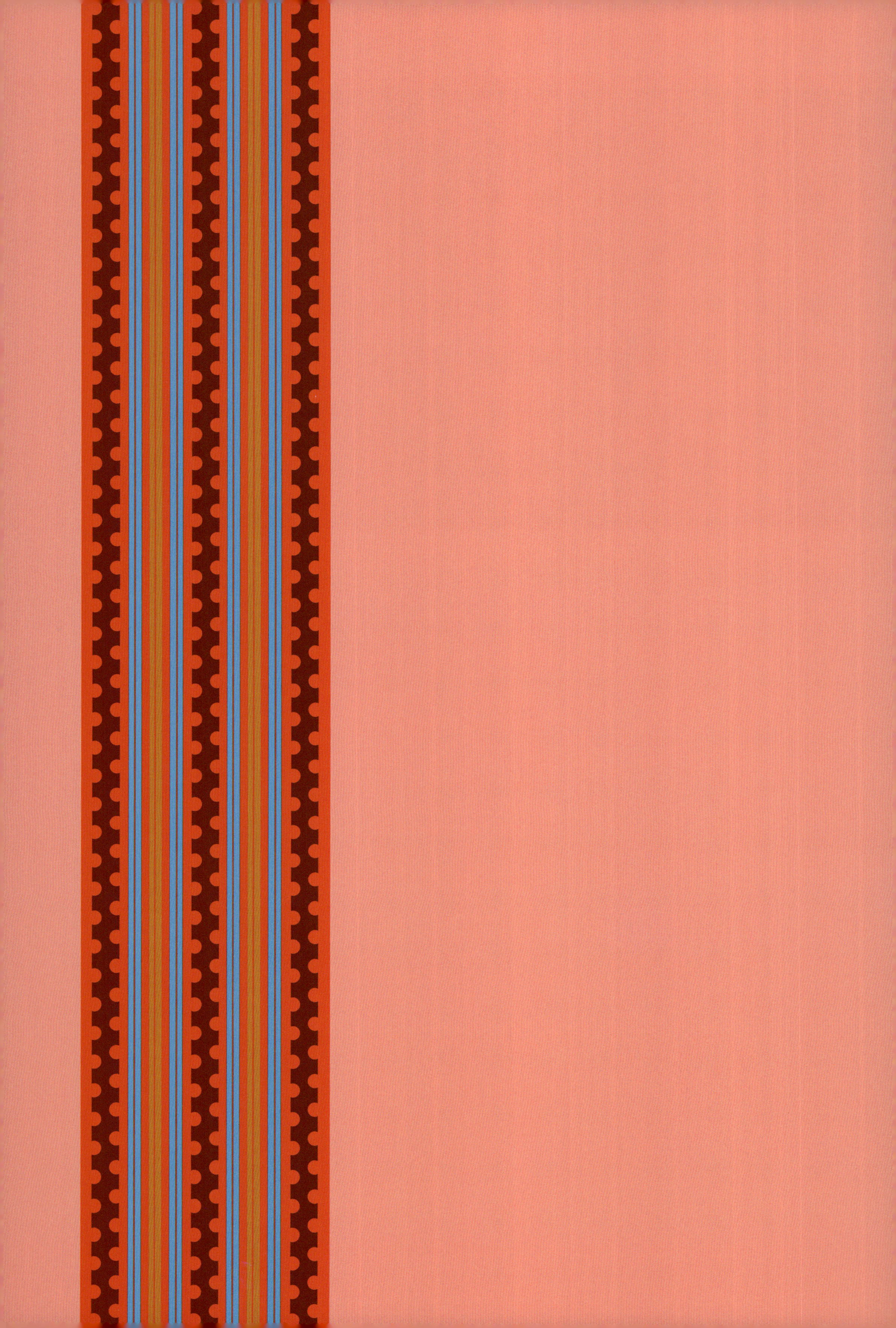

THREADS OF MEMORY

CONFLICT, NATURE AND HEALING

WULAN DIRGANTORO

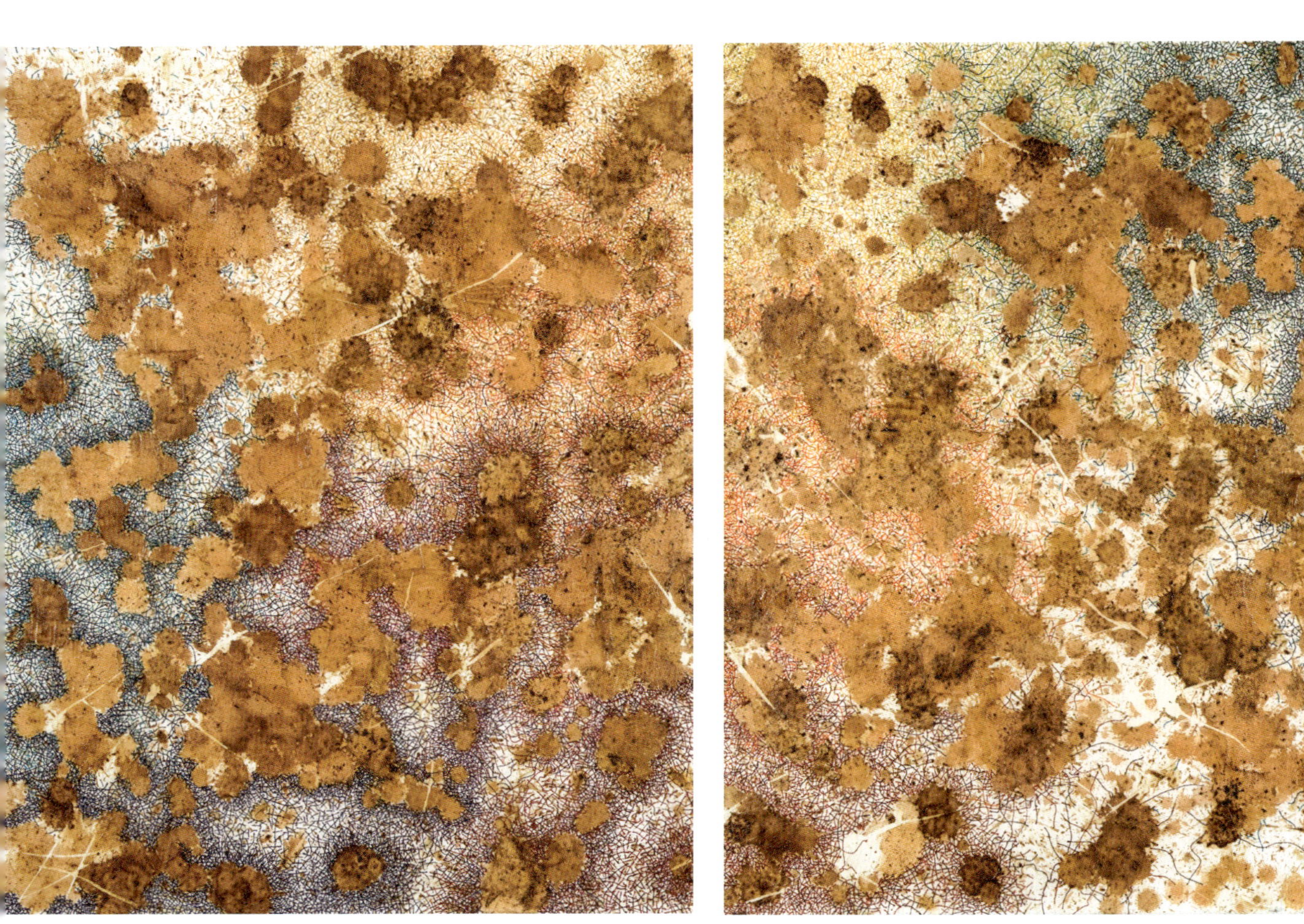

*Renaissance (Moris fila fali), Renascence (Moris foun) and Renascent
(Moris tan)*, 2007

THREADS OF MEMORY:
Conflict, nature and healing[1]

Wulan Dirgantoro

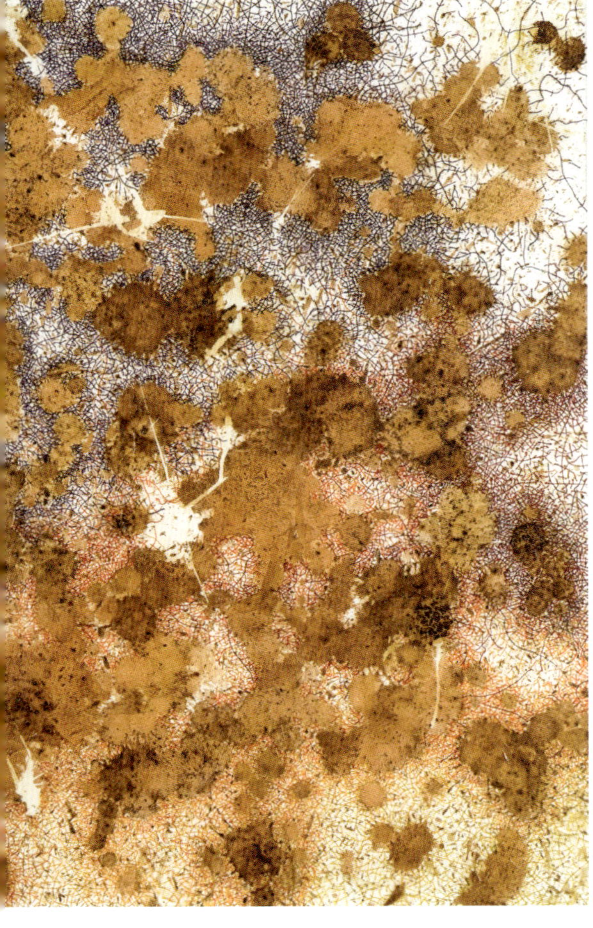

How can communities respond to collective trauma caused by environmental challenges and political, religious or ethnic conflict? Like the bushfires in Australia, disasters created by natural phenomena and human action have caused significant trauma in directly affected communities, particularly Timor-Leste. The intersection of memory and ecology draws from the diversity of imaginary on climate change by human and non-human actors. Memory scholars like Tom Cohen and Sebastian Groes note that the variety of responses in the humanities provides several alternatives for thinking about the future.[2] Firstly, this diversity mimics the changing and evolving nature of imagination that allows creative practitioners to connect us to the past via literary and cultural traditions. Secondly, the emerging responses form a tentative network of relationships between creative practices and nature, whereby the diversity of ideas, connectivity and flexibility, both in form and content, are driven by memory.[3]

This essay discusses memory in relation to human conflict and the role of nature in the work of Maria Madeira, a Timorese artist based in Dili, Timor-Leste and Western Australia. Her artworks highlight how artistic practices operate in and around communities where climate disasters such as extended drought in Timor-Leste have been compounded by the aftermath of political and religious conflict. Her artistic practices show how memory and nature are deeply intertwined to form the basis for community healing.

Timor-Leste experienced traumatic violence during the Indonesian occupation, and in the run-up to and aftermath of the independence referendum in 1999. The works of Maria Madeira highlight how gender shapes the experiences of survivors of conflict by showing how women artists articulate their approach to dealing with difficult past experiences. Madeira plays an important role in witnessing and testifying to the violence through her art practice. Moreover, she draws from nature to reconnect with the land, positive memories and healing processes.

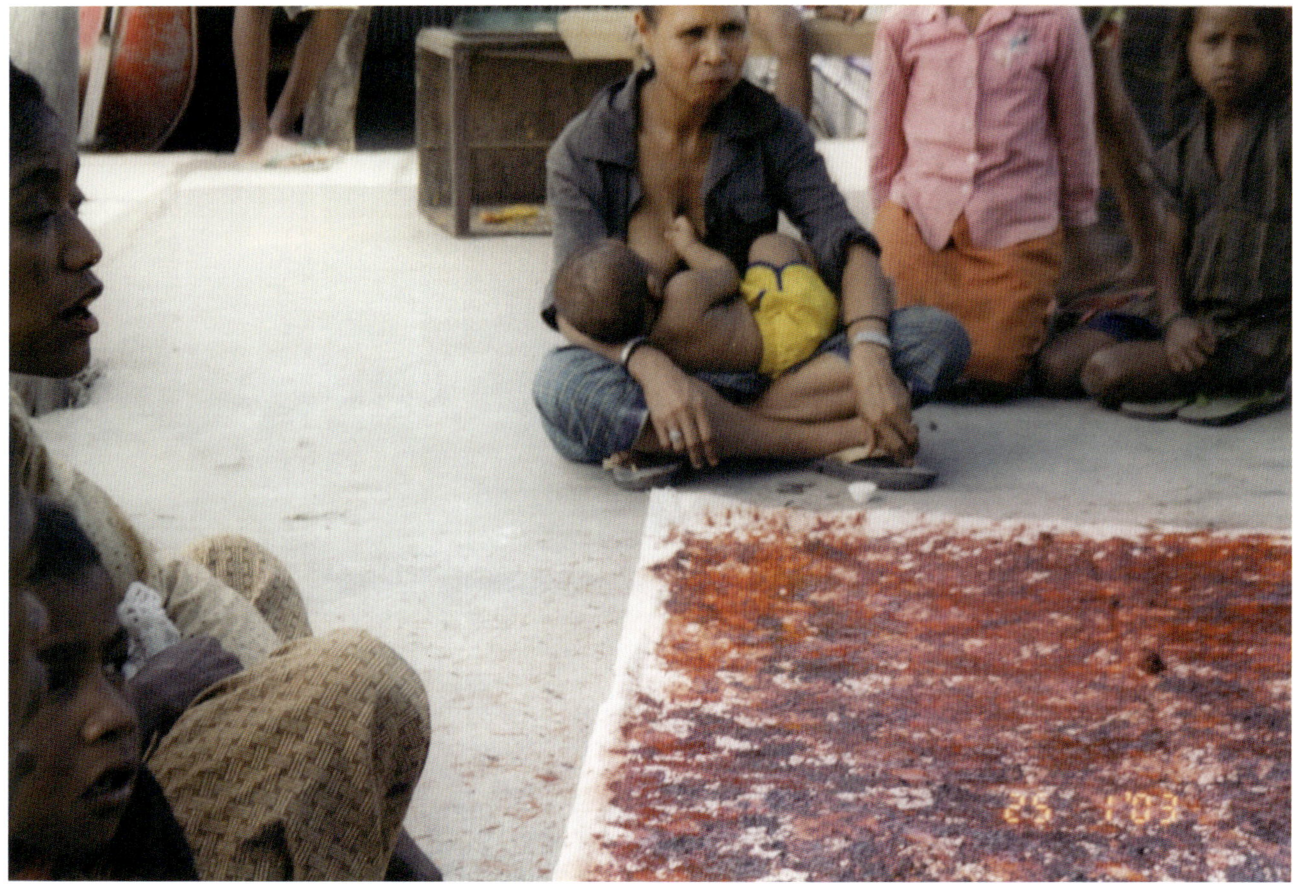

Timor-Leste is a young country that is currently in the process of rebuilding itself after occupations by the Portuguese from the 1600s to 1975, by Japan during a brief interim between 1942 and 1945 and, lastly, by Indonesia from 1975 to 1999. When Timor-Leste gained its independence in 2002, the emerging contemporary artistic practices in the new country and its diaspora reflected stories of resilience and the desire of a people to be free. Maria Madeira was born in the Ermera region of Timor-Leste. In 1976, during the Indonesian invasion, she was evacuated to Portugal, where she spent the next eight years in a refugee camp outside Lisbon. Madeira then migrated to Australia with her family in 1983. She recently completed a doctorate at Curtin University in 2019, and she is currently living in Dili, Timor-Leste and Perth, Western Australia.

Madeira regularly returns to Timor-Leste to maintain connections with her family and the artistic community. In a conversation with the author in January 2020, she recounted the story of her signature betel nut paintings. The first painting that she created from betel nut, *Mama Hamutuk (Chewing Betel Nut Together, Mascar Juntos)* (2003), is a reflection of her search for connection. Madeira stated that the painting is a tribute to her ancestors:

It was achieved through an unrehearsed performance in Gleno (completed in Dili), where up to 14 people chewed

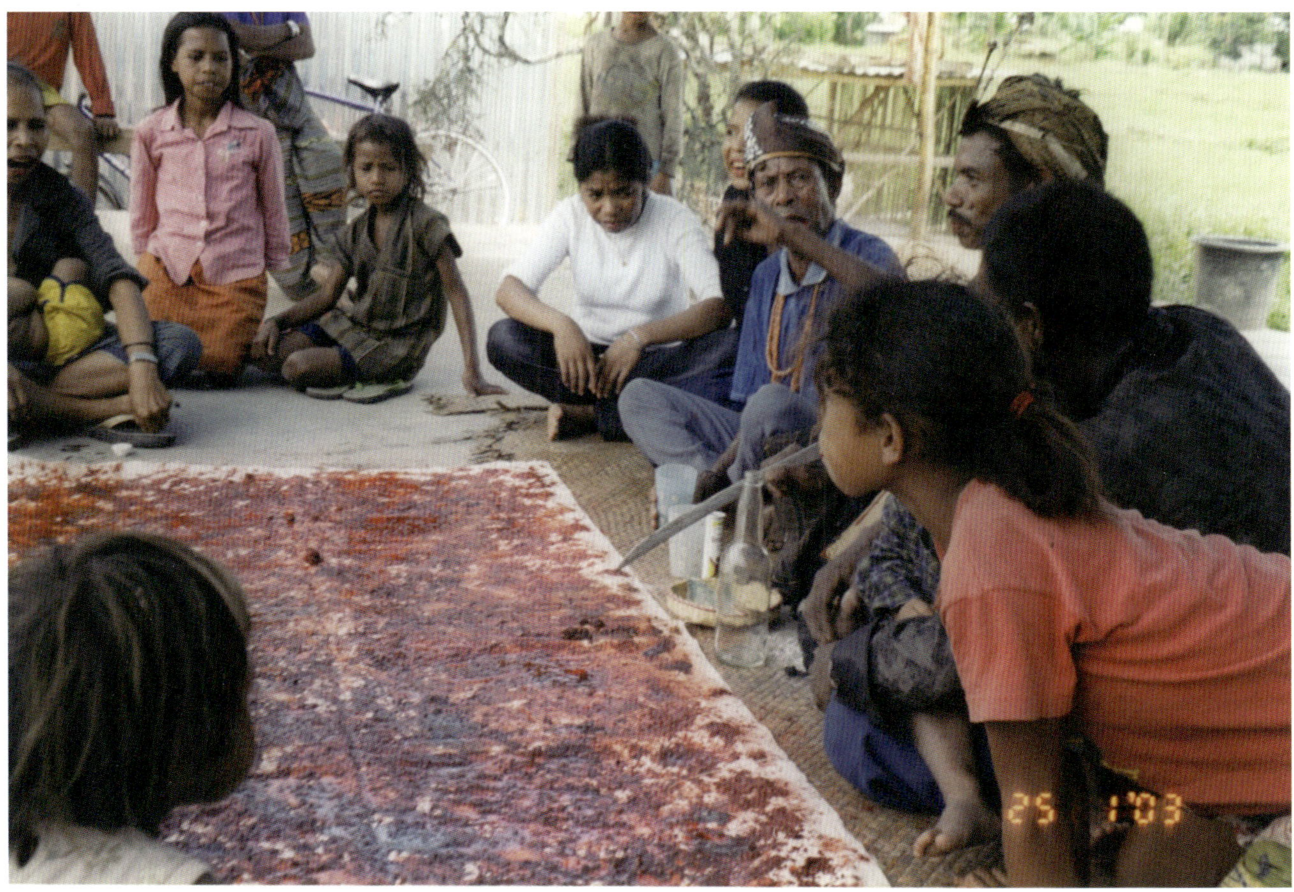

Community participants with *Mama Hamutuk (Chewing Betel Nut Together)*, 25 January 2003

The painting's surface is thickly covered with the betel juice and paste spat out by participants onto the canvas, where the bright red stains of the juice turned a deep shade of brown. The stains blend and bleed into each other, suggesting that they were applied close together in time. The dynamic trajectory of the splatters and drips on the canvas documents the makers' positions and movements around the work. In Timor-Leste it is a common practice for guests to be offered betel quid by the host as a sign of hospitality.[5] For Madeira, partaking in betel nut chewing with the group is an affirmation of her identity as Timorese and her belonging in her community. The painting becomes the artist's personal expression as much as a documentation of community bonding and ritual.

After discovering this new possibility for betel juice, Madeira continues to use it in her paintings while incorporating other media such as tais (traditional woven cloth), synthetic paints and, most recently, red earth. A triptych painted in 2007 entitled *Moris Fila Fali: Renascimento (Renaissance)*, *Moris Foun: Renescença (Renascence)* and *Moris Tan: Renascente (Renascent)* exemplifies the artist's exploration in combining betel nut juice and tais.[6] Tais is a woven cloth made by women for ceremonial use and often given to another as a sign of respect. After Timor-Leste's independence in 2002, tais became a symbol of cultural identity. Madeira has collected tais over the years and has said that her paintings use the cloth with respect, which, in her understanding, means she does not paint over the cloth. Instead of filling the whole space of the triptych with betel paste and juice as she did in *Mama Hamutuk*, in this work Madeira fills the open spaces between dark brown stains of the betel juice with colourful yarns that she has separated from a tais. The yarns are cut in minute pieces and carefully glued onto the surface of the canvas. The resulting image is evocative of an archipelago: a series of dark brown islands surrounded by small radiating lines over sections of red, blue and yellow background.

The titles of the paintings, which centre on the notion of renewal, emphasise the artist's conceptual and political direction; in combining two of the most significant cultural forms, the tais and betel nut, the artist advocates for the important role of art and women in rebuilding Timor-Leste's cultural identity. Furthermore, Madeira also situates her practice within a deep sense of connection to the identity of the land and its people.

Importantly, the dark earth colour from the betel juice evokes the red soil and the rugged landscape around Madeira's hometown in Ermera. The name Ermera derives from the Mambai language and means 'red water'. Madeira recounts that the waterways, lakes and rivers turn a reddish hue caused by the rain and soil erosion during the wet season.[7] Also, as with other parts of Timor-Leste, much of Ermera's landscape has been shaped by human actions, not only the traditional swidden agriculture practices, but also 400 years of Portuguese occupation and 25 years of Indonesian rule. Napalm bombing and forced resettlement practices during the Indonesian occupation heightened the destruction of the environment and have been attributed as the cause of widespread famine in Timor-Leste.[8] The structural damage, human casualties and trauma during times of occupation is the reason that many visual artists foreground tradition and its renewal in their practices, even though in post-independence Timor-Leste the loss of connection between Timorese people and their land is gradually healing.[9]

Madeira's betel nut paintings could be seen as an attempt to reconnect with the damaged and altered landscape through restorative practices. In these paintings, the artist seems to be focusing on how art-making can be a positive social force in responding to the collective challenge of rebuilding lives in Timor-Leste. Madeira suggests that women are often perceived to have little voice, and for this reason she speaks strongly and 'thunderously' through her art ('*No, iha hau nia silensio ne'ebe imi haree, hau nia lian ne'ebe neneik deit,*

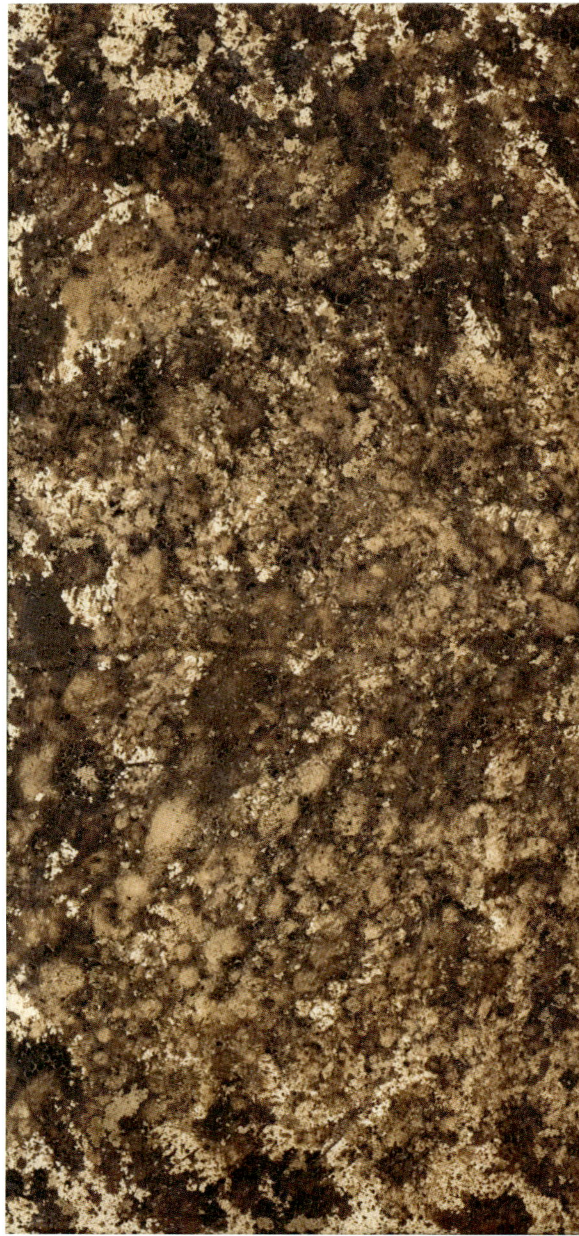

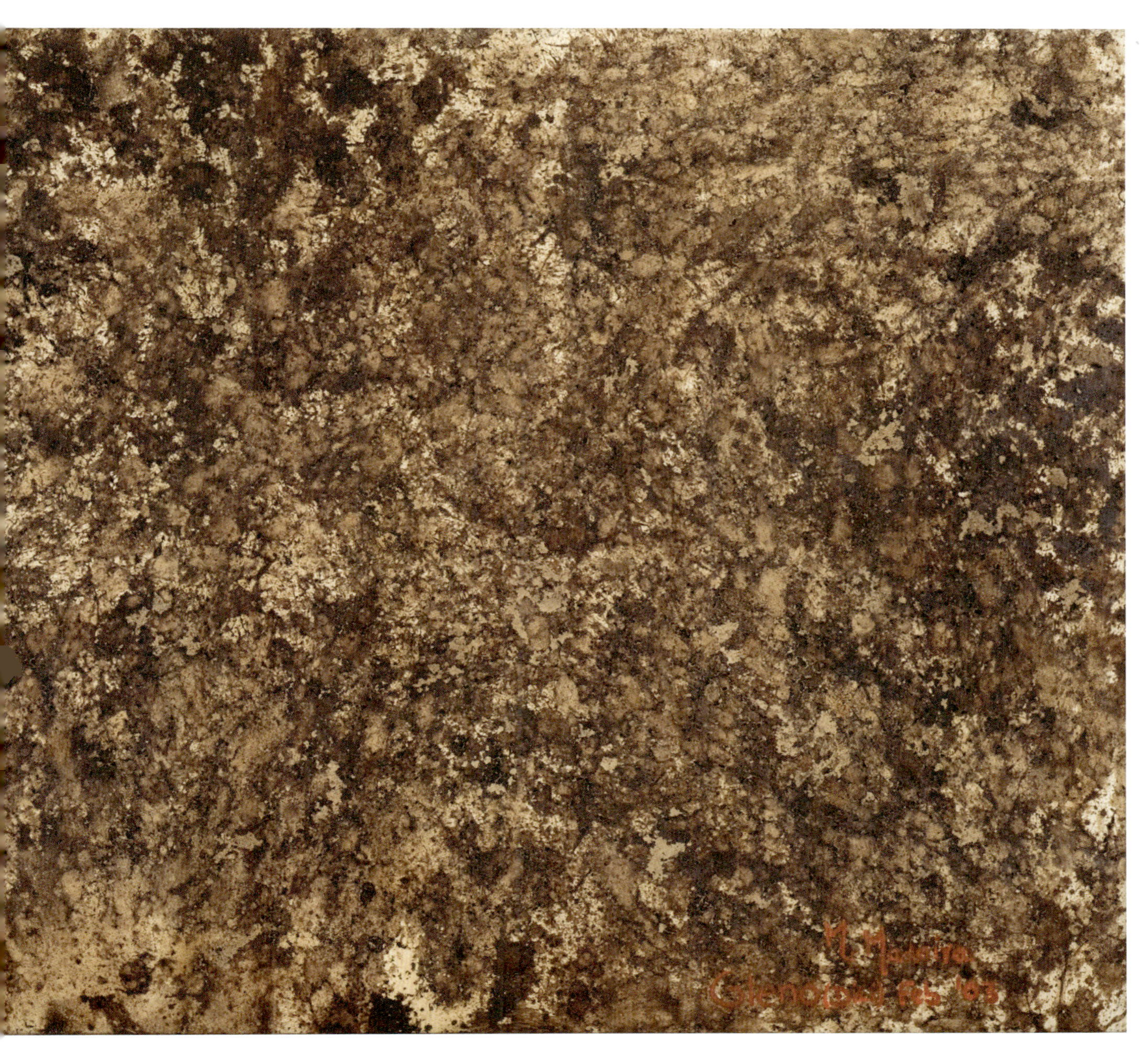

Mama Hamutuk (Chewing Betel Nut Together), 2003

dala barak hanesan rai lakan').[10] Madeira is drawn to giving voice to those who have been neglected or occluded, particularly women and their stories. As such, her paintings of the evocative landscape seem to function in two ways.

On the one hand, the dark brown stains can be understood as representing the dry and parched land, a symbol for the long drought caused by human activities in Timor-Leste and of blood spilled over decades of violence. On the other, the evocative quality created by the betel juice and the tais pattern conjures a dynamic presence and a feeling of place. Madeira's paintings can be understood as an attempt to visualise her memory of the land in Timor-Leste, as shaped by women's stories and the movement of its people.

Madeira's practice exemplifies art's potential to signify gender differently and materialise female subjectivity.[11] As women artists are finding their voices and strengthening their networks, they are also reminding us that the political is inextricably tied with the personal. Some artists actively use their art practice to reflect socio-political issues and effect changes within their community. In doing so, they focus on the collective spirit and art communities outside the dominant urban art centres.[12]

Despite the ongoing conflict and challenges in her home country, Maria Madeira chooses to present alternatives to the violence and the resultant losses caused by political conflicts. Her use of natural materials, from earth to betel nut juice, demonstrates that memory of the land is embedded with the politics of hope; memory is directed to the future, while acknowledging the dark past and the reality of the present time.

Indeed, the experience of loss is expressed through aesthetic strategies that highlight women's resilience, acknowledging that it is women who often suffer the most in spaces of conflict. We may then read the references to nature and beauty in Maria Madeira's artworks as offering reparative potential – as visual texts they may be empowering and regenerative, encouraging personal healing and affecting social change. That is, artistic forms can be employed to deal with politically sensitive and difficult issues that affect communities.

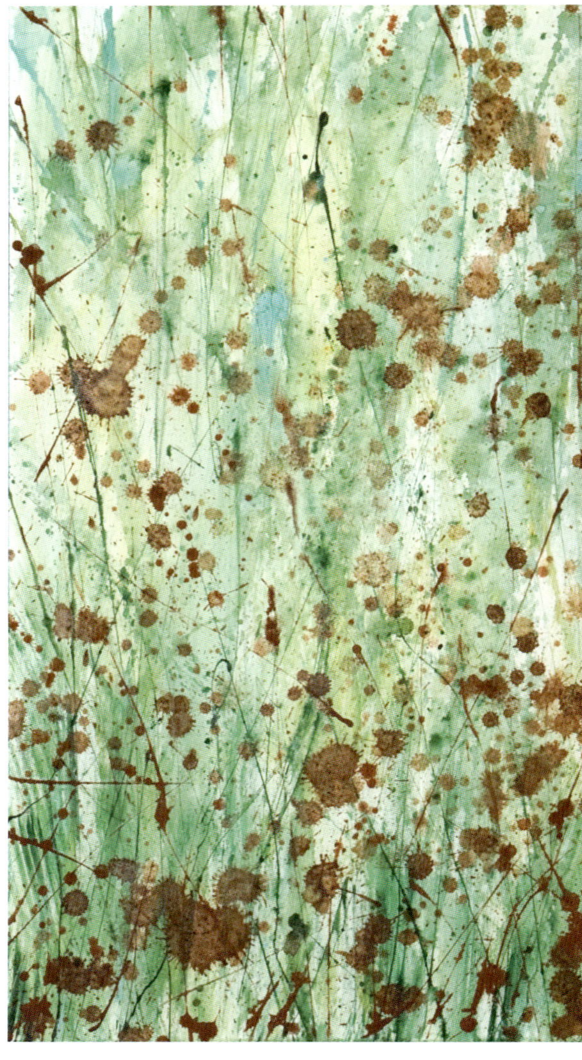

Tebe Hare/Sama Hare/Stepping on Rice Husks, 2008

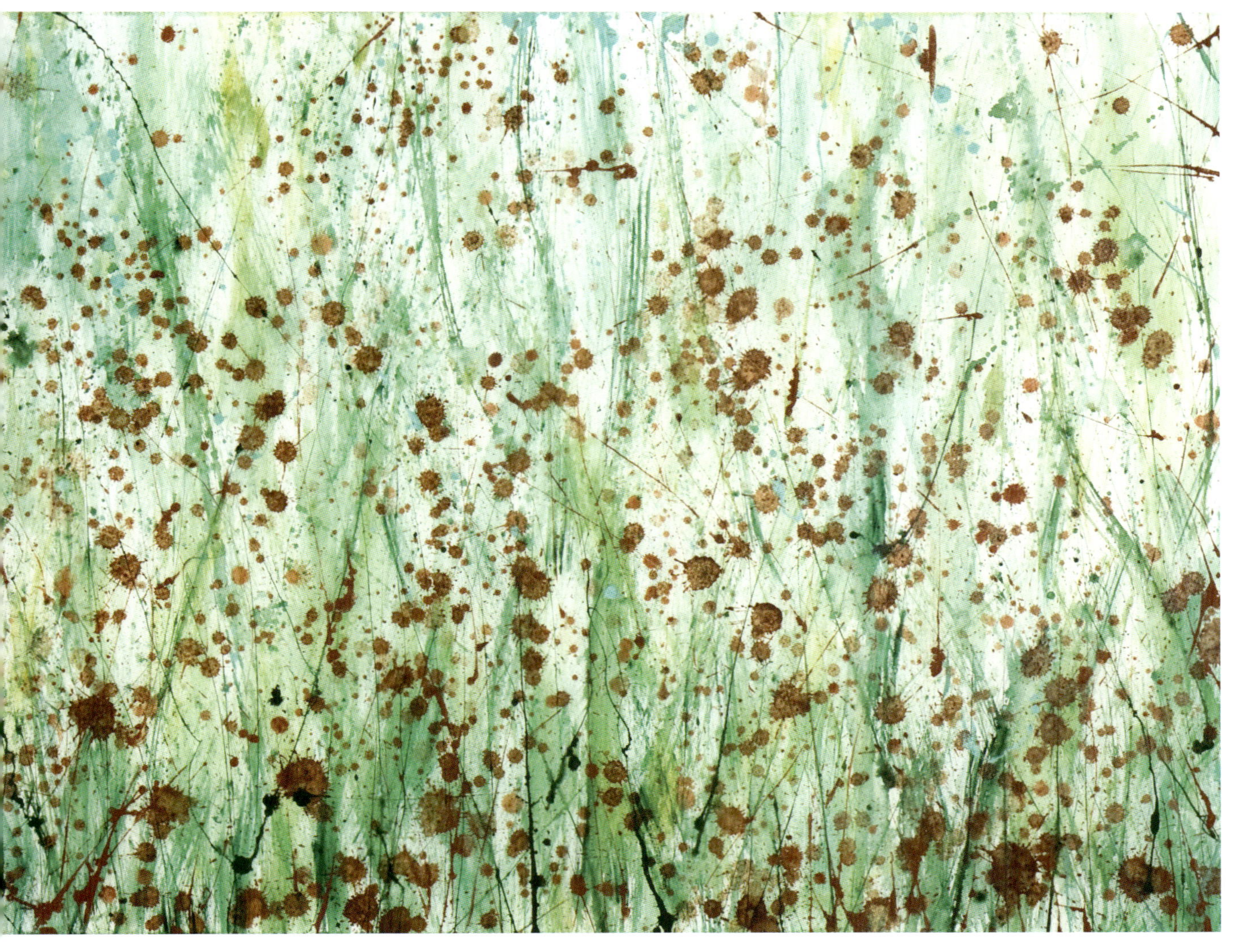

NOTES

1. This essay is adapted from 'Like Planting Flowers in a War Zone: Memory, Conflict and Healing in Contemporary Southeast Asian Art', in *Afterstorm*, Charles Green and Jon Cattapan (eds), Art+Australia and Victorian College of The Arts Publishing, the University of Melbourne, 2014, pp. 195-207.

2. Tom Cohen, *Telemorphosis: Theory in the Era of Climate Change*, Open Humanities Press, Ann Arbor, 2012; Sebastian Groes (ed), *Memory in the Twenty-First Century: New Perspectives from the Arts Humanities and Science*, Palgrave Macmillan, Hampshire, NY, 2016, pp. 175-87.

3. Sebastian Groes, 'Memory in the Twenty-First Century: New Critical Perspectives from the Arts, Humanities, and Sciences', Palgrave Macmillan, 1st ed 2016, pp. 175-87.

4. Maria Madeira, *Maria Madeira Timorese Visual Artist*, <http://mariamadeira.blogspot.com/2007/11/my-artworks-under-construction.html>.

5. Betel quid is a small parcel that typically contains slices of areca nut wrapped in a betel leaf and coated with lime powder. When the small parcel is chewed, the juice will react to saliva, which will turn into a bright red colour. The liquid is not swallowed and is usually spat into a container or on the ground. Chewing betel quid has cultural and social significance throughout Southeast Asia and New Guinea. See Anthony Reid, 'From Betel-Chewing to Tobacco Smoking in Indonesia', *The Journal of Asian Studies*, vol. 44, no. 3, 1995, pp. 529-47; and Dawn Rooney, *Betel Chewing Traditions in South-East Asia*, Oxford University Press, Kuala Lumpur, 1993.

6. See reproduction in Maria Madeira, *Koalia Neneik Deit (Quietly Speaking)*, exhibition catalogue, Casa Europa, 2010, p. 7, <https://issuu.com/incidentaldoc/docs/issuu_maria1>.

7. Maria Madeira, email to the author, 25 September 2020.

8. Sandra Pannell, 'Struggling Geographies: Rethinking Livelihood and Locality in Timor-Leste', in Andrew McWilliam and Elizabeth G. Traube (eds) *Land and Life in East Timor: Ethnographic Essays*, ANU Press, Canberra, 2011, pp. 217-39.

9. Leonor Veiga, 'Movimentu Kultura in East Timor: Maria Madeira's Agency', *Cadernos de Arte e Antropologia*, vol. 4, no. 1, 2011, pp. 85-101.

10. Maria Madeira, 'Artist Statement', in *Koalia Neneik Deit/ Falar Baixanho/Quietly Speaking*, exhibition catalogue, Casa Europa, Dili, State Secretariat of Culture and National Directorate of Culture, Timor-Leste, October 2010, np.

11. Elizabeth A Grosz, *Space, Time and Perversion: The Politics of the Body*, Allen & Unwin, St Leonards, NSW, 1995. See also Imelda Cajipe Endaya, 'Examining Our Roles as Women and as Artists', in 'Identity, Tradition and Change: Contemporary Art of the Asian Pacific Region, The First Asia-Pacific Triennial of Contemporary Art, Brisbane, Australia, 1993', unpublished conference papers & list of attendees, Queensland Art Gallery, South Brisbane, 1993.

12. Jasmine Nadua Trice, 'Gendering National Histories and Regional Imaginaries: Three Southeast Asian Women Filmmakers', *Feminist Media Histories*, vol. 5, no. 1, 2019, pp. 11-38. See also Edwin Jurriëns 'Intertwined Ecologies: Environmental Aesthetics in Indonesian Contemporary Art', *Third Text*, vol. 33, no. 1, 2019, pp. 59-77.

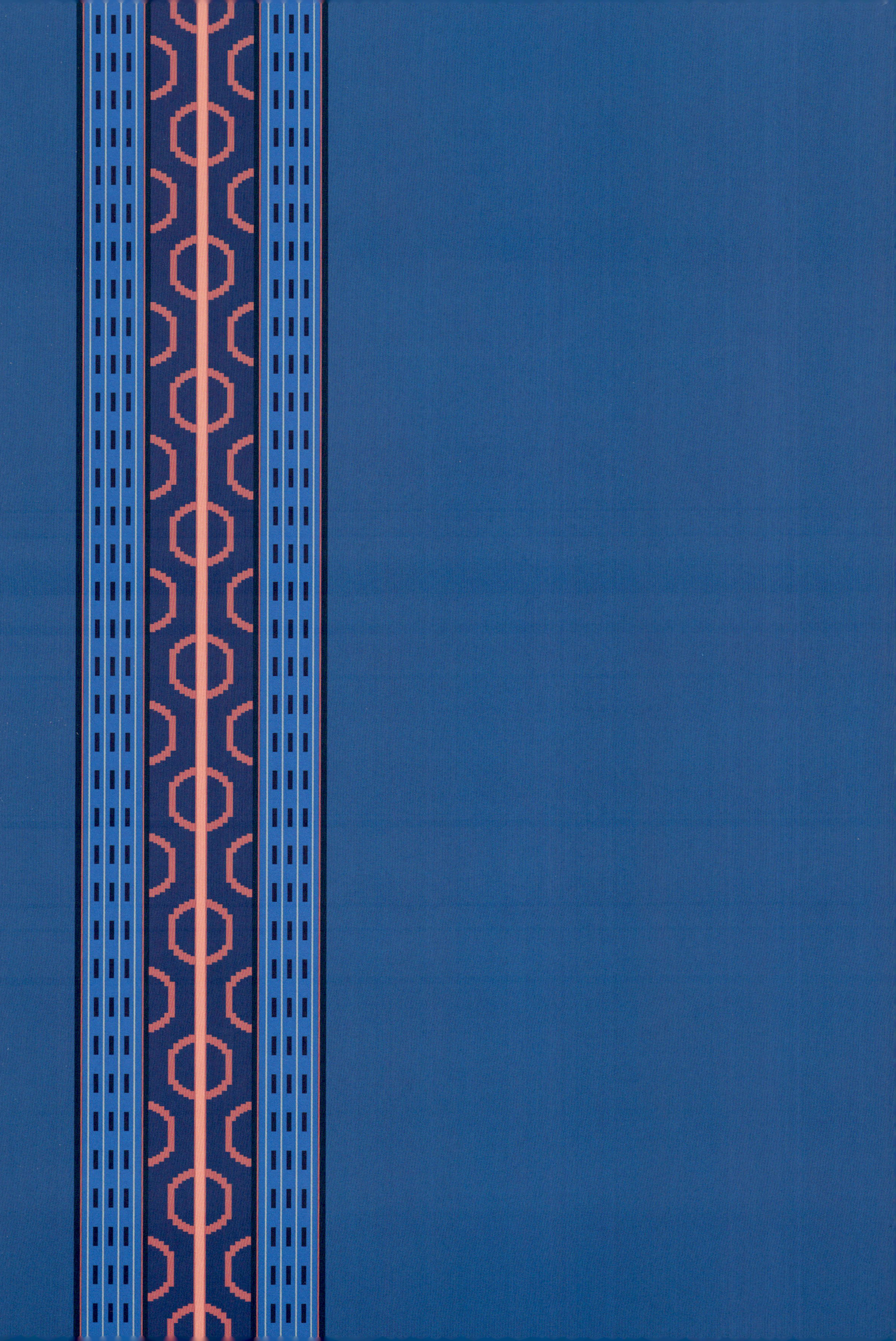

WHO CAN ERASE THE TRACES?

HISTORICAL JUSTICE AND WOMEN'S EMPOWERMENT

CRISTINA BALDACCI

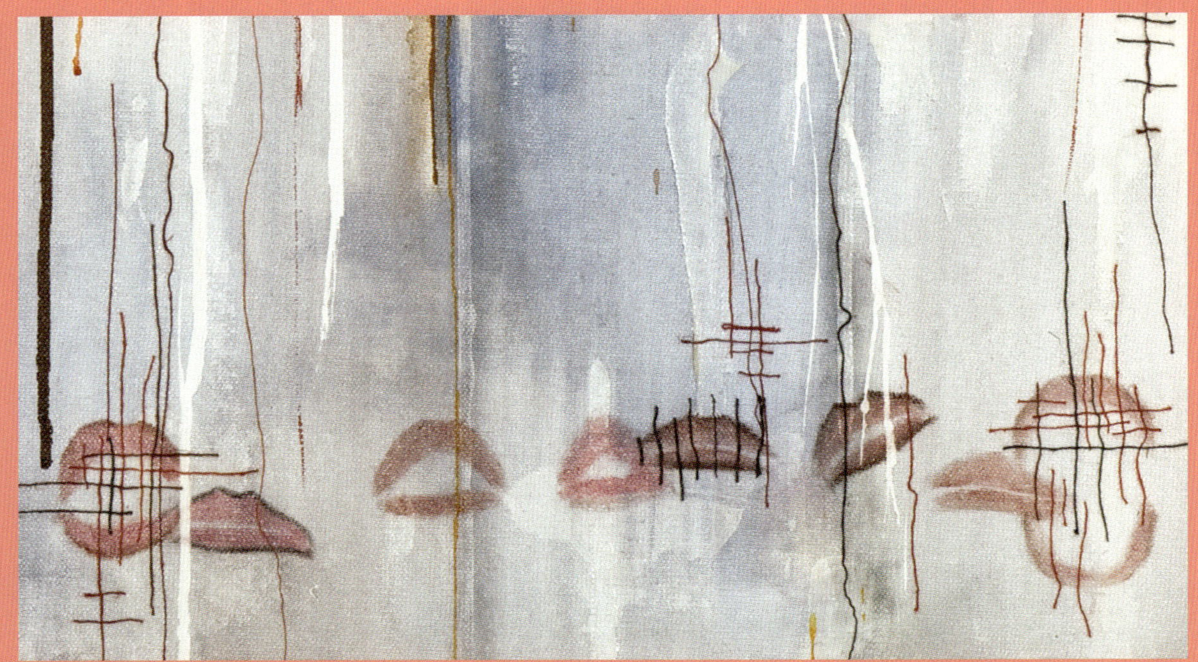

Kiss & Don't Tell II, (a study) (detail), 2007

WHO CAN ERASE THE TRACES?
Historical justice and women's empowerment

Cristina Baldacci

On the morning of 3 July 2003, Regina José Galindo walked barefoot in Guatemala City from the Constitutional Court to the National Palace, leaving behind her bloody footprints which marked the ground both as a symptom of the past and a warning for the future. In doing so, she performed at once an act of political critique (against the presidential candidacy of Efraín Ríos Motti, under whose previous dictatorship civilians experienced brutal violence and the Maya indigenous community was massacred), of memory rewriting and of women's emancipation in a still highly conservative country.

This radical performance was indeed an act of defiance in which the Guatemalan artist asked publicly through her title – 'Quién puede borrar las huellas?' (*Who can erase the traces?*), when the stigmas from the past are made manifest in the present. Galindo's main effort was in trying to exorcise the risk of history repeating itself by giving voice to those whose bodies, souls, identities and rights were violated. She produced a vivid image that left an indelible mark – not so much on the ground, where the human blood in which she dipped her feet was bound to vanish, but on the viewers' consciousness.

Maria Madeira performs a similar political and feminist gesture by imprinting her red lips on the walls of the first Timor-Leste pavilion at the Biennale Arte 2024. She leaves lipstick kiss traces instead of bloody footprints to refer to another act of criminal violence that occurred in her country during the Indonesian occupation (1975-1999). While being abused by the foreign army, Timorese women were forced to kiss the walls of their torture rooms. In an attempt towards mourning and reconciliation, the exiled artist, who left her native country as a child to survive the occupation, revives the silenced voices of her ancestral sisters in the pavilion by performing ritual songs. The installation in Venice also includes other Indigenous materials, such as traditional cloths, betel nut, earth and pigments, that intertwine gender, race and environmental matters into her art practice. The result is a special (hi)story-telling that goes 'beyond a love of change and always with traditions in mind'.[1]

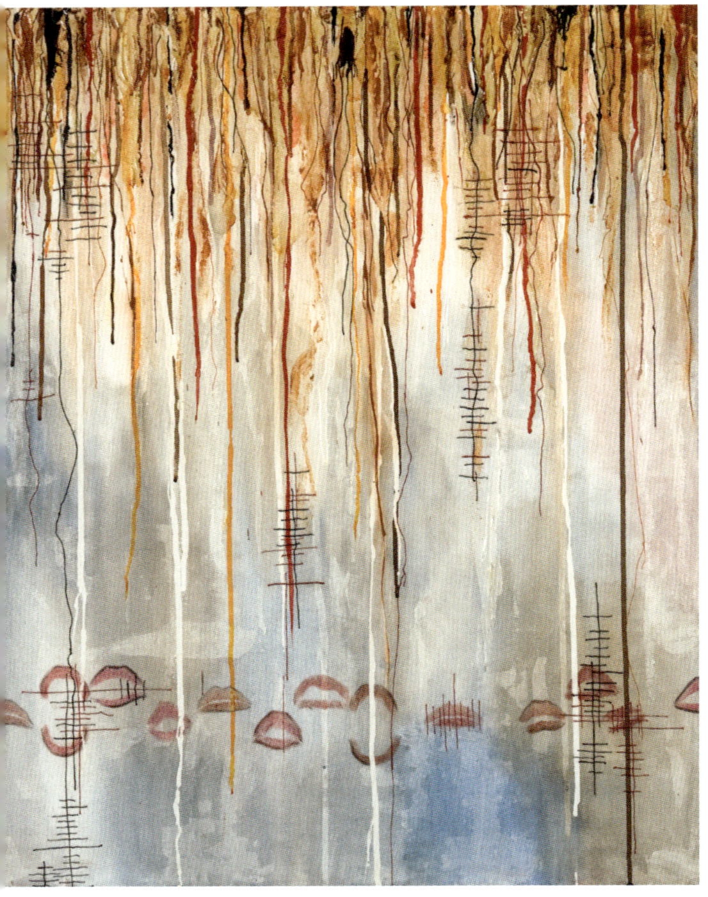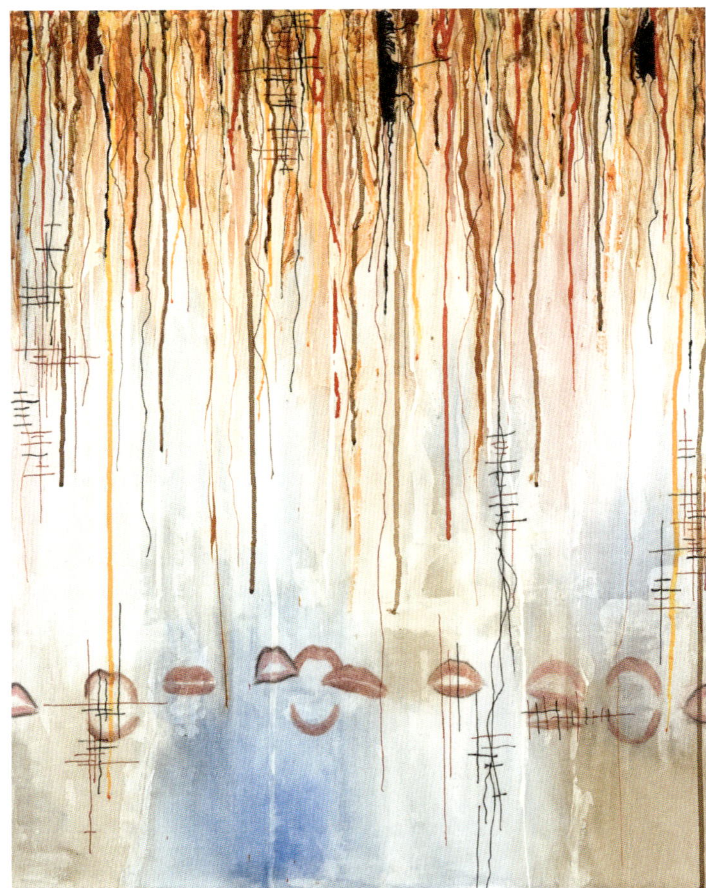

Kiss & Don't Tell II, (a study), 2007

With this performative installation that demands historical justice and women's empowerment, Madeira re-enacts a previous artwork of hers by the same title, *Kiss and Don't Tell* (2007). It is a triptych stemming from an assemblage of different materials on canvas: acrylic, gesso, impasto, gel, glue, lipstick and tais, the traditional East Timorese textile that she often uses in her work. She also remediates the piece from one medium (painting) to another (site-specific installation), relating multiple temporalities, idioms and traditions.[2] Moreover, the visual friction and uncanny feeling that Madeira generates by connecting kisses both to trauma and to intimacy refers to (Western) feminist art by reactivating and updating it to Timorese traditions as 'a voice of resistance in exile'.[3] Madeira received an education in Australia and only returned sporadically to her country after independence (2000) for teaching and periods of community work, intended to promote women's art education and practice in particular.

Madeira shares the feminist urge to confront women's sexual objectification – a pervasive circumstance across cultures – with female agency to engender change within the established order. Thinking for example of the kiss as an image to perform feminism, many comparisons could be made between Madeira's and other women artists' works.[4] From the most literal ones, such as the kisses imprinted with lipstick on paper or wall by Joyce Wieland (*O Canada*, 1970) and Chiyoko

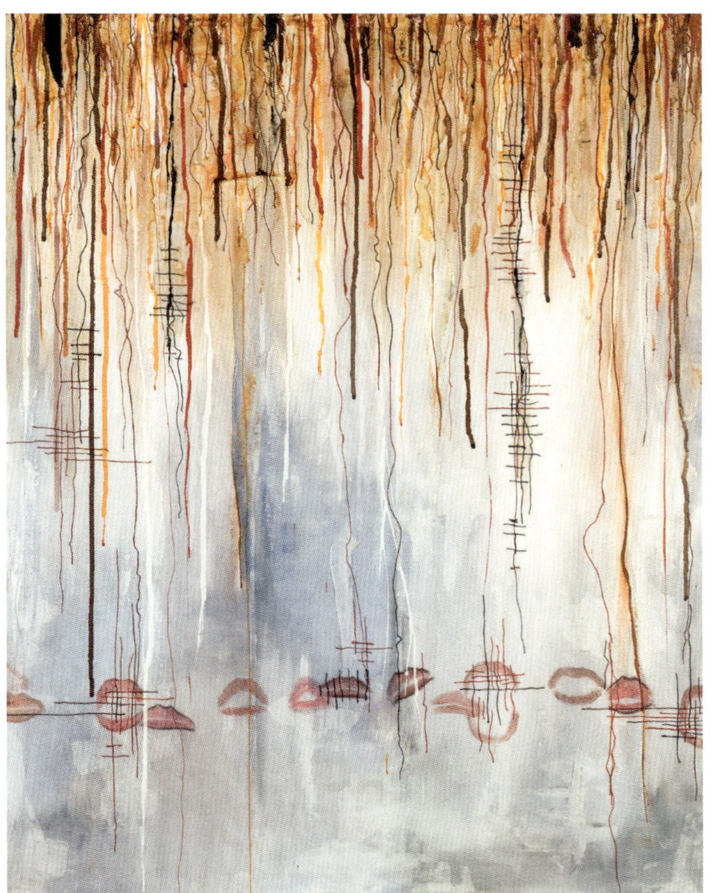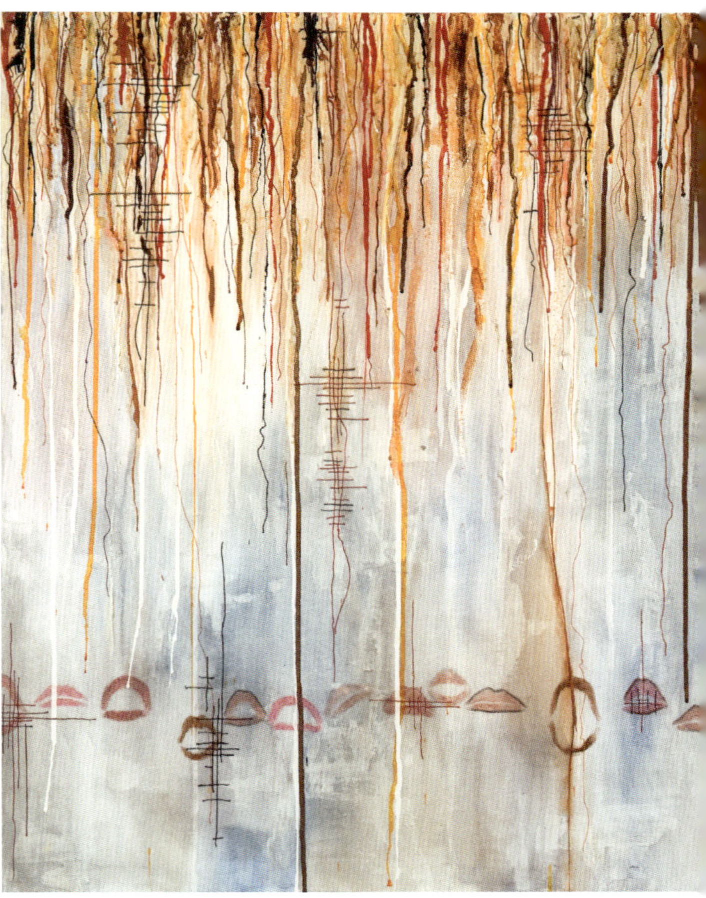

Miura (*Idea non c'è*, 1992) – who respectively question issues of national identity and the role of being a non-Western woman artist in a country of acquisition – to Orlan's famous 1977 subversive action against gender stereotypes and the patriarchal society (*Le baiser de l'artiste*).

By giving voice to the past and present female community of Timor-Leste, with *Kiss and Don't Tell* – and more generally with all of her work – Maria Madeira contributes to ensuring both the survival and vitalism of the culture of her birth country, encouraging the emancipation of women through (art) education. It is no coincidence that she is one of the most committed activists of the Movimentu Kultura, which, starting from independence, marked the rebirth of Timorese art.[5] She also situates herself in the art-historical discourse with great awareness and care, from the distinctive position – as an artist in exile – of a 'foreigner'. This is a privileged perspective, because it allows a double gaze, from the outside and from the inside, with one eye turned to contemporaneity and one to tradition, a necessary condition for 'looking back to the future'.[6]

NOTES

1. Maria Madeira, 'Women's Contribution to Timor-Leste's Art and Culture', in *Southeast of Now: Directions in Contemporary and Modern Art in Asia*, vol. 6, no. 2, October 2022, p. 123.

2. In terms of cultural mirroring and amalgamation, it is interesting to note, in this context, how fabrics and colouring techniques, such as tais for Timor-Leste or batik for Africa, that were chosen as symbols of the local tradition, and are mainly women-made, are both of Indonesian origins.

3. Leonor Veiga, 'Movimentu Kultura in Timor-Leste: Maria Madeira's "agency"', in *Cadernos de Arte e Antropologia*, vol. 4, no. 1, 2015, p. 85.

4. Javier Arakistan (ed), *Kiss Kiss, Bang Bang: Arte Eta Feminismoaren 45 Urte/45 años de arte y feminism/45 Years of Art and Feminism*, Museo Bellas Artes De Bilbao, Bilbao, 2007.

5. Leonor Veiga, "Movimentu Kultura: Making Timor-Leste", in *The Routledge Handbook of Contemporary Timor Leste*, Routledge, New York, 2019, pp. 256–70.

6. Griselda Pollock, *Looking Back to the Future: Essays on Art Life and Death*, Routledge, London and New York, 2014 [first published in 2001].

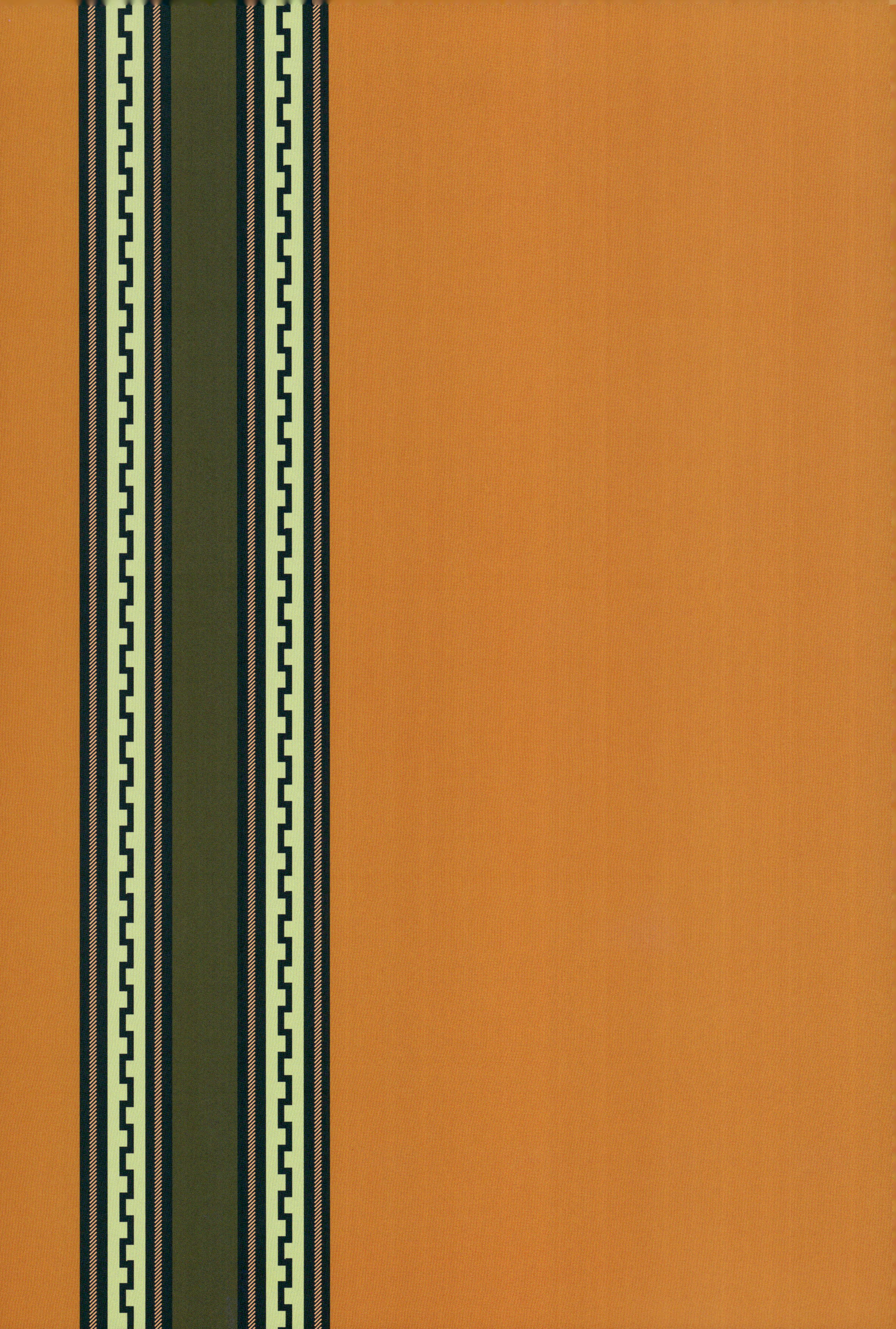

HASORU MALU

MEETING, WEAVING AND CONNECTING

JOANA SARAIVA

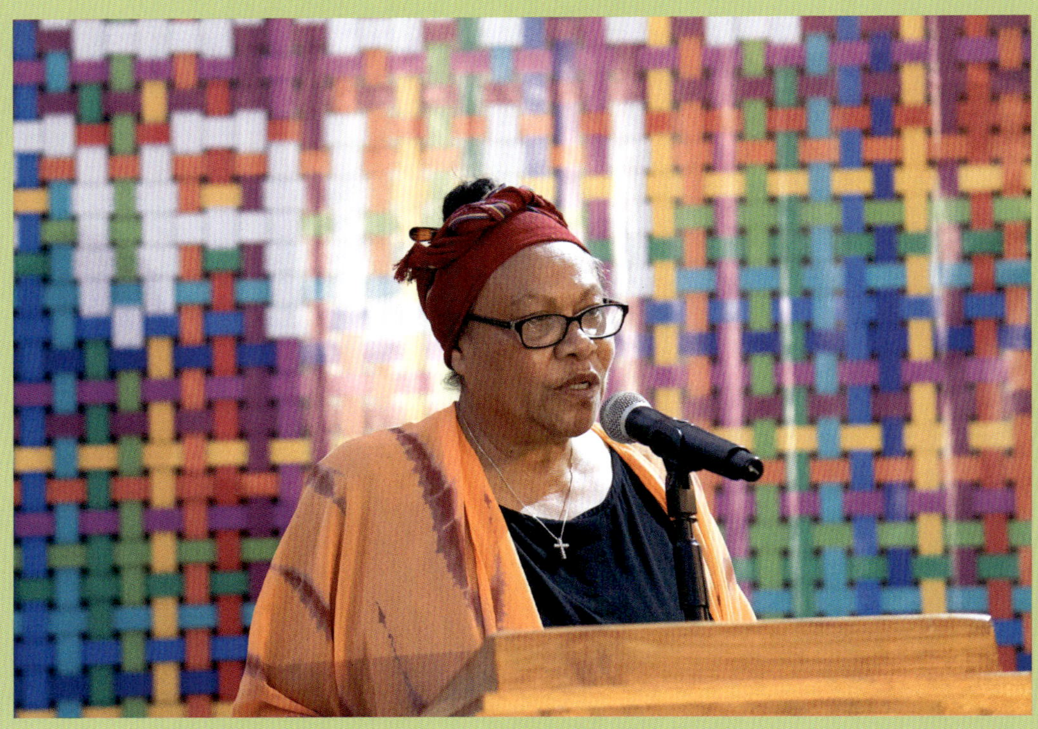

Maria Madeira giving an opening speech at *Hasoru Malu*,
September 2023

HASORU MALU:
Meeting, weaving and connecting

Joana Saraiva

In the national language Tetun, *hasoru malu* means to meet, while *soru* is 'to weave' and *soru-malu* means 'to connect' or 'interlace'. The associative range of *Hasoru Malu* was the impetus for a contemporary art enhancement programme developed by Fundação Oriente in Timor-Leste. The multifacted project was initiated as a collective exhibition to celebrate the twentieth anniversary of Timor-Leste's Restoration of Independence in 2022, highlighting artists' views on society, culture, identity; past, present and future. Beyond promoting and nurturing individual artistic expression, the aim was to bring the role of the arts – and artists – to the forefront of contemporary Timorese collective identity, with the immeasurable, cross-sectoral effect of culture on individuals, communities and societies.

From this initial impetus, *Hasoru Malu* has become a creative movement, constantly active, bringing together over 200 artists and other creative professionals. Maria Madeira was pivotal in this process since its inception. She was an early supporter of the exhibition project, which was under her curatorship, as well as a key participant in the talks that engendered an ongoing action-based programme for advancing Timor-Leste's contemporary arts ecology, by addressing broader issues. To these, she contributed her unique knowledge from her nearly three-decade experience as a visual artist, curator, teacher and arts mentor.

To the participating artists, some of whom were also involved in the programme coordination, such as Alfeo Sanches Pereira (Alfe RM), Etson Caminha, Simão Cardoso Pereira (Mong) and Tony Amaral, this has been an opportunity to come together and (re)unite in a joint effort to contribute to the development of the creative industry in their country. In a context where there are virtually no art schools or galleries, *Hasoru Malu* facilitates, supports and produces a multitude of contemporary arts events with the overarching ambition to build a dynamic and lively cultural scene in Timor-Leste.

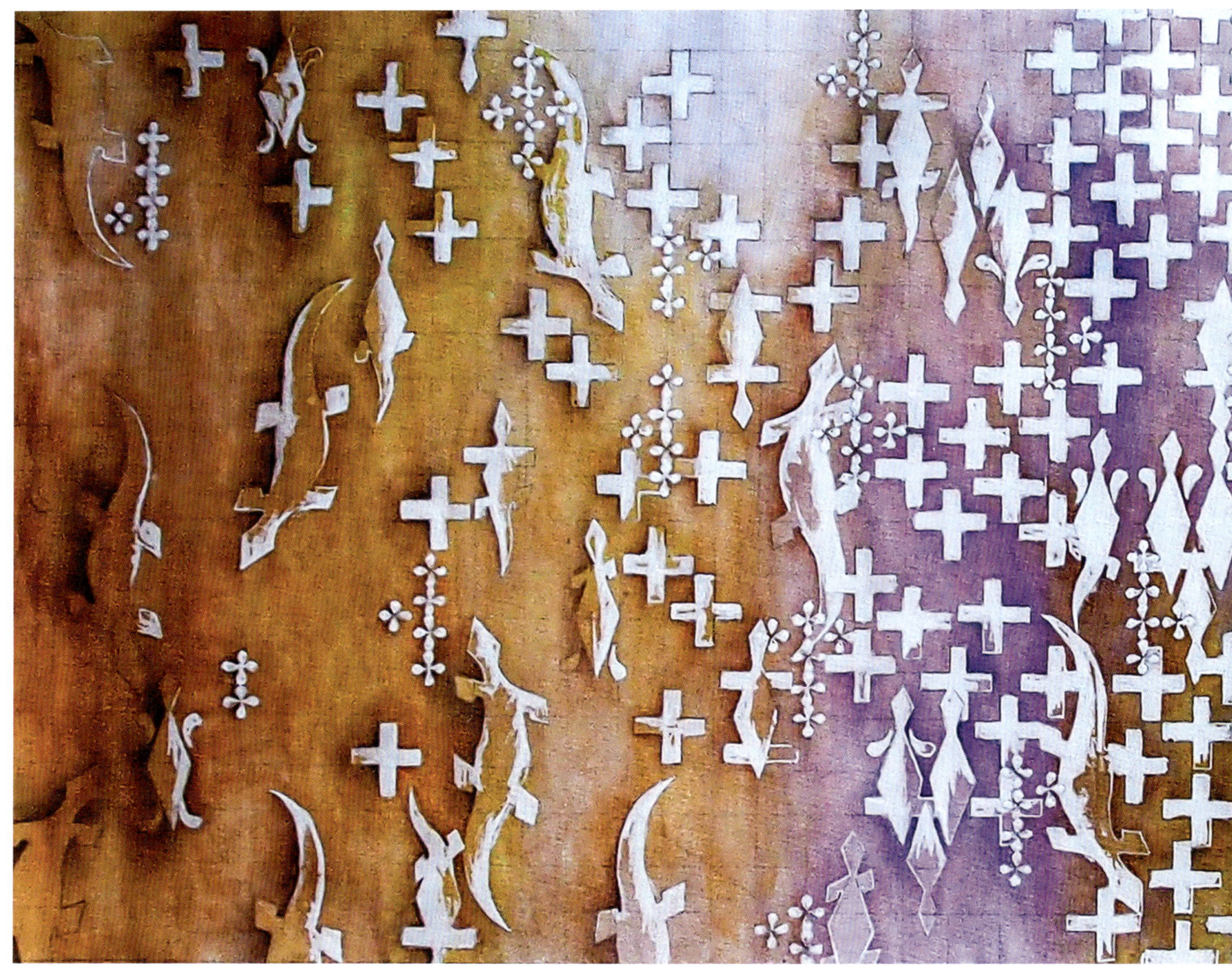

Hasoru Malu is now consistently promoting learning, experimentation, collaboration, exchange, creation, production, diffusion and distribution across all disciplines of artistic practice. Since May 2022 we have presented the work of nearly 40 Timorese visual artists through several exhibitions, and in 2023 held the inaugural Visual Arts Award in Timor-Leste. The programme also hosted and funded performances and concerts with 20 different groups and has organised over 30 art talks and workshops, with national and international speakers and trainers. Although still evolving, *Hasoru Malu* has gained attention and support both nationally and internationally, aspiring to be the beginning of a shift in the recognition and understanding of contemporary art in Timor-Leste.

Contemporary arts in Timor-Leste largely draws inspiration from Timorese traditions and history. As Madeira does with the betel nut, red soil and tais (traditional woven cloth), so too do most Timorese artists make extensive use of traditional symbology to express themselves through unique cultural signifiers, altering and reinterpreting the original symbolic meaning, which

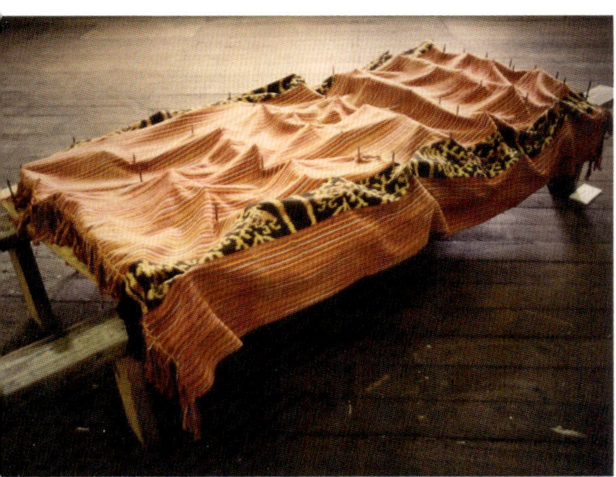

largely remains unnoticed in the international art circuit. The world has everything to gain from knowing their inspirations and artworks.

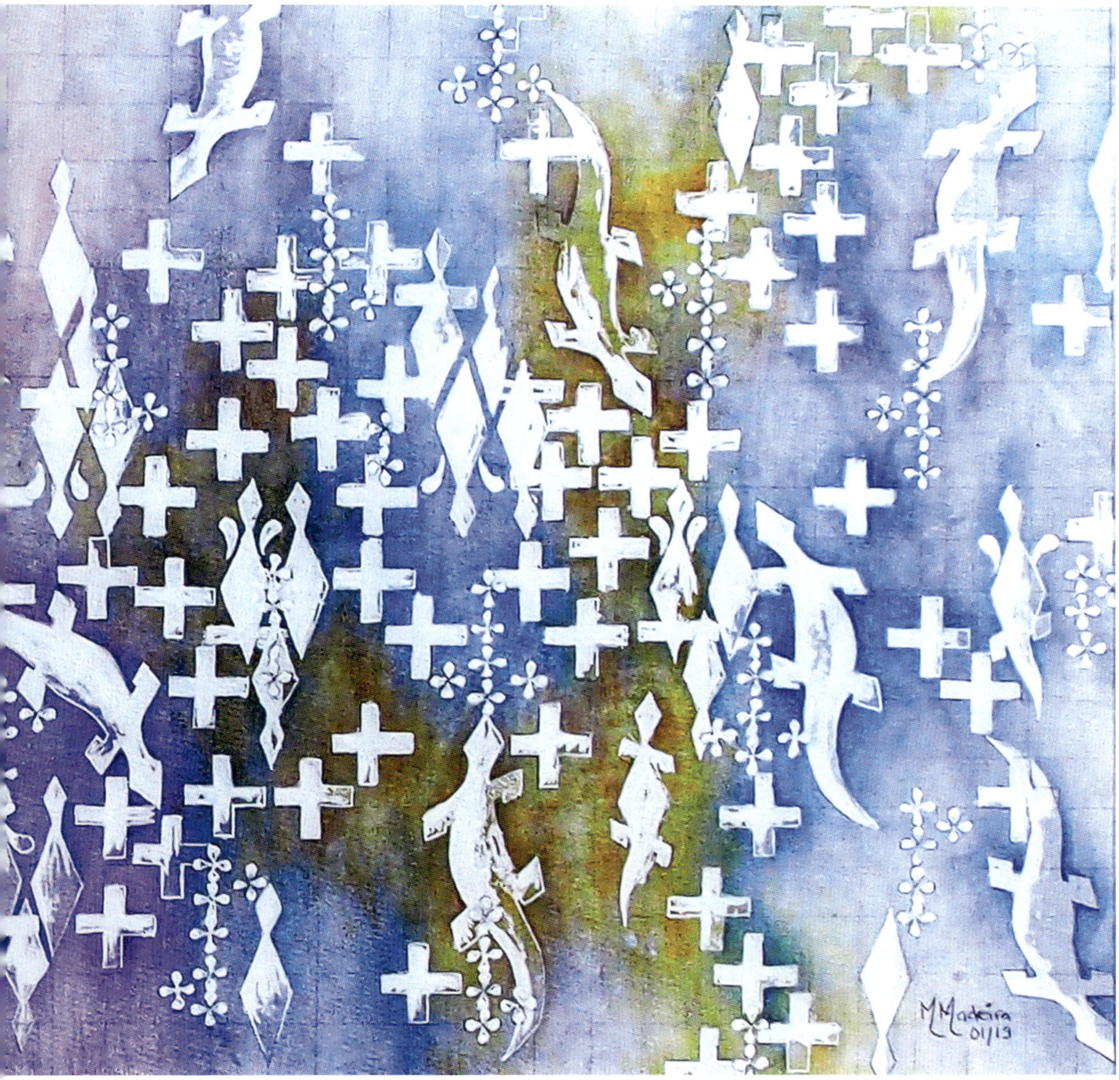

Madeira's presence in the Venice Biennale is as much a mammoth step for an individual artist as it is for Timor-Leste, which as a nation participates in the prestigious event for the first time. Moreover, it will also be an impulse and inspiration to all Timorese towards realising the full contribution of the arts to this young, post-conflict country in advancing firmly into the future.

MONTANHAS

XANANA GUSMÃO

Montanhas
        que estremecem as mentes
        das vozes que não se ouvem

Montanhas
        de chuvas pinceladas de verde
        dos suores que se derramam

Montanhas
        que calam nas alturas
        dos combates que não se ouvem

Montanhas
        de sóis queimados de azul
        das lágrimas que se derramam

Montanhas
        montanhas de Timor Leste!

Montanhas
        grávidas de sangue
        parindo a dor

Montanhas
        enlutado de ossos
        gemendo a luta

Montanhas das nuvens
Montanhas dos ventos
Montanhas do frio
Do frio da Pátria...
Montanhas – santuário
        do guerrillheiro
        que não tombou!

(Em seis minutes, pensando em vós...)

MOUNTAINS

XANANA GUSMÃO

Mountains
     that stir up the minds
     of voices that go unheard

Mountains
     of shedding sweats
     that smear the rains green

Mountains
     that silence in their heights
     unheard battles

Mountains
     of suns burnt blue
     by spilt tears

Mountains
     mountains of Timor-Leste!

Mountains
     pregnant with blood
     giving birth to pain

Mountains
     mournfully dressed with bones
     bemoaning the struggle

Mountains of the clouds
Mountains of the winds
Mountains of the cold
The cold of the homeland …
Mountains – the sanctuary
     of the warrior
     who has not fallen!

(Written in six minutes, thinking of you all…)

Xanana Gusmão, *To resist is to win!: The autobiography of Xanana Gusmão with selected letters & speeches*, Aurora Books with David Lovell Publishing, Melbourne, 2009, p. 183, translation by Elizabete Lim Gomes, 1999.

CHRONOLOGY

compiled by Leah Batterham

1966

Maria Madeira is born in the village of Gleno, in what was then Portuguese Timor. She is the third youngest of eight children to mother Terezinha de Jesus Madeira and father Matias Madeira. Her parents are agricultural workers who look after coffee plantations, vegetable and rice fields.

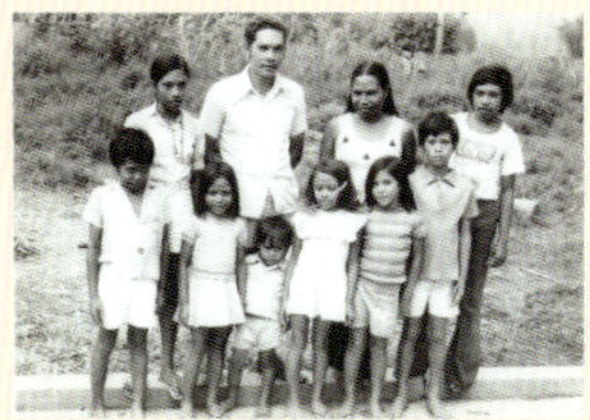

Maria Madeira (front row, fourth from left), parents and siblings in their Gleno backyard, c.1972

Her mother is a skilled cook, her father and grandfather carve wooden *surik* (traditional sword) covers and drums, and her brothers play guitar and write music.

Growing up in this environment, young Madeira develops a natural creativity.

1974

In Lisbon, Portugal's authoritarian Estado Novo regime is overthrown in a peaceful coup known as the Carnation Revolution. The new government announces an end to Portuguese colonialism, putting Portuguese Timor on a pathway to independence after four centuries of Portuguese rule. Political associations quickly form in Dili including Fretilin, the Revolutionary Front for an Independent East Timor.

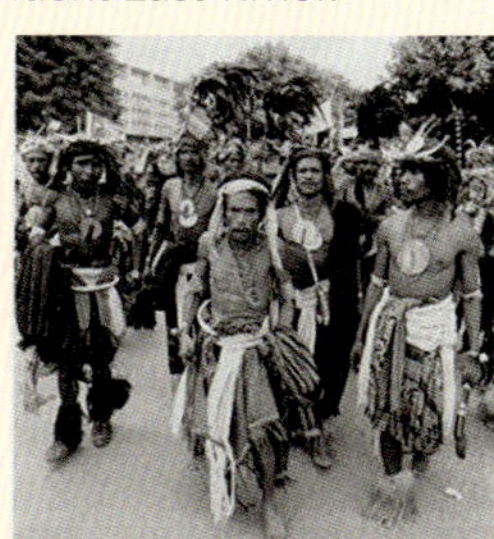

Villagers come to Dili to celebrate the first anniversary of Fretilin, 1975

1975

In August, internal armed conflict breaks out in Dili and spreads across the territory. Thousands escape to the mountains or across the border to Indonesian West Timor. In September, Madeira and her family flee during the middle of the night in the back of a truck. After pausing to collect children from a nearby orphanage, they cross the border into Indonesia. They live in a West Timor refugee camp for a year.

In October, five international journalists are killed at Balibo in Portuguese Timor by Indonesian troops.

On 28 November, Fretilin declares independence from Portugal. Nine days later Indonesia invades by land and sea, violently taking control of Dili. This begins a twenty-four year illegal occupation that is met with armed resistance by Fretilin.

1976

At the age of nine, Madeira and her family are evacuated from Indonesia by the Portuguese Air Force and spend the next seven years in a refugee camp run by the Red Cross, on the outskirts of Lisbon, Portugal. Over 4,000 Timorese people flee to Portugal or Australia between 1975-76.

Displaced families from different communities take turns performing music and dance for each other in the camp, sparking Madeira's interest in multicultural performance.

At the refugee camp, Madeira meets skilled tais-weaver Dona Veronica Pereira Maia, who inspires her artistic practice and with whom she later exhibits.

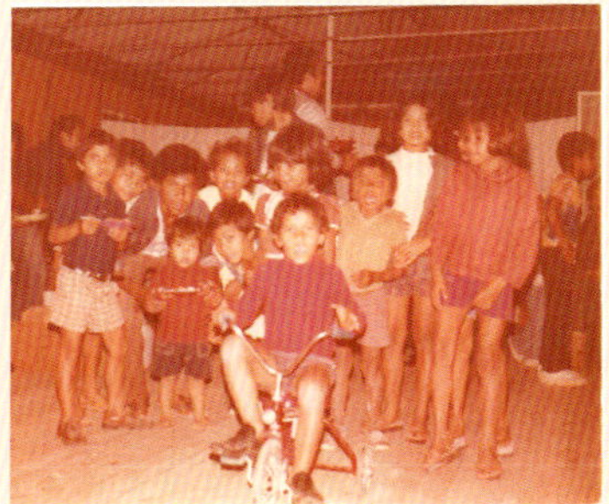

Maria Madeira (standing right) and other children arrive at refugee camp, c.1977

1977

The Indonesian military begins a campaign of 'encirclement and annihilation'. Over 300,000 Timorese are forced into internment camps where they suffer famine, sickness and death.[1]

1981

Xanana Gusmão is elected leader of a reorganised resistance, Forces for the National Liberty of East Timor (Falintil).

1982

As a teenager Madeira studies at the Lisbon Catholic College Lar D. Pedro V. She joins the dance group 'Grupo Dança Folklórico' with her sister Celina Diana Madeira and other East Timorese refugee girls.

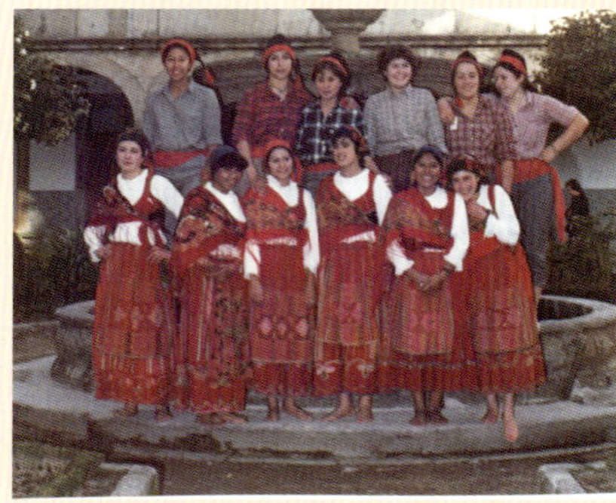

Maria (front row, second from left) and sister Celina (front row, second from right) with Grupo Dança Folklórico, 1982

While still living in the refugee camp Madeira joins Coro Loro Sa'e, a traditional Timorese dance and choir organised by the local Catholic church. They travel and perform around Portugal, England and Wales.

Coro Loro Sa'e opens up a new world for Madeira and allows her to celebrate Timorese culture. The choir provides welcome breaks from the refugee camp.

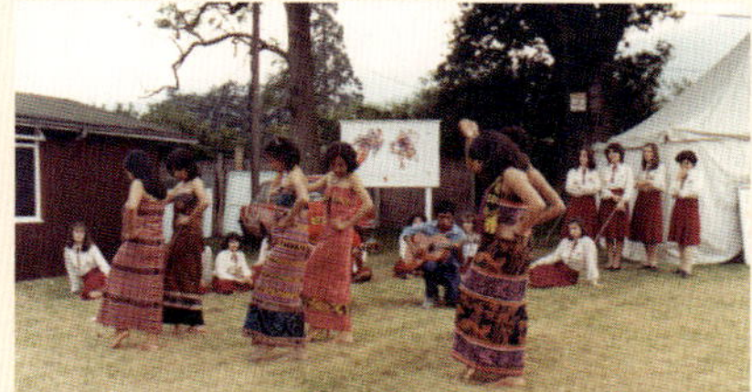

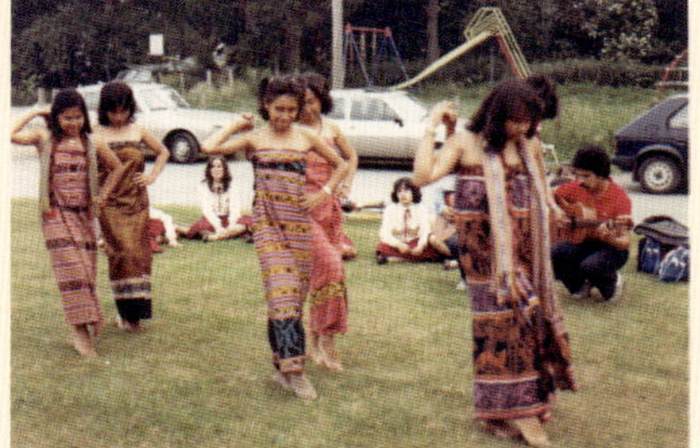

Maria Madeira (front right) and Coro Loro Sa'e at Wales Choir Festival, 1982

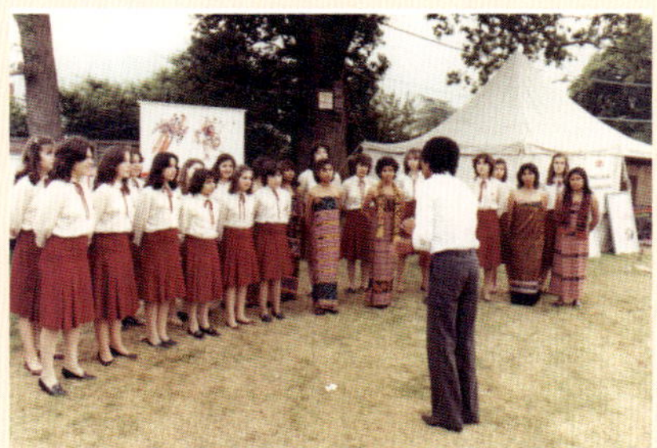

Maria Madeira (back row, middle) with Coro Loro Sa'e and the Portuguese girls choir, 1982

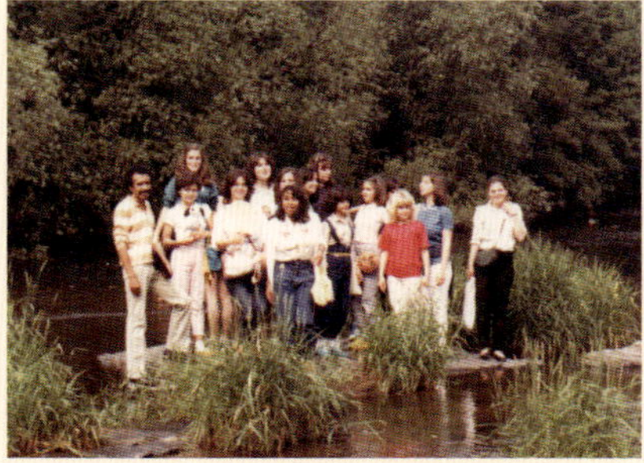

Maria Madeira (front centre) with choir group, England,1982

1983

Madeira and her family migrate to Perth in Western Australia, where her parents work in factories.

At sixteen, and knowing little English, Madeira enrols into Swanbourne High School to study art and English as a second language.

1986

Exiled leader of the international diplomatic independence campaign, José Ramos-Horta publishes *'Funu: The Unfinished Saga of East Timor'*, about the Timorese people's resistance struggle and the indifference of other countries.

1991

Madeira graduates from Curtin University with a Bachelor of Fine Arts and two years later with a Graduate Diploma of Education majoring in art.

On 12 November, Indonesian military open fire on mourners at the Santa Cruz cemetery in Dili, killing more than 270 young people.

Graphic footage of the massacre filmed by British journalist Max Stahl is smuggled out of the country by Dutch activist Saskia Kouwenberg, who hides the film in her underwear smeared with blood. The footage is broadcast around the world and becomes a turning point in the struggle for self-determination.

Madeira presents her graduation installation two weeks after the Santa Cruz massacre. Her sculptural work confronts the sustained violence and hopelessness experienced by the Timorese and reflects on her own displaced and dislocated identity.

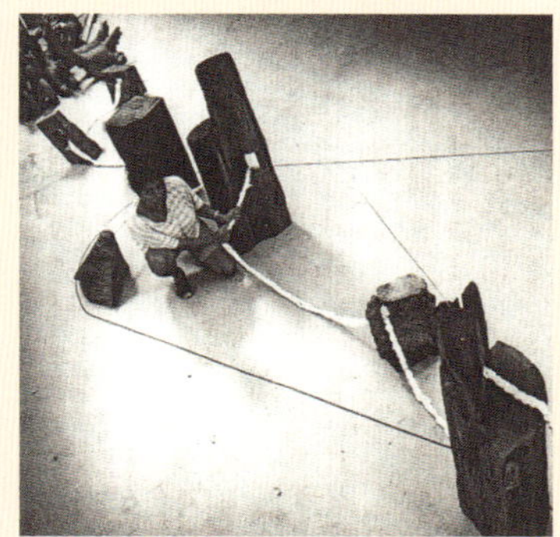

Maria Madeira and her installation at graduation exhibition, Curtin University, 1991

Madeira protests and speaks out publicly against the Indonesian military regime.

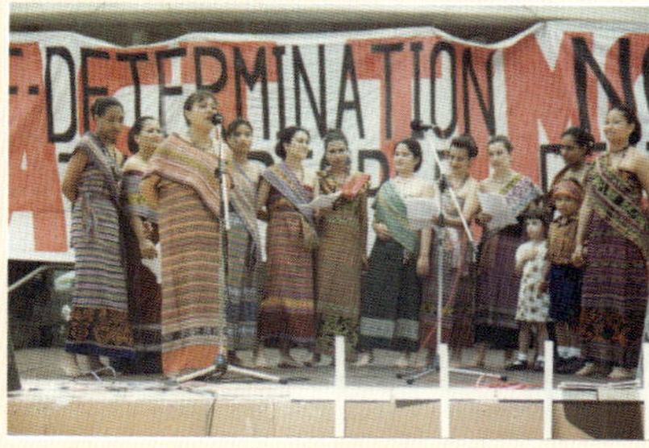

Madeira speaks at a protest in Perth, 1991

1992

Works as Research Assistant in Curtin University School of Fine Arts, where she debuts *Dislocation* in her first major group exhibition.

In collaboration with her mentor David Jones, Professor of Sculpture and Fine Arts, *Dislocation* is made of Timor-Leste newspapers and red earth, which signifies her birthplace Ermera. It references her experience as a refugee and all those who are dislocated, the endlessly mobile and the homeless.

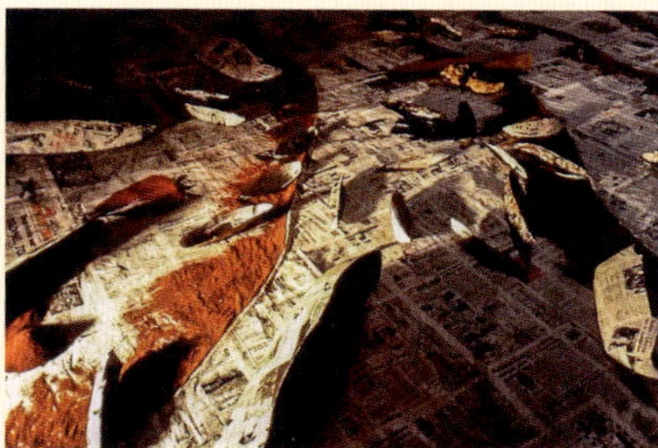

Dislocation installation, 1992

1992

In November, Xanana Gusmão is captured near Dili. He is later convicted of subversion and imprisoned in Jakarta. He continues to lead the resistance from prison.

1994

Exhibits in the group exhibition *Junction* at the Kalla Yeedip Arts in Midland, Western Australia in August.

1995

Guest teaches 'East Timor Exploring the Culture and Exploding the Myths' at University of Western Australia for two months over spring term, also interpreting and translating for East Timorese participants.

1996

Graduates with a BA in Political Science from Murdoch University.

Leads public protests against illegal occupation of East Timor.

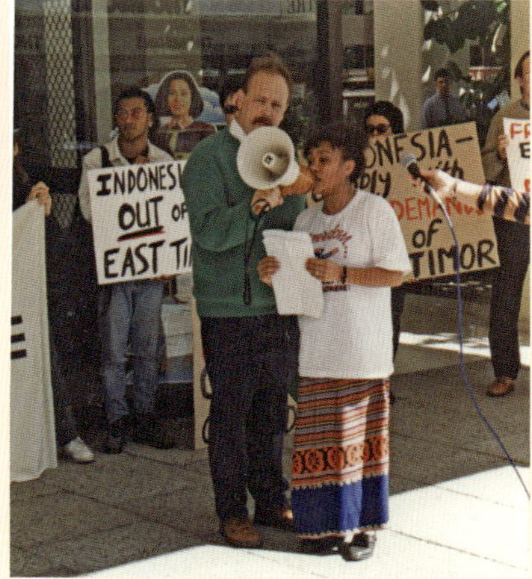

Madeira speaks at protest with Peter Stewart, who runs the Christian Centre for Social Action, 1996

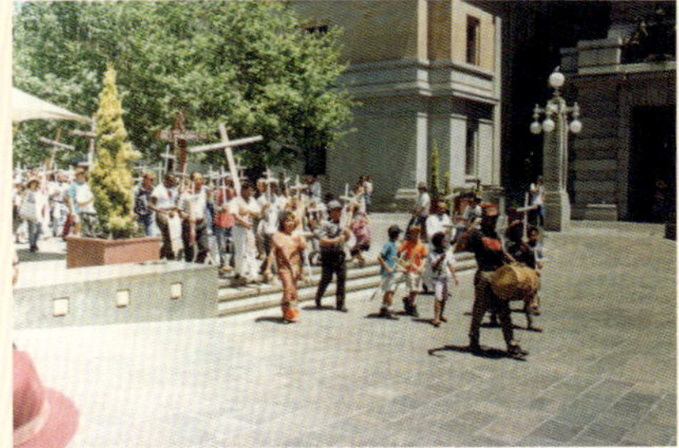

Protest in Perth, 1996

Nobel Peace Prize is awarded to José Ramos-Horta and Archbishop of Dili, Bishop Carlos Ximenes Belo for their combined efforts to bring peace to East Timor.

Madeira debuts her first solo exhibition *East Timor – Land of Crosses* at Perth Institute of Contemporary Arts in Western Australia. Sculpture work *270+ The Santa Cruz Massacre* honours the Timorese who died in the 1991 massacre by depicting them as warriors, symbolised by the handmade moon-shaped *kaibuk,* a traditional and sacred headdress.

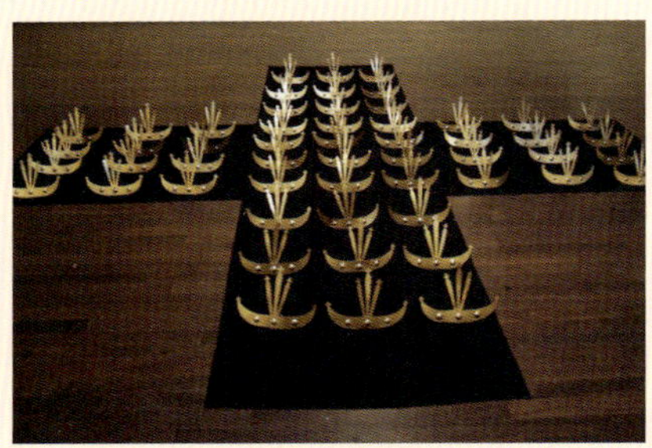

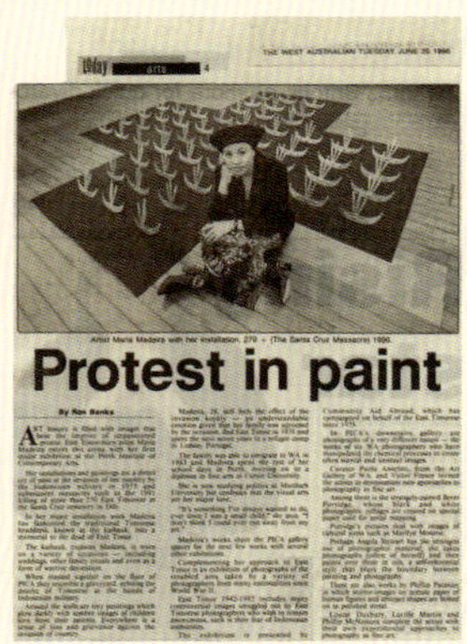

270+ The Santa Cruz Massacre, 1996
Madeira features in West Australian, 1996

Creates installation work *Silence at What Price?* Madeira uses traditional tais cloth on a bed of nails to reference the torture and killing of young East Timorese Fernando Boavida by the Indonesian military four years earlier.

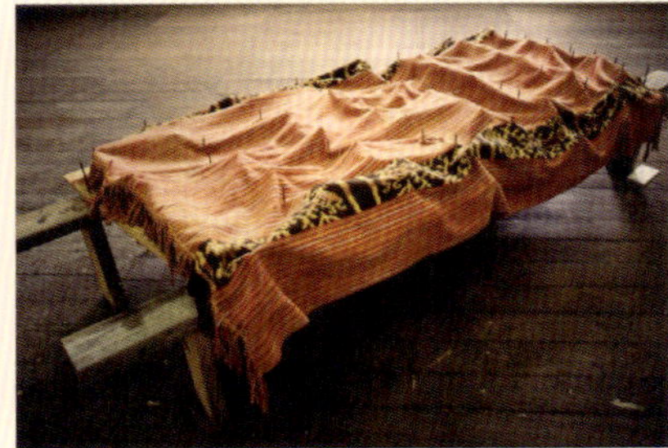

Silence at What Price?, 1996

Presents in group exhibition *Memory & Reality* at Kalla Yeedip Gallery, Midland in Western Australia.

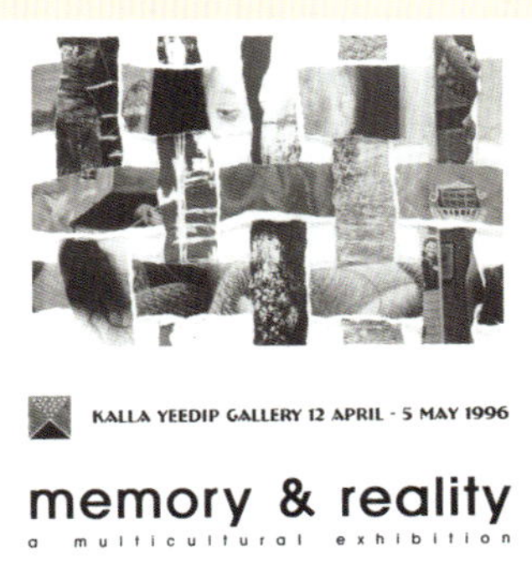

Poster *Memory & Reality*, 1996

Works from 1996 to 2000 in Western Australia as a high-school art teacher, visual artist and cultural advisor for several arts and cultural organisations.

1997

Presents solo works at *Hamutuk (Together)* and curates the exhibit *Uma Knua* at the Kalla Yeedip Gallery in Western Australia.

Features in the newspaper *Hills Gazette* for *Hamutuk* which 'speaks out about her homeland's fight for freedom and justice'.

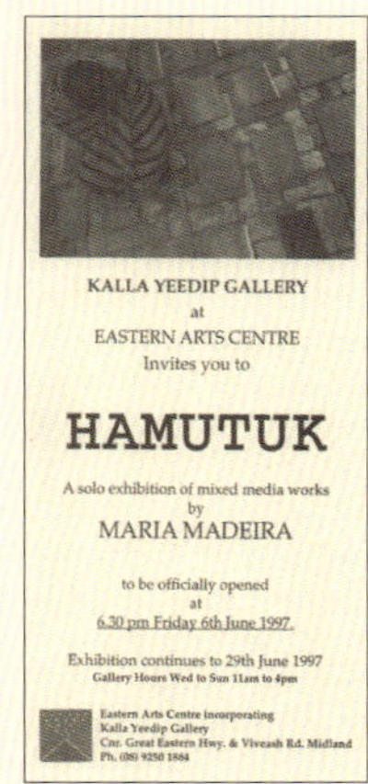

Invitation to *Hamutuk*, Kalla Yeedip Gallery WA, 1997

Presents solo exhibition *Visual Kulcha* and is awarded 'Artist of the Month' at Kulcha, a venue dedicated to promoting multicultural arts in Western Australia.

Takes on the role of Arts Coordinator at Kulcha, Multicultural Arts of Western Australia

Madeira finds an outlet of musical expression singing with Perth band Jah Era alongside her lead guitarist brother, Angelo Madeira. Their sound is a multicultural mix of merengue, reggae and marrabenta music, and their lyrics speak of war and loss.

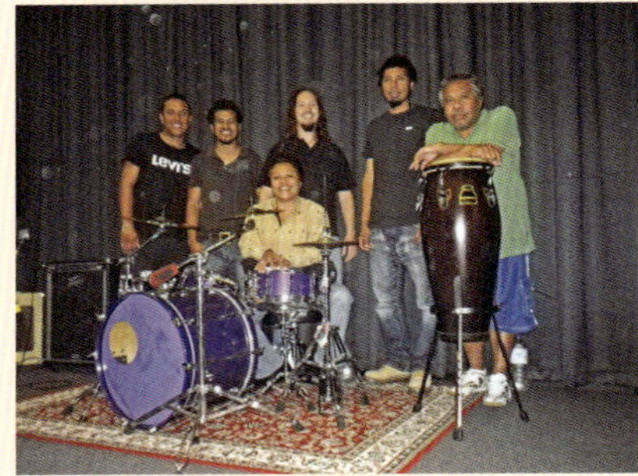

Maria Madeira (singer) and band Jah Era, c.1997

FOKUPERS (East Timor Women's Communication Forum) is established by activists in East Timor under the leadership of Maria Domingas 'Micato' Alves. It is run by communities of womens' groups who address violence and human rights violations against women and children.

1998

Suharto resigns on 21 May 1998 following a collapse of support and Habibie becomes president of Indonesia. He agrees to a referendum.

Madeira presents in Portugal at her first international group exhibitions *East Timor Cultural Week* at the University of Aveiro and *Mar de Timor, Mar de Paz (Timor Sea, Sea of Peace)* at the World Expo98 held at the University of Lisbon.

1999

In August a United Nations supervised referendum is held in East Timor offering a choice between autonomy within Indonesia or independence.

Despite months of intimidation and violence by Indonesian-backed militia, 98.6% of registered voters come out to vote.

On 4 September 78.5% of voters reject the proposal for special autonomy and vote for independence.

The result triggers a campaign of violence by East Timorese pro-integration militias supported by factors of the Indonesian military.

Power, water and transport infrastructure and over three-quarters of buildings are destroyed along with the collection of the Timor-Leste National Museum.[2]

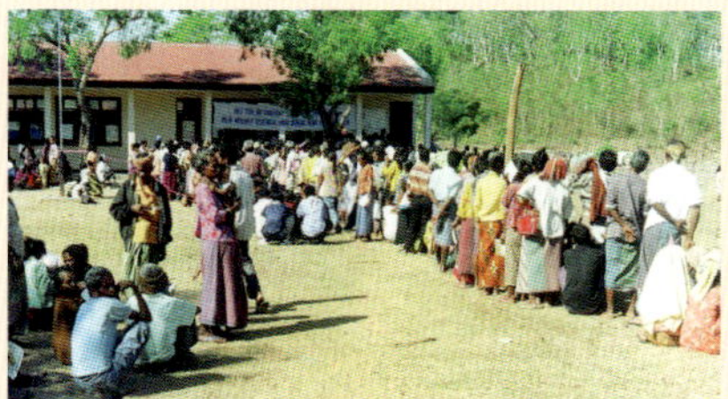

Voting in Bobonaro District, Timorese queue for hours exercising their right to self-determination, 1999

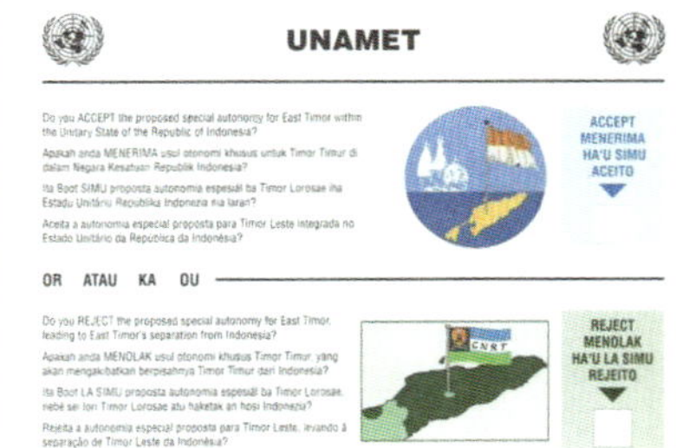

Independence referendum ballot paper, 1999

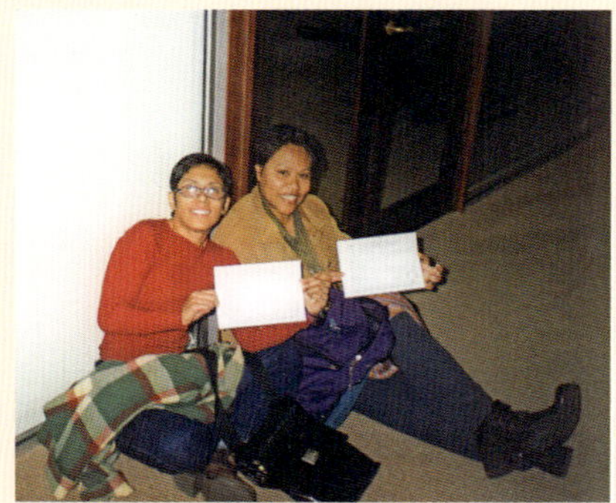

Maria Madeira and cousin Lumena Madeira vote on Referendum Day, 1999

Madeira speaks as Guest Artist at the 'National Convention of East Timorese Abroad', Worldwide Convention in Portugal.

Conducts art workshop for the Western Australian Department of Culture & the Arts.

Teaches art and cultural programmes at Merredin Senior High School and Kambalda High School in Western Australia. Also teaches art and music at West Coast College of Technical and Further Education, Western Australia.

2000

Madeira returns to Timor-Leste to live and help with the recovery, rebuilding and development of her country.

Speaks at Vancouver Arts Centre in Western Australia at the opening of *As it Was – East Timor 1971*, an exhibition of photographs capturing East Timor everyday life before the Indonesian invasion.

Presents at the National Conference 'Different Stories' in Esperance, Western Australia.

Conducts an artist residency at Lockridge Primary School in Perth, Western Australia.

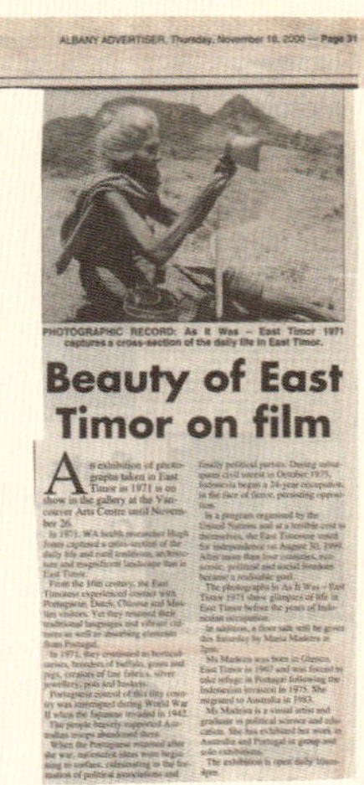

Article in Albany Advertiser on '*As It Was – East Timor 1971*' exhibition, 2000

In Timor-Leste, a Timor Aid Textile Collection is assembled in the years following 2000 'to assist in the preservation of an endangered culture'.[3]

2001

Madeira's first job in Timor-Leste is with Aus-Aid creating distinctive logos for ambulance teams in the district of Los Palos. She also works in Dili as an interpreter and translator.

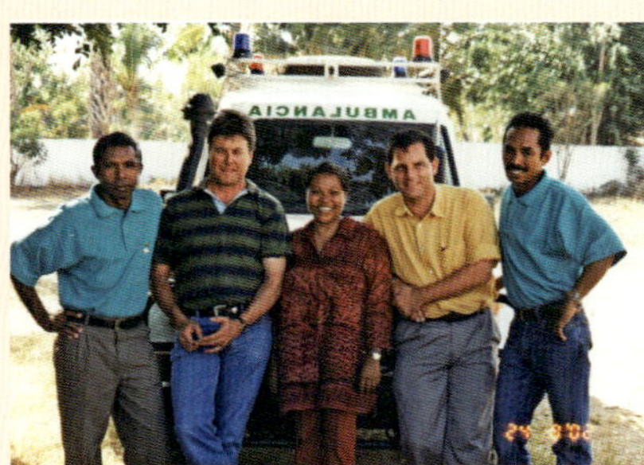

Madeira with her boss Craig Hopper (second from right) and Los Palos Ambulance team, 2002

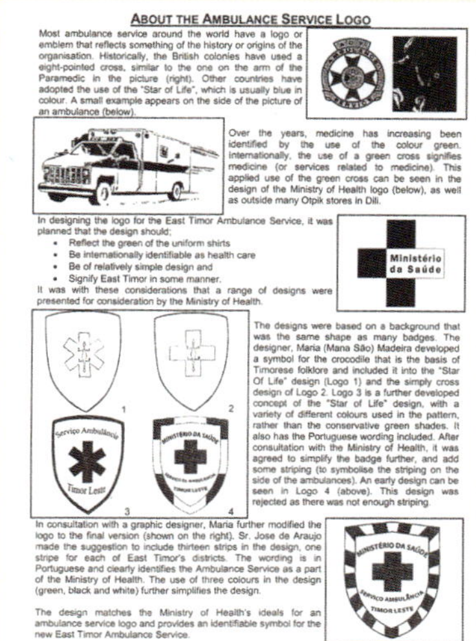

ABOUT THE AMBULANCE SERVICE LOGO

Most ambulance service around the world have a logo or emblem that reflects something of the history or origins of the organisation. Historically, the British colonies have used a eight-pointed cross, similar to the one on the arm of the Paramedic in the picture (right). Other countries have adopted the use of the "Star of Life", which is usually blue in colour. A small example appears on the side of the picture of an ambulance (below).

Over the years, medicine has increasing been identified by the use of the colour green. Internationally, the use of a green cross signifies medicine (or services related to medicine). This applied use of the green cross can be seen in the design of the Ministry of Health logo (below), as well as outside many Otpik stores in Dili.

In designing the logo for the East Timor Ambulance Service, it was planned that the design should:
- Reflect the green of the uniform shirts
- Be internationally identifiable as health care
- Be of relatively simple design and
- Signify East Timor in some manner.

It was with these considerations that a range of designs were presented for consideration by the Ministry of Health.

Ministério da Saúde

The designs were based on a background that was the same shape as many badges. The designer, Maria (Mana São) Madeira developed a symbol for the crocodile that is the basis of Timorese folklore and included it into the "Star Of Life" design (Logo 1) and the simply cross design of Logo 2. Logo 3 is a further developed concept of the "Star of Life" design, with a variety of different colours used in the pattern, rather than the conservative green shades. It also has the Portuguese wording included. After consultation with the Ministry of Health, it was agreed to simplify the badge further, and add some striping (to symbolise the striping on the side of the ambulances). An early design can be seen in Logo 4 (above). This design was rejected as there was not enough striping.

In consultation with a graphic designer, Maria further modified the logo to the final version (shown on the right). Sr. Jose de Araujo made the suggestion to include thirteen strips in the design, one stripe for each of East Timor's districts. The wording is in Portuguese and clearly identifies the Ambulance Service as a part of the Ministry of Health. The use of three colours in the design (green, black and white) further simplifies the design.

The design matches the Ministry of Health's ideals for an ambulance service logo and provides an identifiable symbol for the new East Timor Ambulance Service.

Ambulance logos designed by Madeira, 2001

In August 2001 the Timorese people vote in their first election to choose members of the Constituent Assembly. The following year these members approve the Constitution of the Democratic Republic of Timor-Leste.

First Lady Kirsty Sword Gusmão establishes the Alola Foundation, a not-for-profit government organisation in Timor-Leste which advocates for women by addressing problems relating to education, economic development, maternal and child health.

2002

Xanana Gusmão is inaugurated Timor-Leste's first elected president in April.

On 20 May 2002, the Democratic Republic of Timor-Leste becomes the 191st member state of the United Nations.

Timor-Leste begins the slow process of reconstruction and development.

Timor-Leste's Commission for Reception, Truth and Reconciliation (CAVR) is established to document the experiences of Timorese people during the occupation.

The full evidence to the CAVR Inquiry fills two large rooms at the Comarca Prison, a unique and irreplaceable record.

Madeira travels around Timor-Leste doing field research for 'Tatoli Ba Kultura' (Passing on Culture) a collaborative project between the Secretary of State for Arts & Culture in Timor-Leste and Griffith University in Australia. It gathers knowledge and materials for a future Academy of Arts Creative Industries in Timor-Leste.

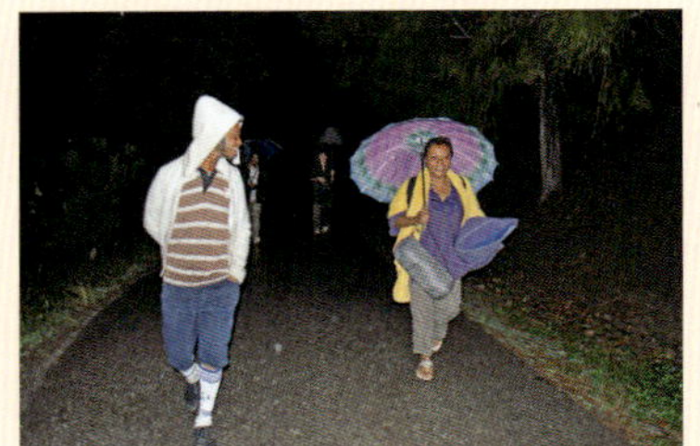

Madeira and local guide look for accommodation in the district of Ainaro, 2002

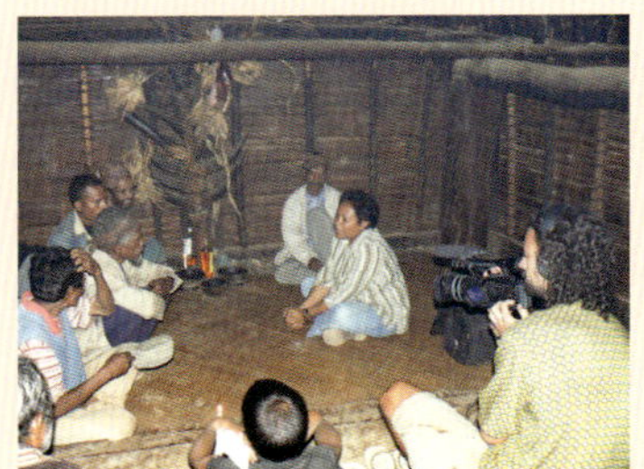

Madeira interviews with *Lian Nain* (Elders) in *Uma Lulik* (Sacred House) of Estado Hatu Mautei, Letefoho in Ermera, 2002

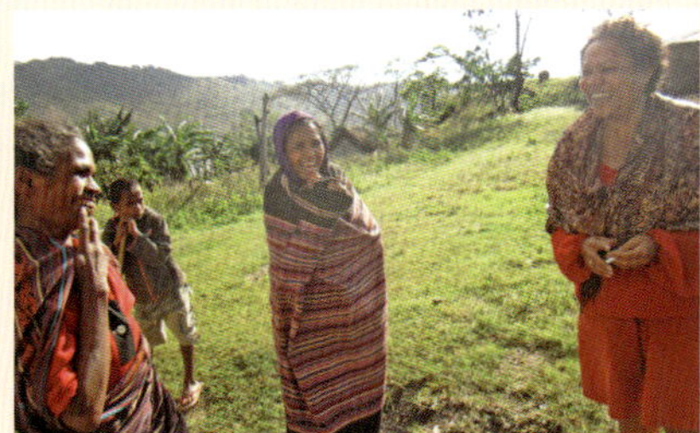

Madeira with locals in the village of Hau Tio, Maubisse, Ainaro, 2002

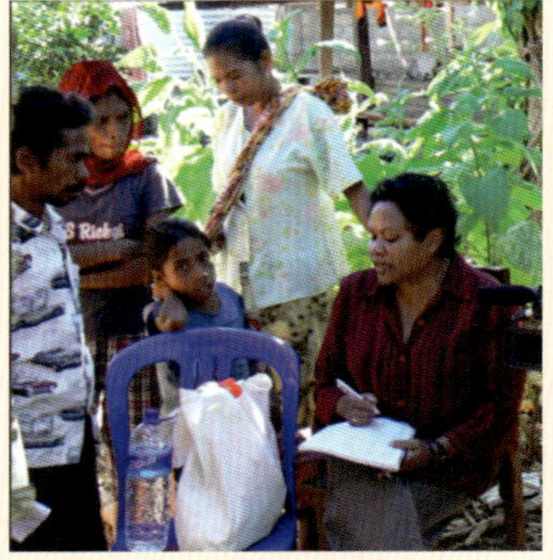

Madeira interviewing locals, Ermera, 2002

Madeira acts as a cultural advisor and teaches East Timorese songs for musical Theatre production *Mavis Goes to Timor* at Deckchair Theatre, Western Australia.

Based on the true story of 86-year-old Mavis Taylor who moves to Timor-Leste to help the people and builds sewing centres. The production tours to Victoria and Tasmania in Australia.

2003

Madeira presents her interactive installation *Hili Batar, Picking Corn* at the group Trade Fair Exhibition held in the Instituto Camões in Dili. She challenges viewers to spell their names by picking corn seeds with the alphabet written on them.

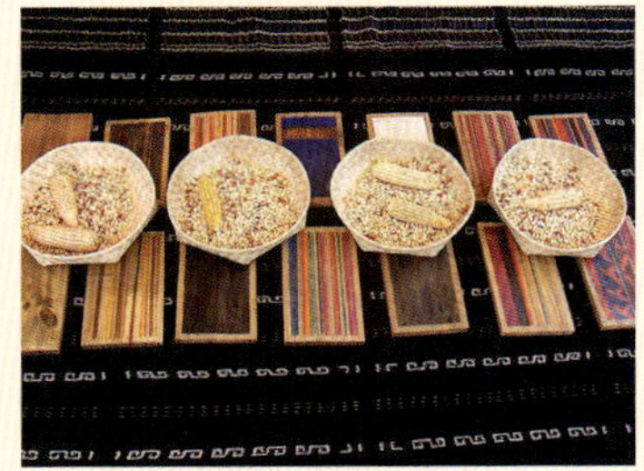

Picking corn (Hili Batar), 2003

This work responds to the frustration felt by East Timorese people engaging with UN officials for the recovery and rebuilding of Timor-Leste, even in the seemingly simple task of spelling Timorese names.

Arte Moris opens in the former premises of the National Museum in Comoro, Dili. It is the only art school in Timor-Leste, is free, and shares its premises with a camp for internally displaced people. Many of the artist students squat on-site.

Madeira lives and teaches at Arte Moris with other art teachers.

2004

Madeira works as an interpreter, translator and cultural adviser for the United Nations Serious Crimes Unit, investigating Crimes Against Humanity committed in 1999 and 2000. She encourages and helps Timorese people convey their experiences, exonerating a number of East Timorese people wrongly accused of committing crimes.

Madeira stays in a bedroom in Dili with her brother and sister-in-law, where she discovers lipstick stains along the walls. She learns that this room, and others throughout Timor-Leste, were used by Indonesian military to torture and rape women. Madeira later uses elements and symbols in her art to speak out about the traumas endured by Timorese women.

2005

Debuts *A Dream Come True* in Hotel Timor, Dili, and becomes the first ever artist to present a solo exhibition in Timor-Leste. The exhibition is opened by First Lady, Kirsty Sword Gusmão.

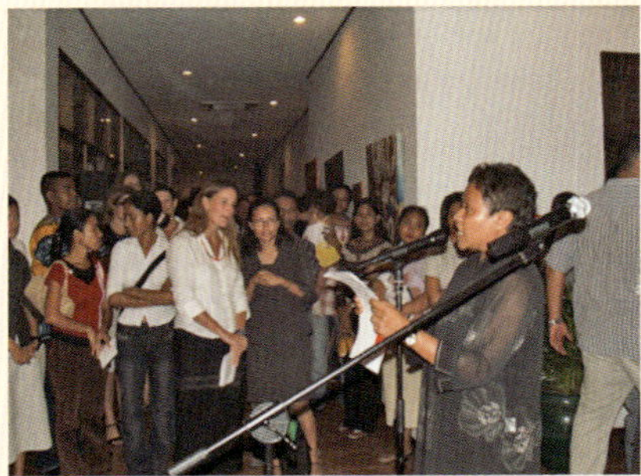

Madeira speaks at the opening of *A Dream Come True*, 2005

While the exhibition is deemed a great success, some of the Timorese public are shocked to see the art works are by a woman, since most public events are carried out by men. This response surprises Madeira and prompts her to investigate issues faced by East Timorese female visual artists.

CAVR publishes the Executive Summary of 'Chega! The Report of the Commission for Reception, Truth and Reconciliation'. It finds that the Indonesian occupation was directly responsible for the deaths of approximately 183,000 East Timorese over the period 1975–99.[4]

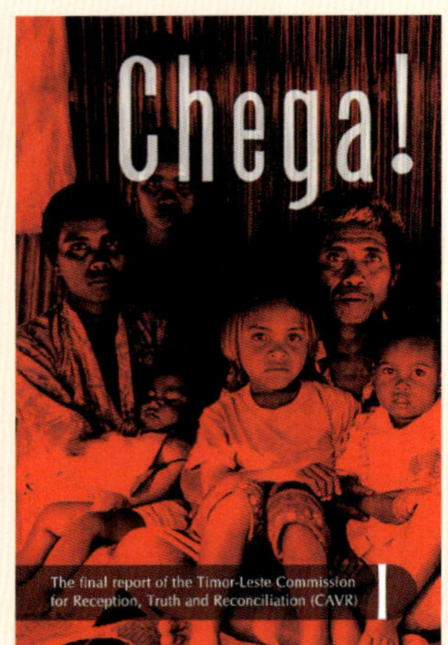

'Chega!' (Meaning 'Enough!'), the CAVR Final Report, 2013

2006

Exhibits in major group exhibition *Picturing the Sea* at Lawrence Wilson Art Gallery, University of Western Australia, alongside artists including Patricia Piccinini, Polixeni Papapetrou and Narelle Autio.

Leads talk 'East Timor and The Sea' exploring the politics of oil and gas reserves in the Timor Sea.

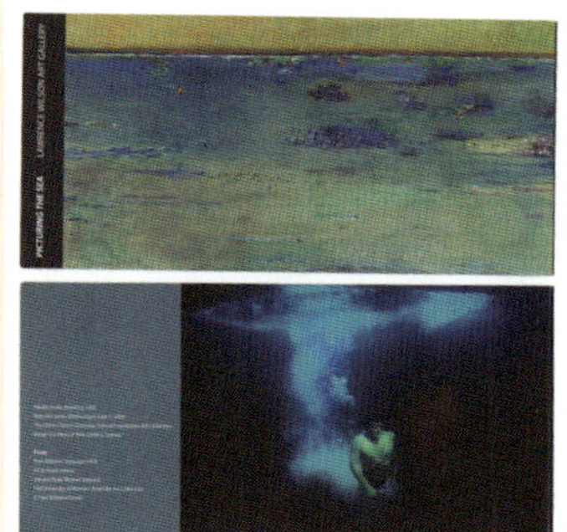

Catalogue cover for exhibition *Picturing the Sea*, 2006

Riots erupt in Dili following the dismissal of former soldiers. At least 25 people are killed and about 150,000 take refuge in makeshift camps. Prime Minister Alkatiri resigns over his handling of the violence and José Ramos-Horta is appointed Prime Minister.

Artists undertake a peace campaign of posters and murals throughout Timor-Leste.

2007

Presents solo exhibition *Silent Voices* at Cannery Arts Centre in Esperance, Western Australia during a two month residency. The exhibition tells stories of oppression and resilience in Timor-Leste, particularly those of women.

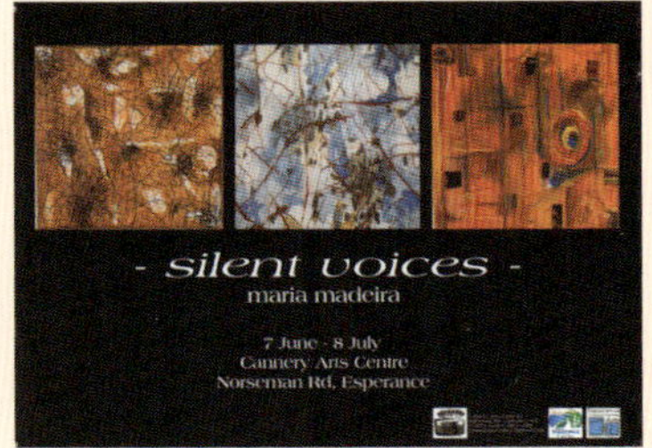

Advertisement for *Silent Voices*, 2007

Showcases 30 works in solo exhibit *Lian Tatoli* held at Kulcha in Fremantle, Western Australia.

Performs with her band Jah Era for opening night a fusion of East Timorese, African and Reggae music.

Participates in 'Glass with the Artist', monthly art discussions through Rockingham Regional Art Gallery, Western Australia. Maria highlights her art and the art of Timor-Leste, and her friends attend to sing and play traditional East Timorese music.

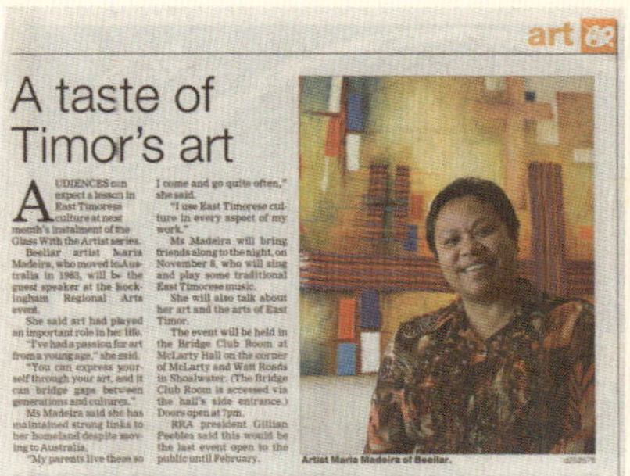

Newspaper Article of Madeira 'Glass with the Artist', 2007

2008

In February, President José Ramos-Horta is shot in the stomach in an assassination attempt by renegade soldiers at his Dili residence. Rebel leader Alfredo Reinado is killed in the attack.

Participates in a residency at the Centre for Sustainable Living in Western Australia, where she debuts the solo exhibition *Threads of Culture, Brave New Works*.

Awarded an Arts grant from Department of Culture & the Arts, Western Australia.

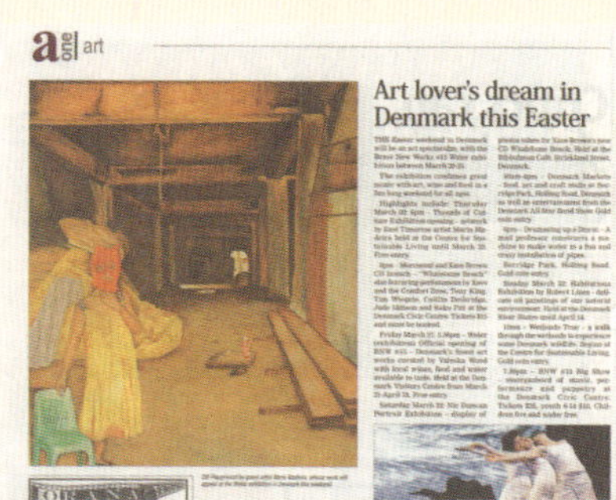

Newspaper article for *Brave New Works*, 2008

Spends 3 month residency at Arte Moris in Dili. She teaches introductions to art theory and global art history, and runs filmed workshops teaching students how to paint using betel juice.

Out of the thirty or so students, only one is female.

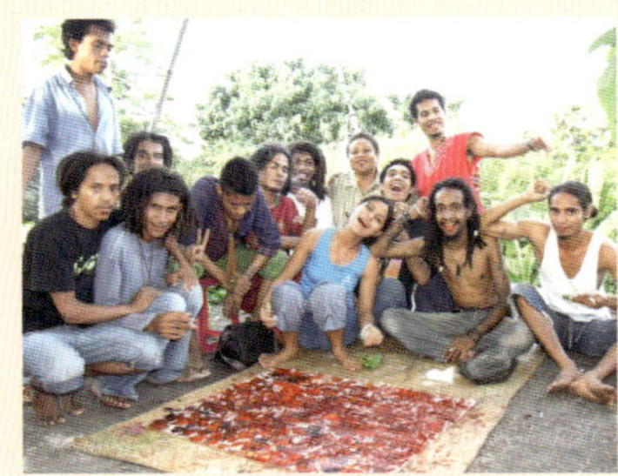

Madeira (middle) and Arte Moris students paint using betel nut, 2008

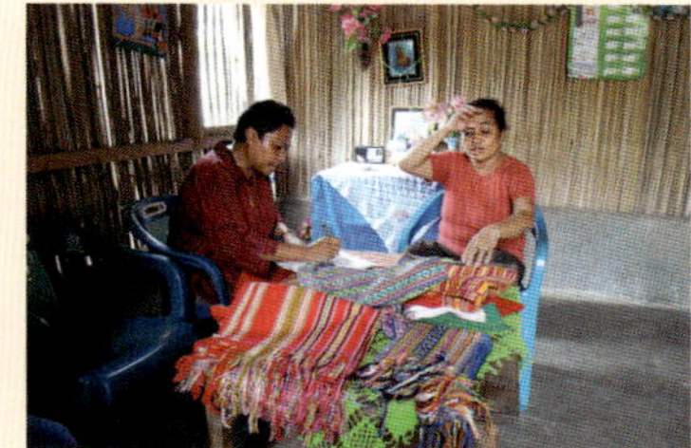

Madeira with tais weaver in Viqueque, Timor-Leste, 2008

2009

The film *Balibo* is released. Directed by Robert Connolly, it tells the story of five international Australian based journalists captured by Indonesian militia and killed while reporting activities just prior to the Indonesian invasion of Portuguese Timor.

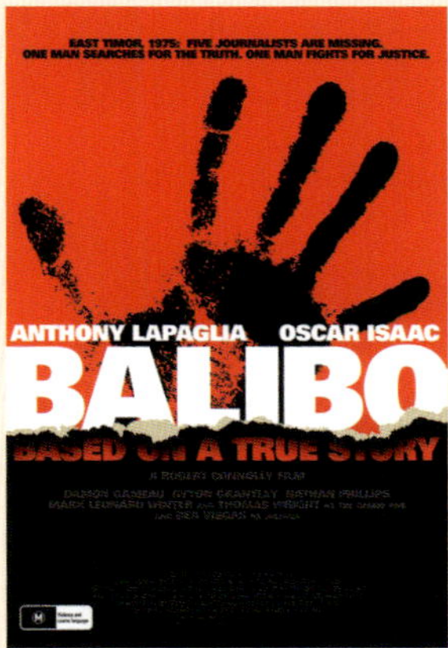

Poster for *Balibo*, 2009

Madeira's 2006 painting on tais *Troubled Spots* features on the book cover for Belton et al.'s 'Maternal Mortality, Unplanned Pregnancy and Unsafe Abortion in Timor-Leste'.

Receives the Australian Postgraduate Award Scholarship which allows her to research and more deeply study contemporary art in Timor-Leste.

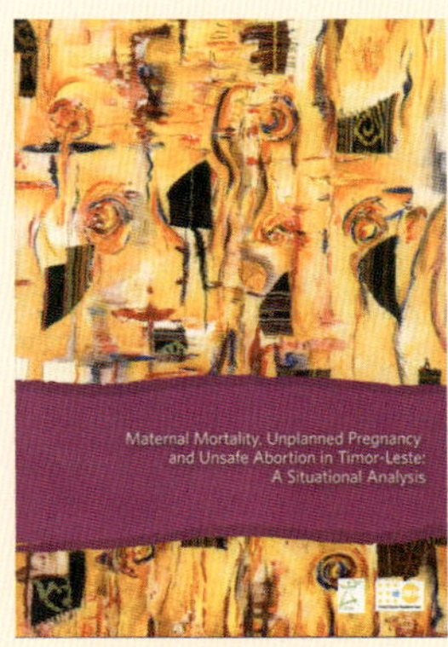

Book cover features *Troubled Spots*, 2009

2010

Presents solo exhibition *Koalia Neneik Deit (Quietly Speaking)* in historic building Casa Europa in Dili.

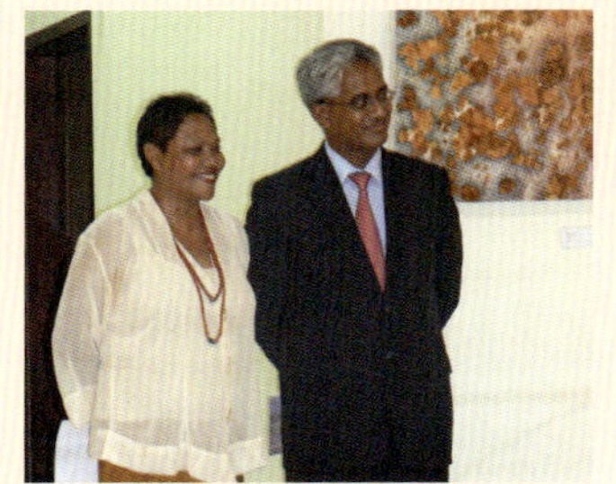

Dr Maria Madeira with Dr Zacarias Albano da Costa at opening of *Quietly Speaking*, 2010

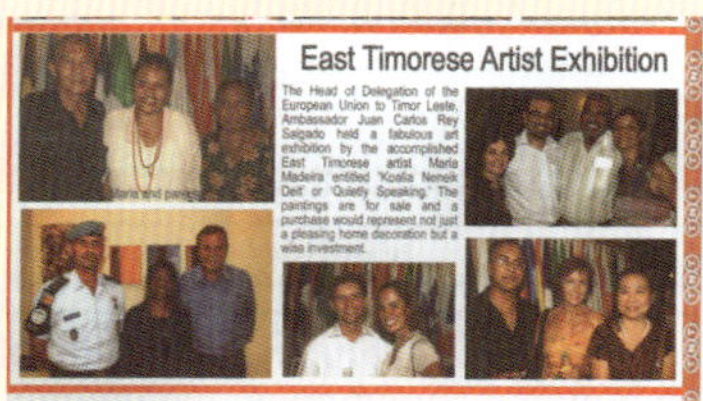

Magazine article on *Quietly Speaking*, Maria top left with parents, 2010

Acts as Cultural Advisor and Researcher for the project 'Tatoli ba Kultura' (Messenger for Culture) a collaboration between Griffith University and Secretary of State for Culture in Timor-Leste.

Creates interactive installation *Traveller (Lao Rai)*. Participants play the prominent Timorese game *lao rai* while moving around the installation work. It reflects Madeira's desire to be distinctly contemporary while also speaking to Timorese tradition.

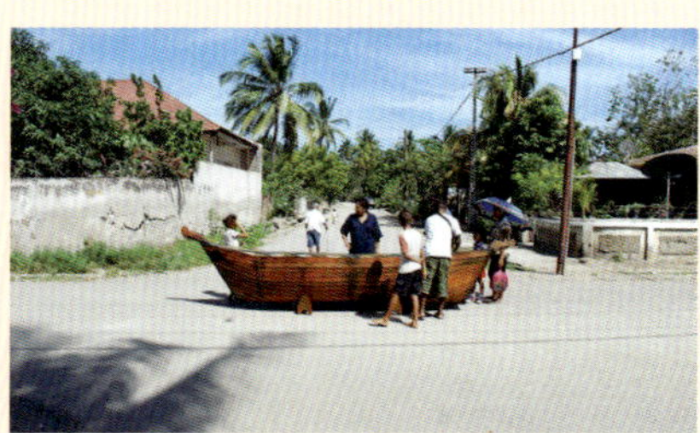

Madeira and locals in Dili with *Traveller (Lao Rai)*, 2010

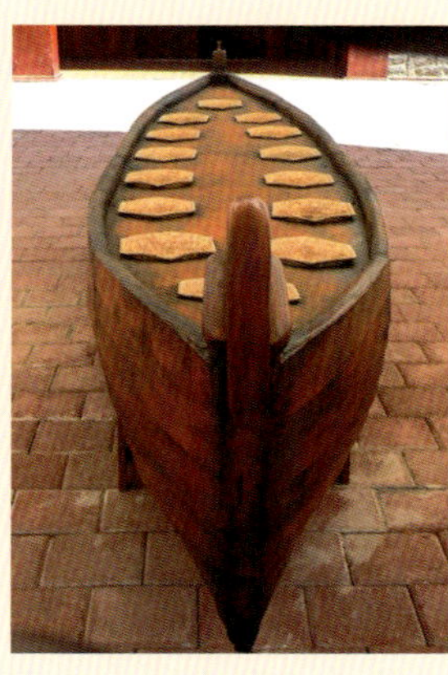

Traveller (Lao Rai) (detail), 2010

The award-winning documentary *Uma Lulik* is released. It follows the construction of an *Uma Lulik* (sacred house) in Venilale. It is directed by Timor-Leste artist and filmmaker Victor de Sousa, with whom Madeira travels two years later on an arts residency.

2011

Participates in *Macau City Fringe Festival* alongside fellow East Timorese artist Mario Dorosario Mira Da Costa. From a mobile street vendor cart she distributes small gift boxes which contain positive aspects of daily life for people in Timor-Leste. The installation aims to encourage cultural and artistic exchange between Timor-Leste and Macau.

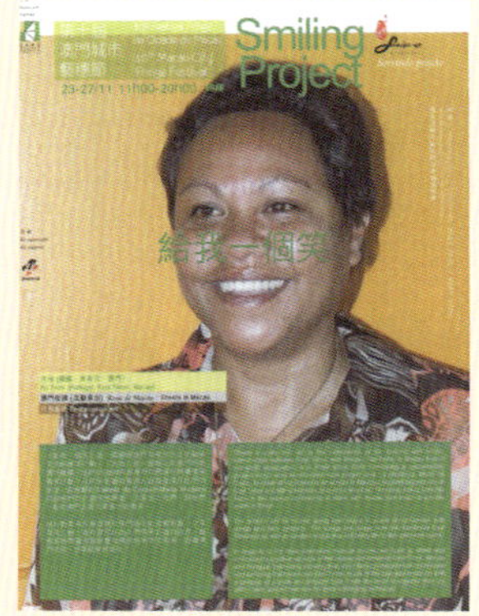

Poster of Madeira for Smiling Project Macau, 2011

While in Macau, Madeira also presents the solo exhibit *Familiar Steps* at the Festival da Lusofonia.

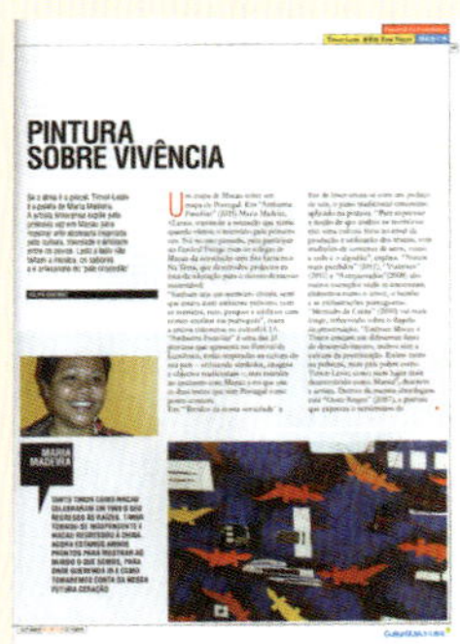

Article CulturGUIA, Festival Da Lusofonia, Macau, 2011

Presents in group exhibition *Arte Lusófona Contemporânea* in Galeria Marta Traba, São Paulo, Brazil. Brings together artists from Portuguese-speaking countries to initiate and deepen dialogue around Latin American artistic expression.

Serves as moderator for the Creative Industries Conference in Dili. It explores and celebrates the works of current Timorese artists and creatives and discusses the future Academy of Creative Industries in Timor-Leste.

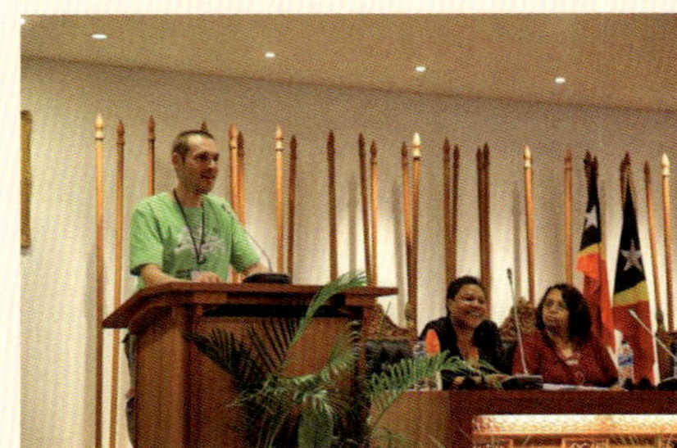

Madeira (centre) at the Creative Industries Conference, Dili 2011

2012

Travels to 11 of Timor-Leste's 13 regions with Fiona Macdonald, Narelle Jubelin and Victor De Sousa, as part of mobile art residency *Cross Arts Projects*. Records aspects of everyday life in Timor-Leste and in particular the traditional textiles of women weavers.

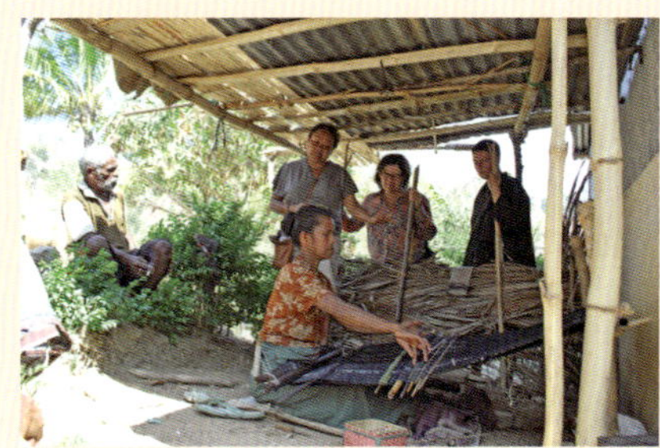

Maria Madeira with artists Narelle Jubelin, Fiona MacDonald and a tais weaver in Ilat Lau, Marobo, Bobonaro, Timor-Leste, 2012

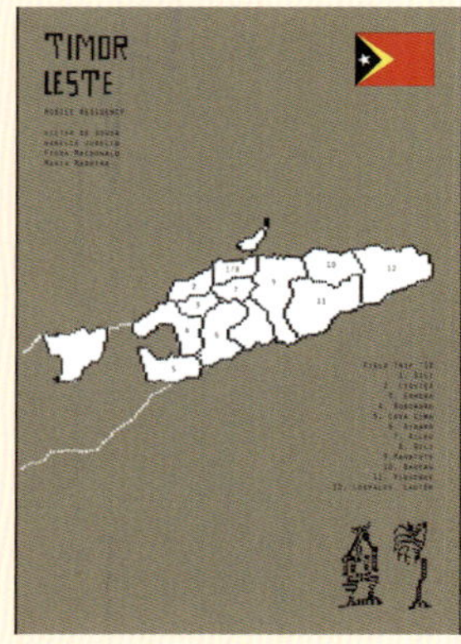

Poster for mobile residency, 2012

Acts as Cultural Advisor for exhibition *Debt of Honour* at the Western Australian Museum. The exhibit highlights the support that the East Timorese people gave to Australian soldiers in East Timor during World War II.

The World Development Report 2011 finds that on average, post-conflict countries take between 15 and 30 years, a full generation, to transition out of fragility and to build resilience. 'It is against this backdrop that Timor-Leste's social and economic development can be seen as remarkable'.[5]

2013

The first full-length feature film produced in Timor-Leste, *Beatriz's War* premieres in Dili. It shows how women in Timor-Leste resisted and coped with the Indonesian occupation. The film wins the Golden Peacock (Best Film) at the 44th International Film Festival of India.

2014

Presents solo exhibition *Ina Lou (Dear Mother Earth)* at Galeri Cipta II in Central Jakarta. She is the first female artist from Timor-Leste to have a solo exhibition in Indonesia.

Ina Lou includes Madeira's mixed media painting *Foremothers Fingerprints*. It references tais weaver's from Bobonaro who identify their own tais by "fingerprints" left on each cloth, a metaphor for stylistic and technical individuality.

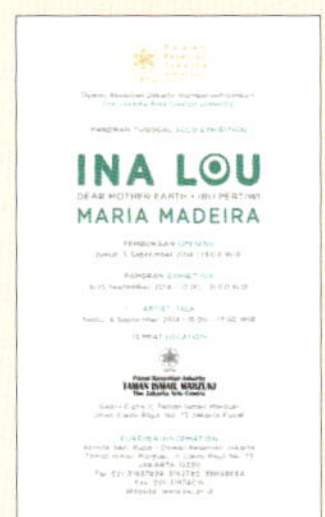

Ina Lou invite , 2014

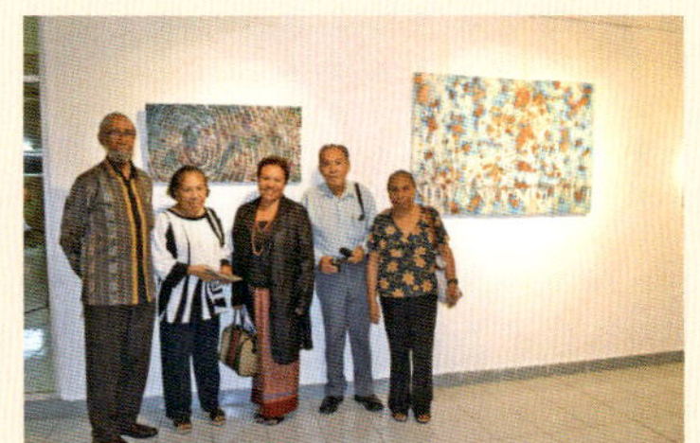

Madeira at opening of *Ina Lou* with parents (right) and family friends (left), Jakarta Arts Centre, 2014

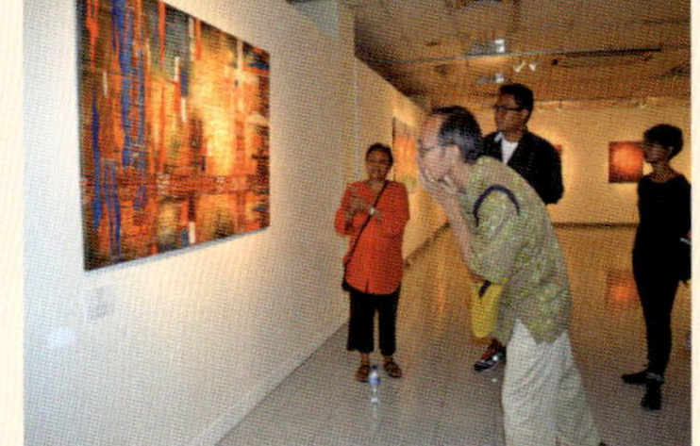

Madeira gives tour of *Ina Lou*, 2014

Exhibits in group exhibition *Elastic/Borracha/Elastico* at Contemporary Art Space in Darwin, Australia. The exhibition presents the outcomes of the 2012 mobile residency when Maria Madeira and fellow Timorese and Australian artists travelled around Timor-Leste witnessing the country's reconstruction and art practices such as tais weaving.

Along with weaver and performer Veronica Pereira Maia and curator Jo Holder, the artists in *Elastic/Borracha/Elastico* present an important archive and appreciation for Timor-Leste contemporary arts.

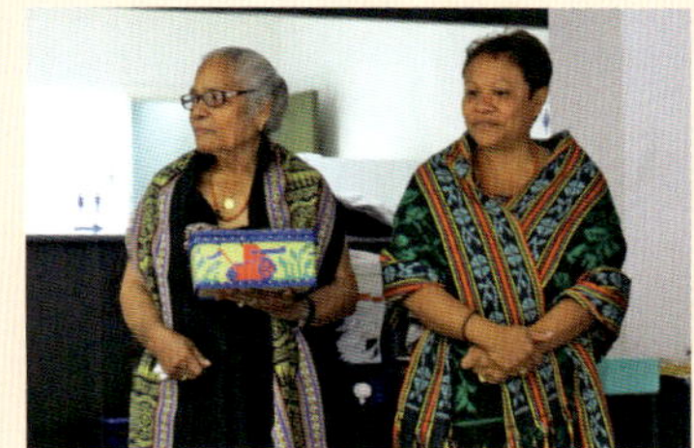

Left: Maria Madeira with Dona Veronica Pereira Maia at the opening of *Elastic*, 2014

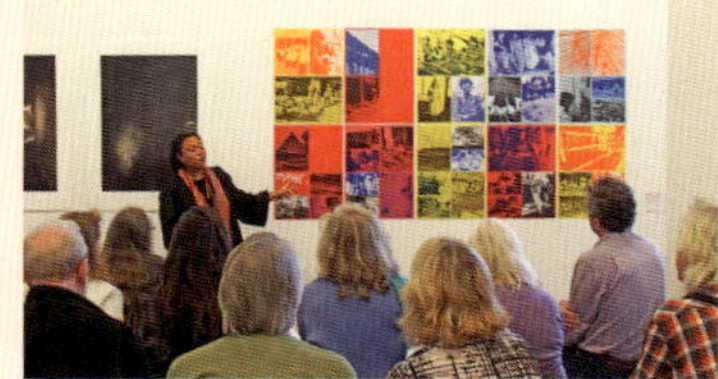

Madeira talks in front of award-winning print *Elastic/Borracha/Elastico (2012 Timor-Leste Mobile Residency Archives)* at Fremantle Arts Centre, 2014

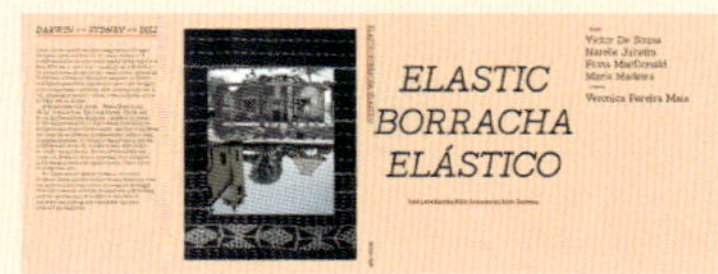

Cover for book *ELASTIC/BORRACHA/ELÁSTICO*, 2014

2015

Madeira delivers a talk on TED, a channel for influential and expert speakers from around the world. She presents "Art Can be Traditional and Contempcrary", expressing a desire for more contemporary female artists in Timor-Leste and her understanding of the union between the traditional and contemporary.

Wins the Fremantle Arts Centre Print Award jointly with artists Narelle Jubelin, Victor De Sousa and Fiona MacDonald for their collaborative work *Elastic/Borracha/Elastico (2012 Timor-Leste Mobile Residency Archives)*. The work documents their meetings with women weavers and cultural builders throughout Timor-Leste.

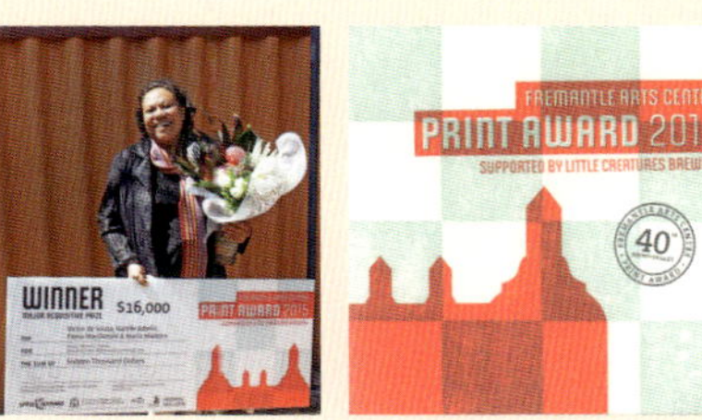

Madeira (left) receives the Fremantle Arts Centre Print Award (right), 2015

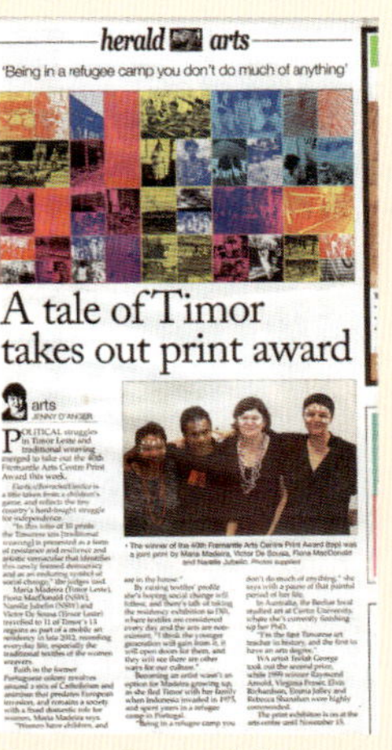

Herald Arts features Fremantle Print Award, 2015

Foremothers Fingerprints features on album cover for Jen Shyu and Jade Tongue's *Sounds and Cries of the World*. The music, sung in both English and Tetum, reflects upon the musical traditions of Shyu's mother's birthplace of Timor-Leste.

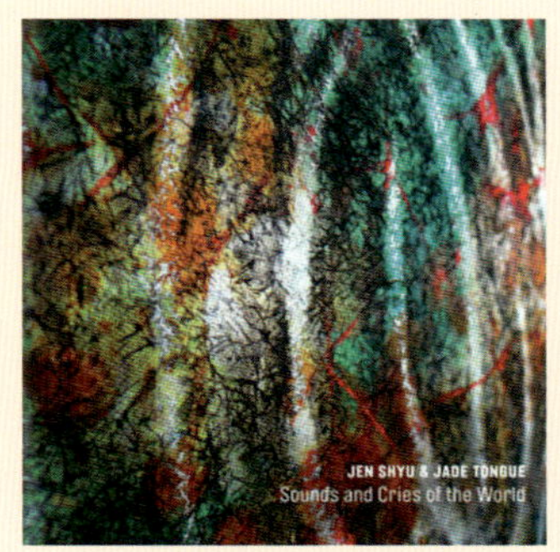

Album cover 'Sounds and Cries of the World' with Madeira's *Foremothers Fingerprints*, 2015

2018

Art work *Peskiza* features on the cover of Alterman et al's 'Independence Movements and Their Aftermath: Self-Determination and the Struggle for Success'.

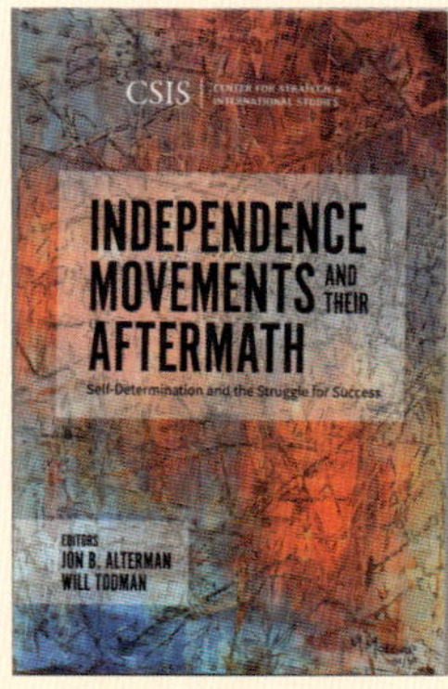

'Independence Movements and their Aftermath' featuring *Peskiza*, 2018

2019

Obtains a Doctor of Philosophy from Curtin University, Australia. Her thesis 'Women's Contribution to Timor-Leste's Art and Culture' explores the significant and under-recognised influence of women on the arts and culture in Timor-Leste.

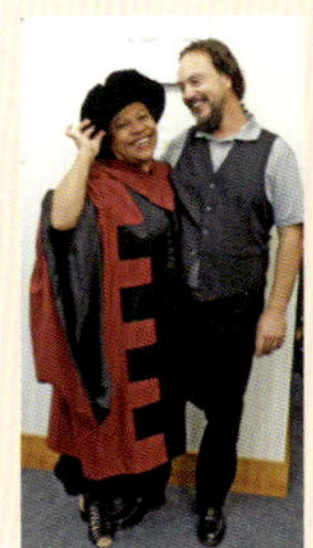
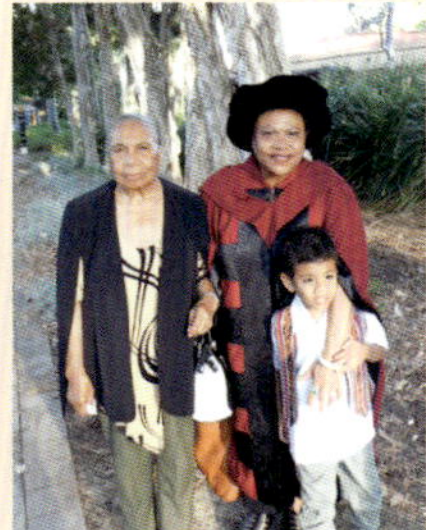

Madeira at graduation ceremony with partner Dennis Phillip Irwin (left) and with mother Terezinha de Jesus Madeira and son Ohara Madeira Irwin (right), 2019

Presents solo exhibition *Timor-Leste: An Artistic Perspective* at the University of Colorado, United States.

Participates in round-table discussions exploring art in political spaces, including 'Art in Contested Political and Cultural Terrains, Asia' at Columbia University, New York, and 'Arts Under Military Occupation' at the Association for Asian Studies Annual Conference in Denver, Colorado.

Presents at workshop *Politics of Visual Arts* at Columbia University, New York.

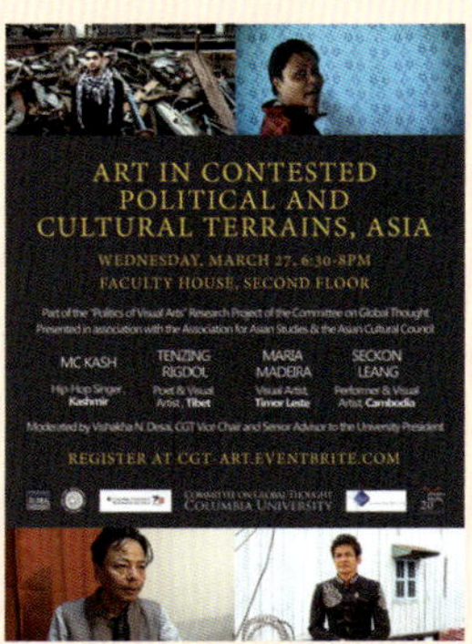

Madeira in Columbia University Poster, 2019

Madeira's art features on the cover of two books: McWilliam et al.'s *Routledge Handbook of Contemporary Timor-Leste* and Loney's *In Women's Words: Violence and Everyday Life during the Indonesian Occupation of East Timor, 1975-1999*.[6]

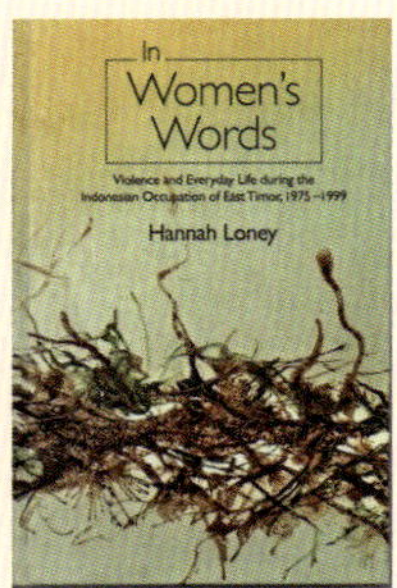

Book Cover *In Women's Words* featuring *Laclo River (Mota Laclo)*, 2019

2020

Exhibits at *ARTFEM Women Artists 2nd International Biennial of Macau* in the Natura Albergue SCM in Macau. It showcases art by 98 influential female artists from around the world.

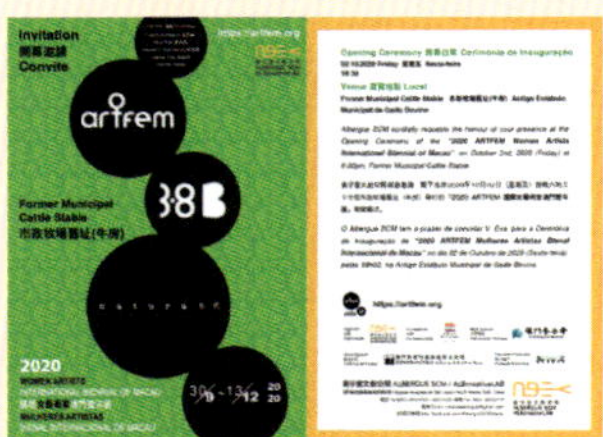

Invite to *ARTFEM, Women Artists International Biennale*, Macau, 2020

2021

The International Symposium 'Santa Cruz Massacre, 1991: 30 years on' is held by the Timor-Leste Studies Association and the Centro Nacional Chega in Dili. It is dedicated to filmmaker Max Stahl, whose footage of the Santa Cruz massacre played a pivotal role in raising awareness about the Indonesian occupation of East Timor.

Over two days almost thirty research papers and first-hand accounts are presented in English, Tetun and Portuguese, exploring topics such as the organisation of the protest, the impact of the massacre, and how these events have been remembered.

Exhibits a number of art works in Indonesia at the *Biennale Jogja XVI Equator #6*, the Jogyakarta National Museum, an international biennale which showcases contemporary art practice and discourse in Indonesia and Southeast Asia.

Red Water II features on award-winning composer Jen Shyu's Album cover for *Zero Grasses: Rituals for the Losses*.

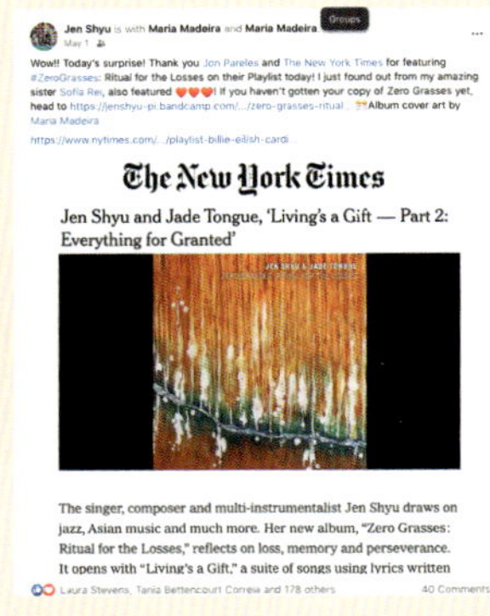

New York times on album 'Zero Grasses' with artwork *Red Water II*, 2021

2022

Tais officially becomes UNESCO Intangible Heritage. This safeguards tais as a cultural tradition including the establishment of the supportive body Tais National Committee.

Curates the exhibition *Hasoru Malu* which showcases the work of 15 Timorese artists. Held in Fundação Oriente, Dili, it marks the 20th anniversary of the Restoration of Independence in Timor-Leste.

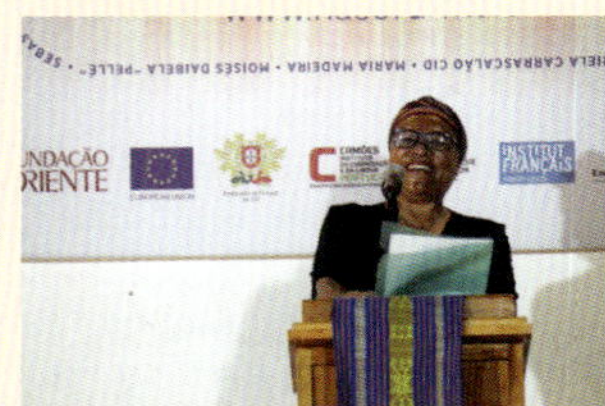

Madeira gives speech at opening of *Hasoru Malu*, 2022

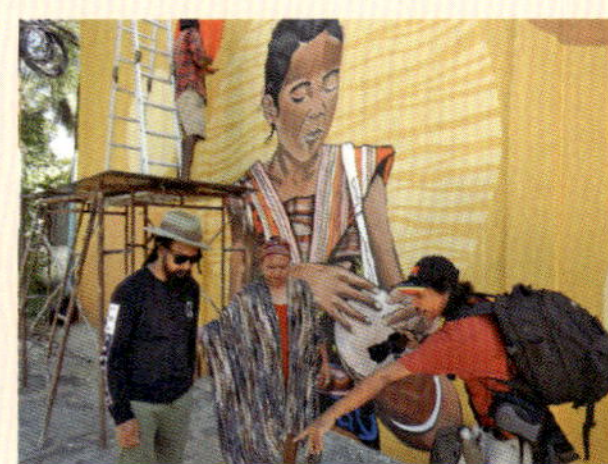

Madeira with artist Tony Amaral in front of his mural for *Hasoru Malu*, Dili, 2022

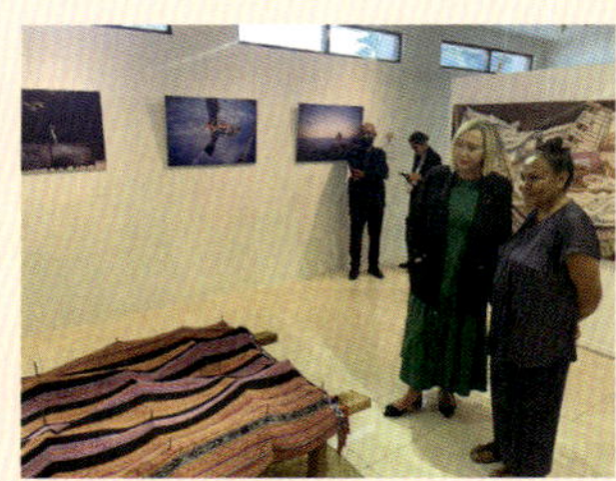

Madeira at *Hasoru Malu* with the Honourable Administrator of Northern Territory, Vicki O'Halloran, 2022

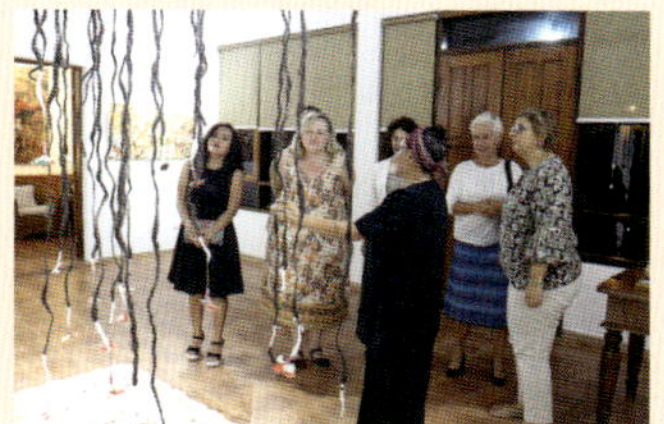
Madeira gives artist floor talk at *Hasoru Malu*, 2022

Presents the major solo exhibition *A Place in the Sun* at the Fundação Oriente in Dili.

Presents solo exhibit *Mana Maria* at the symposium 'Addressing the Multiple Marginalities of South and Southeast Asia' at Chiang Mai University in Thailand. Participates in the concurrent workshop 'Gender and Women's participation in Higher Education'.

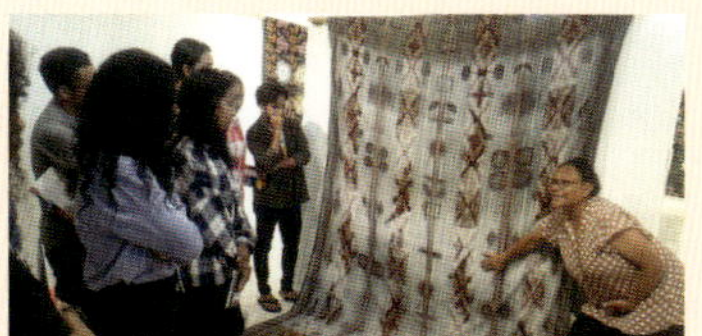
Madeira talks to Timorese high school students at *A Place in the Sun*, Fundação Oriente, 2022

2023

As an artist-in-residence, Madeira develops the major solo exhibition *Ko'alia Funan-Funan (Flowery Talk)* at Fundação Oriente, Dili. She centres the female voice and highlights the fundamental contribution of women to the contemporary arts in Timor-Leste.

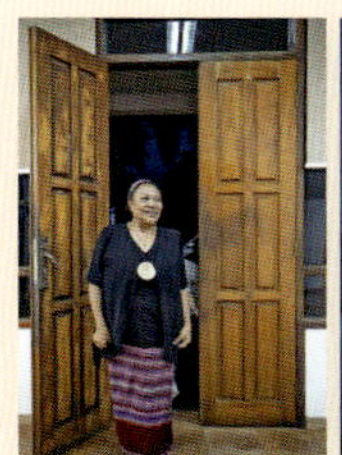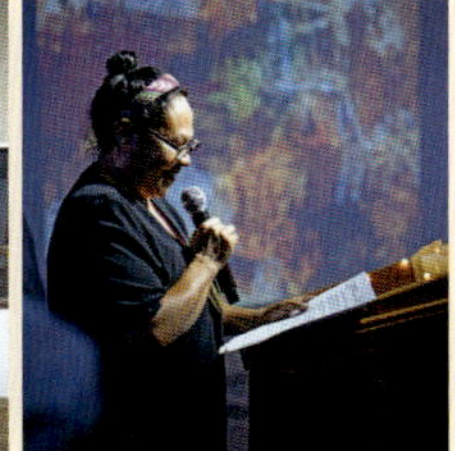
Left: Madeira opens *Ko'alia Funan-Funan (Flowery Talk)*, 2023
Right: Madeira gives speech at opening night, 2023

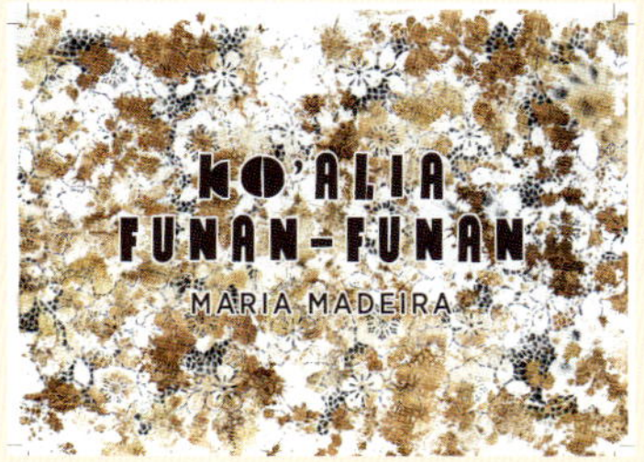
Catalogue cover *Ko'alia Funan-Funan*, 2023

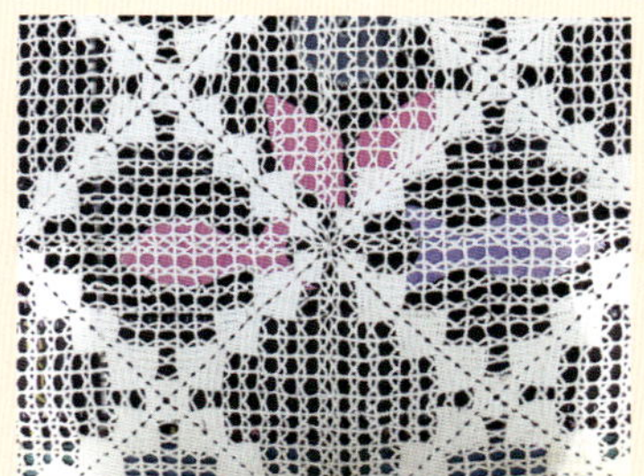
Detail of *Grupo Coral Sol Nascente* exhibited at *Ko'alia Funan-Funan*. Created by placing crochet, made and gifted by Madeira's mother, over the top of tais and baking in sunlight, 2023

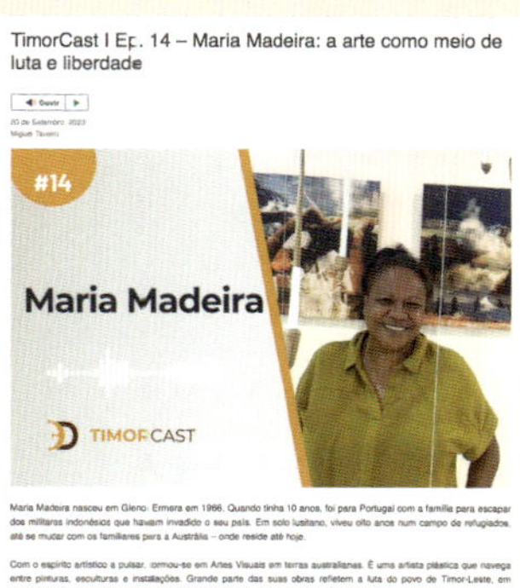

Madeira interviews on TimorCast, 2023

Unanimously selected by the Government of Timor-Leste to represent the country at the 60th International Art Exhibition La Biennale di Venezia, curated by Natalie King with assistant curator Leah Batterham.

2024

Professor Natalie King OAM, Anna Schwartz AM and Dr Kim McGrath spend time in Dili and make plans with Maria Madeira for the Venice Biennale.

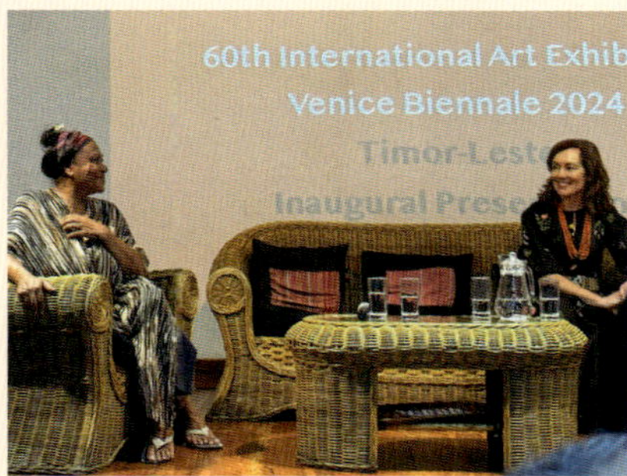

Maria Madeira and Natalie King present ideas for Timor-Leste at Venice Biennale, 2024

Travels to Venice with the Commissioner to select a venue for the Timor-Leste pavilion and meet with the La Biennale team.

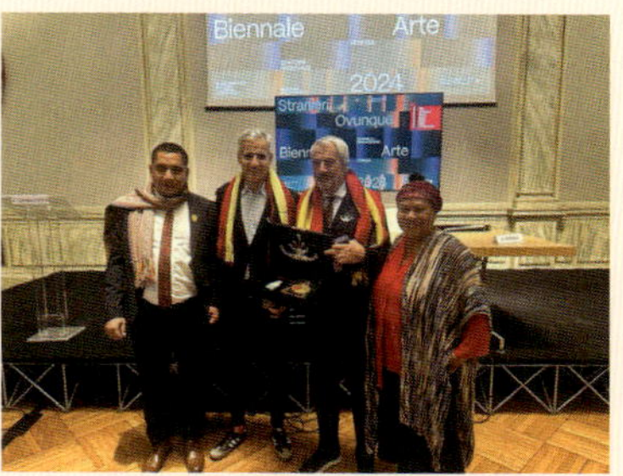
Maria Madeira meets with (from left) Jorge Soares Cristovão, Timor-Leste's Secretary of State for Art and Culture, Adriano Pedrosa, Curator of the Biennale Arte and Roberto Cicutto, President of La Biennale Di Venezia, Venice, Italy, 2024

Presents solo exhibition *Kiss and Don't Tell*, Timor-Leste's inaugural exhibition at the Biennale Arte 2024.

NOTES

1. Balibo Fort Veterans Museum, 'History of Timor-Leste', p. 39.

2. Jo Holder (ed.), *Elastic Borracha Elástico: Timor-Leste/Australia Mobile Contemporary Artists' Residency*, Northern Centre for Contemporary Art, Darwin and The Cross Art Projects, 2016, p. 114.

3. Jo Holder (ed.), 2016, p. 114.

4. *Chega! The Report of the Commission for Reception, Truth and Reconciliation (CAVR)*, executive summary, Government of Timor-Leste, 2005, p. 73.

5. World Bank, *World Development Report 2011: Conflict, Security and Development*, Published by The World Bank, 2011.

6. Andrew McWilliam & Michael Leach, *Routledge Handbook of Contemporary Timor-Leste (1st ed.)*, Routledge, 2019; Hannah Loney, *In Women's Words: Violence and Everyday Life during the Indonesian Occupation of East Timor, 1975-1999*, Liverpool University Press, 2018.

GLOSSARY

Arte Moris	first art school in Timor-Leste, based in Dili
Atis	(Tetun) backstrap loom used to weave tais
Balibo	town in Timor-Leste near the Indonesian border
Betel nut	seed of the areca palm grown and chewed in tropical Pacific, South and Southeast Asia, and parts of East Africa
Betel quid	mixture of tobacco, crushed betel nut and spices
CAVR or CRTR	Comição de Acolhimento Verdade e Reconciliação, Commission for Reception, Truth and Reconciliation est. 2001 to promote East Timorese reconciliation
Centro Nacional Chega	museum dedicated to promoting human rights and communicating experiences during the occupation
Chega!	(Tetun meaning 'enough!') report on human rights violations during the Indonesian occupation
CNRT	Conselho Nacional da Reconstrucão Timorense, National Council of Timorese Resistance 1998–2001
CTF	commission of truth and friendship
Ermera	village in Timor-Leste, in Mambai means 'red water'
FALINTIL	Forças Armadas de Libertação Nacional de Timor-Leste, the armed force of FRETILIN 1975–2001
Fataluku	(Tetun) people from the eastern tip of Timor
F-FDTL	Forças de Defesa de Timor-Leste, Defence Forces of Timor-Leste, formed 2001 as substitute for Falintil
Firaku	(Tetun) people from the eastern part of Timor-Leste
FRETILIN	Frente Revolucionário Timor-Leste Independente, Revolutionary Front for an Independent East Timor est. 1974
Futus	(Tetun) wrap resistant dye used in making tais
INTERFET	UN-authorised armed force led by Australia to East Timor in 1999
Kaibauk	(Tetun) traditional headdress in the shape of a buffalo horn
Katuas	(Tetun) term of respect for a veteran or elder
Lafaek or Abo	(Tetun) crocodile, represents grandparents or ancestors. In Timorese belief the crocodile is the transformation of the ancestors' body or spirit
Leste	(Portuguese) east
Liurai	(Tetun) the king in traditional kingdoms of Timor
Loromonu	(Tetun) where the sun sets, western part of Timor-Leste
Lorosa'e	(Tetun) where the sun rises, eastern part of Timor-Leste
Lulik	(Tetun) sacred
Luta	(Portuguese) the fight for independence
Mambai	language spoken by the Mambai people, the second largest ethnic group in Timor-Leste
Palapa or Ai-tali nia tahan-kain	(Portuguese/Tetun) local palm leaf used in building and weaving
Soru-Nain	(Tetun) traditional textile weavers
Surik	(Tetun) traditional carved sword
Tais	(Tetun) traditional handwoven textile
Tais-Feto	(Tetun) woman's cloth
Tais-Ki'ik	(Tetun) cloth sash
Tais-Mane	(Tetun) man's cloth
Tebe-Hare/Sama-Hare	(Tetun) traditional rice-harvesting ceremony
Tetun/Tetum	one of the official and most commonly used languages of Timor-Leste
UDT	União Democrática de Timorense, Timorese Democratic Union
Uma-Lulik	(Tetun) sacred house, in villages throughout Timor-Leste
UN	United Nations

LIST OF WORKS

All works are courtesy of Maria Madeira and Anna Schwartz Gallery, Australia

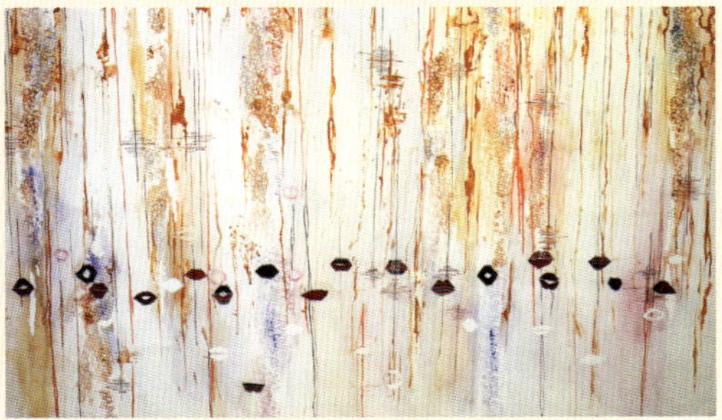

Kiss and Don't Tell, 2024
Painting installation of acrylic, betel nut, tais, lipstick, pigment, diluted earth and antiseptic on canvas with earth
Dimensions variable

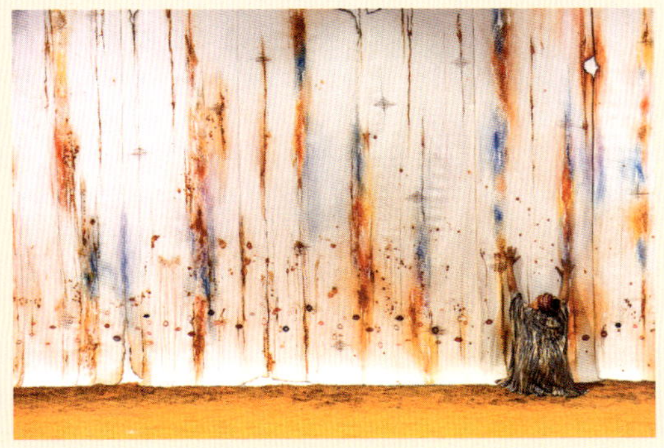

Kiss and Don't Tell, 2024
Performance video
Duration: 13–17 minutes

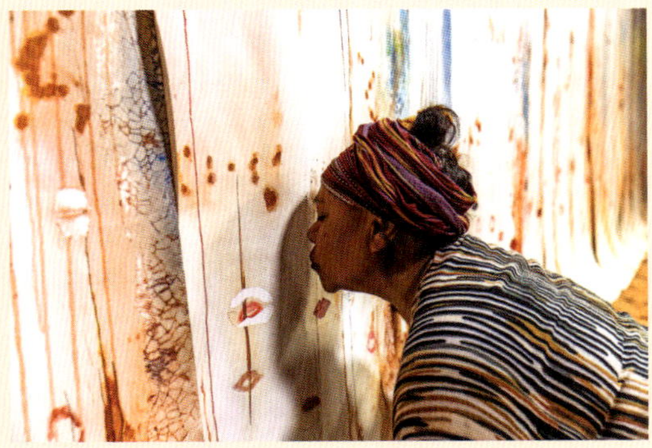

Kiss and Don't Tell, 2024
Live performance
Duration: 12–15 minutes

Kiss and Don't Tell, 2024
Site-specific installation of lipstick on window
Dimensions variable

FURTHER READING

Barrkman, Joanna, 'Binding Identities' in *From The Hands of Our Ancestors*, Museum and Art Gallery Northern Territory, with Direcção Nacional da Cultura, Timor-Leste, 2008.

Balibo Veterans Museum, *History of Timor-Leste,* Balibo Veterans Museum, Balibo, Timor-Leste, pp. 1–82.

Bovensiepen, Judith, 'Visions of prosperity and conspiracy' in *Timor-Leste Journal of Global and Historical Anthropology*, vol. 75, 2016, pp. 75–88.

Brown, Lyndell, Green, Charles & Cattapan, Jon, *Framing Conflict: Contemporary War and Aftermath*, Macmillan Art Publishing, Australia, 2014.

Dirgantoro, Wulan, 'Like Planting Flowers in a War Zone: Memory, Conflict and Healing in Contemporary Southeast Asian Art' in *Afterstorm*, (eds.) Charles Green and Jon Cattapan, Art+Australia & Victorian College of The Arts Publishing, University of Melbourne, Australia, 2021, pp. 195–207.

Dunn, James, 'Genocide in East Timor' in *Century of Genocide, Critical Essays and Eyewitness Accounts,* (eds) Samuel Totten & William S Parsons, Routledge, New York, 2004, pp. 263–94.

Fry, Tony & Palazón, David, *Academy of Arts and Creative Industries in Timor-Leste,* Griffith University, Brisbane, 2011.

Gusmão, Xanana, *To resist is to win!: The autobiography of Xanana Gusmão with selected letters & speeches,* Aurora Books with David Lovell Publishing, Melbourne, 2009.

Holder, Jo (ed), *Elastic Borracha Elástico: Timor-Leste/Australia Mobile Contemporary Artists' Residency,* Northern Centre for Contemporary Art, Darwin & The Cross Art Projects, Sydney, 2016.

Madeira, Maria, *Women's Contribution to Timor-Leste's Art and Culture,* Doctoral Thesis, Curtin University, Western Australia, 2019.

Madeira, Maria, 'Women's Contribution to Timor-Leste's Art and Culture' in *Southeast of Now: Directions in Contemporary and Modern Art in Asia*, vol. 6, no. 2, 2022, pp. 103–31.

McGrath, Kim, *Crossing the Line: Australia's Secret History in the Timor Sea,* Black Inc. Redback, Melbourne, 2017.

Molnar, Katalin, *Timor-Leste: Politics, History, and Culture*, Routledge, New York, 2009.

Niner, Sara, *Xanana: Leader of the Struggle for Independent Timor-Leste*, Australian Scholarly Publishing, Melbourne, 2000.

Palmer, Lisa, *Island Encounters: Timor from the outside in,* ANU Press, The Australian National University, Canberra, 2021.

Secretary of State for Arts & Culture, Timor Aid, Alola Foundation & National Commission of Timor-Leste, *Tais: Traditional Textile*, Government of Timor-Leste, 2023.

The Timor-Leste Commission for Reception, Truth and Reconciliation (CAVR), *Chega! The Final Report of the Timor-Leste Commission for Reception, Truth and Reconciliation (CAVR)*, Government of Timor-Leste, 2013.

Totten, Samuel, Parsons, William and Israel, Charney, *Century of Genocide, Critical Essays and Eyewitness Account,* Second Edition, Routledge, New York, 2004.

Veiga, Leonor, 'Movimentu Kultura in Timor-Leste: Maria Madeira's "agency"', in *Cadernos de Arte e Antropologia*, vol. 4, no. 1, 2015, pp. 85–101.

IMAGE CREDITS

All images of Maria Madeira's works are courtesy of Anna Schwartz Gallery, Australia. All measurements list height before width.

pp. 6-7
Timor-Leste and the region
Courtesy of the Timor-Leste Land and Maritime Boundary Office
Palácio do Governo, West Wing Building
Dili, Timor-Leste

No more lipstick
Natalie King

p. 22
Shush … Labele Koalia (Shush … Do Not Tell), 2009
Mixed media on paper: acrylic, pencil, ink
30 x 20 cm
Courtesy of Maria Madeira
Photo: David Palazón

pp. 24-25
Tais weaving from *Tais: Traditional Textile*, Government of Timor-Leste, 2023
Courtesy of the Secretary of State for Arts & Culture, Timor Aid, Alola Foundation & National Commission of Timor-Leste

Map of tais styles in Timor-Leste from *Tais: Traditional Textile*, Government of Timor-Leste, 2023
Courtesy of the Secretary of State for Arts & Culture, Timor Aid, Alola Foundation & National Commission of Timor-Leste

p. 26
Abut- Ama nia Fuk (Raizes-Cabelos Da Mãe; Roots-Mum's Hair), 1990
Mixed media on paper: pencil, charcoal, ink
20 x 30 cm
Courtesy of Maria Madeira
Photo: David Palazón

p. 27
Coro Loro Sa'e, 2023
Tais and sunlight
89 x 123 cm
Courtesy of Maria Madeira
Photo: David Palazón

Coro Loro Sa'e (detail), 2023
Tais and sunlight
Courtesy of Maria Madeira
Photo: David Palazón

pp. 28-29
Ko'alia Funan-Funan I/Conversa Floreada I/Flowery Talk I, 2023
Mixed media on paper: betel nut, red earth, charcoal, pencil, ink, glue and sealer
56 x 77 cm
Courtesy of Maria Madeira
Photo: David Palazón

p. 30
Still images from film *Halo Pintura ho Bua Malus (Painting with Betel nut)*, by Victor de Sousa, Dili, 2008
Courtesy of Maria Madeira

p. 31
Hamutuk/Juntos/Together, 2009
Mixed media on canvas
91 x 152 cm
Courtesy of Maria Madeira
Photo: David Palazón

p. 33
Traveller (Lao Rai), 2010
Installation in collaboration with Matias Madeira
Mixed materials
80 x 115 x 400 cm
Courtesy of Maria Madeira
Photo: David Palazón

From foreignness to fraternity
Kim McGrath

p. 50
Chips Mackinolty, *East Timor Fights On*, 1978
Screenprint on paper, Earthworks Poster Collective
Courtesy of Chips Mackinolty and National Gallery of Australia, Canberra

p. 53
Poster art, *Balibo*, directed by Robert Connolly, 2009
Courtesy of Robert Connolly

José Ramos-Horta speaking at the United Nations on the 'Question of East Timor', 20 August 1982
Courtesy of Balibo Fort Museum, Balibo, Timor-Leste

p. 54
Traveller (Lao rai), 2010
Installation in collaboration with Matias Madeira
Mixed materials
80 x 115 x 400 cm
Courtesy of Maria Madeira
Photo: David Palazón

p. 57
Asuntus Kontemporáneus/ Contemporary Issues/ Masalah Comtemporary, 2014
Mixed media on canvas: acrylic, gesso, impasto gel, red earth, lipstick, pencil, charcoal, betel nut, shellac, ink, glue, tais
42 x 30 cm (series of 16)
Courtesy of Maria Madeira
Photo: David Palazón

The day after tomorrow
Antonio Sampaio

pp. 60-63
Maria Madeira performing with *Kiss and Don't Tell*, 2024
Mixed media on canvas: acrylic, gesso, impasto, gel, glue, lipstick, tais
Courtesy of Maria Madeira
Photo: Juventino Madeira

Songs Performed by Maria Madeira

p. 66
Armonia I/Harmony I, 2010
Mixed media on canvas
25 x 30 cm
Courtesy of Maria Madeira
Photo: David Palazón

p. 67
Kdadalak/River Streams/Sungai Mengalir, 2014
Mixed Media on canvas: rock powder, red earth, glue, shellac and sealer
100 x 130 cm
Courtesy of Maria Madeira
Photo: David Palazón

p. 69
Ina Lou I, II & III/Dear Mother Earth I, II & III/Ibu Pertiwi I, II & III, 2010
Mixed media on canvas: acrylic, gesso, impasto gel, pencil, betel nut, glue and sealer
91 x 46 cm (series of 3)
Courtesy of Maria Madeira
Photo: David Palazón

Maria Madeira in conversation with
Natalie King

p. 72
Untitled I, 2023
Mixed media on paper: betel nut, tais, ink, glue, sealer
29 x 22 cm
Courtesy of Maria Madeira
Photo: David Palazón

p. 75
Lips to Kiss and Don't Tell (Ibun Kulit ba Rei no Labele Koalia)-Study III, 2023
Mixed media on paper: tais, red earth, glue and sealer
22 x 29 cm
Courtesy of Maria Madeira
Photo: David Palazón

pp. 76-77
Bee Matan (Water Source) (detail), 2022
Mixed media on paper: acrylic, betel nut, red earth, cotton, pencil, ink, glue, shellac, sealer
50 x 70 cm
Courtesy of Maria Madeira
Photo: David Palazón

p. 79
Fan Na'an Fatin/Mercado de Carne/Meat Market, 2010
Mixed media on canvas
70 x 90 cm
Courtesy of Maria Madeira
Photo: David Palazón

pp. 80-81
270+ Massakre Santa Cruz Nian (270+ Massacre de Santa Cruz; The Santa Cruz Massacre) (and details), 1996
Mixed media: sculpture in metal
350 x 350 cm
Courtesy of Maria Madeira
Photo: David Palazón

pp. 82-83
Jerasaun Feto Nian/Female Generation, 2014
Mixed media on canvas: acrylic, gesso, impasto gel, red earth, pencil, betel nut, shellac, ink, glue and sealer
52 x 197 cm
Courtesy of Maria Madeira
Photo: David Palazón

Threads of memory: conflict, nature and healing
Wulan Dirgantoro

pp. 86-87
Renaissance (Moris fila fali), Renascence (Moris foun) and *Renascent (Moris tan)*, 2007
Mixed media on canvas
76 x 61 cm (series of 3)
Courtesy of Maria Madeira
Photo: David Palazón

pp. 88-89
Community participants in Gleno, Timor-Leste with *Mama Hamutuk (Chewing Betel Nut Together)*, 25 January 2003
Mixed media on canvas: betel nut, glue, shellac and sealer
Courtesy of Maria Madeira
Photo: David Palazón

pp. 90-91
Mama Hamutuk (Chewing Betel Nut Together), 2003
Mixed media on canvas: betel nut, glue, shellac and sealer
Courtesy of Maria Madeira
Photo: David Palazón

pp. 92-93
Tebe Hare/Sama Hare/Stepp. ing on Rice Husks, 2008
Mixed media on canvas: acrylic, diluted red earth, impasto gel, glue, betel nut, shellac and sealer
91 x 183 cm
Courtesy of Maria Madeira
Photo: David Palazón

Who can erase the traces? Historical justice and women's empowerment
Cristina Baldacci

p. 96
Kiss & Don't Tell II (a study) (detail), 2007
Mixed media on canvas: acrylic, gesso, impasto, gel, glue, lipstick, tais
76 x 61 cm (series of 4)
Courtesy of Maria Madeira
Photo: David Palazón

pp. 98-99
Kiss & Don't Tell II (a study), 2007
Mixed media on canvas: acrylic, gesso, impasto, gel, glue, lipstick, tais
76 x 61 cm (series of 4)
Courtesy of Maria Madeira
Photo: David Palazón

Hasoru Malu: meeting, weaving and connecting
Joana Saraiva

p. 102
Madeira giving opening speech at *Hasoru Malu*, Dili, September 2023
Courtesy of Maria Madeira
Photo: Mariano Gonçalves

pp. 104-105
Kolonizasaun/Colonização/Colonisation, 2019
Mixed media on canvas: acrylic, impasto gel, diluted red earth, betadine, pencil, ink and sealer
70 x 155 cm
Courtesy of Maria Madeira
Photo: David Palazón

Silensiu Folin Hira? (Silencio a Que Preço? What Price Silence?), 1996
Sculpture in metal, wood, wire, tais
100 x 200 cm
Courtesy of Maria Madeira
Photo: David Palazón

Chronology

p. 108
Madeira with her family in Gleno, Timor-Leste, c. 1972
Artists collection

Villagers celebrate the first anniversary of Fretilin, Dili, 1975
Courtesy of Balibo Veterans Museum, Timor-Leste
Photo: Oliver Strewe

Madeira and other children at refugee camp, Quinta da Graca, Portugal, c. 1977
Artist's collection

Maria Madeira with sister Celina Madeira and Grupo Danca Folklorico, Portugal, c. 1982
Artist's collection

p. 109
Two images of Madeira with Coro Loro
Sa'e, Wales Choir Festival, c. 1982
Artist's collection

Madeira with Coro Loro Sa'e and the
Portuguese girls choir, Wales Choir
Festival, c. 1982
Artist's collection

Madeira with Sunshine/Sunrise Choir,
England, 1982
Artist's collection

Madeira with installation, Curtin
University, Western Australia, 1991
Courtesy of Maria Madeira

Madeira speaks at protest, Perth, 1991
Courtesy of Maria Madeira

Dislocation, 1992
Room installation in collaboration with
David Jones
Mixed media: newspaper, glue, earth
and rope
Perth Institute of Contemporary Arts,
Western Australia
Courtesy of Maria Madeira

Madeira delivers speech with the late
Peter Stewart, Perth, Western Australia,
1996
Artist's collection

p. 110
Protest for an Independent Timor, Perth,
c. 1996
Artist's collection

270+ The Santa Cruz Massacre, 1996
Room installation: metal sculpture and
cloth
Perth Institute of Contemporary Arts,
Western Australia
Courtesy of Maria Madeira

The West Australian 'Protest in Paint' by
Ron Banks, Perth, 25 June 1996
Artist's collection

*Silence at what Price? (Silensiu folin
hira?)*, 1996
Mixed media: metal sculpture, wood,
wire and tais
100 x 200 cm
Courtesy of Maria Madeira
Photo: David Palazón

Poster for *Memory & Reality*, Kalla Yeedip
Gallery, Midland, Western Australia, 1996
Artist's collection

Invitation to *Hamutuk (Together)*, Kalla
Yeedip Gallery, Midland, Western
Australia, 1997
Artist's collection

Madeira with band Jah Era, Perth, 1997
Artist's collection

p. 111
Voting in Bobonaro District, Timor Leste,
30 August 1999
Courtesy of Balibo Veterans Museum,
Timor-Leste

East Timor's independence referendum
ballot paper, 1999
Courtesy of Balibo Veterans Museum,
Timor-Leste

Maria Madeira with cousin Lumena
Madeira voting on referendum day,
30 August 1999
Artist's collection

Albany Advertiser 'Beauty of East Timor
on Film', 16 November 2000
Artist's collection

Madeira with Craig Hopper and Los
Palos Ambulance team, Los Palos, Timor-
Leste, 2002
Artist's collection

Ambulance logos designed by Madeira,
Timor-Leste, 2002
Artist's collection

p. 112
Madeira and local guide, Ainaro, Timor-
Leste, 2002
Artist's collection
Photo: David Palazón

Madeira interviews with the *Lian Nain*
(Owner of Words/Elders) in *Uma Lulik*
(Sacred House) of Estado Hatu Mautei,
Ermera, Timor-Leste, 2002
Artist's collection

Madeira with locals, Hau Tio, Ainaro,
Timor-Leste, 2002
Artist's collection

Madeira interviews locals, Ermera, Timor-
Leste, 2002
Artist's collection

Picking corn (Hili Batar), 2003
Mixed media: wood, corn, acrylic, shellac
and traditional East Timorese basketry
60 x 130 cm
Courtesy of Maria Madeira
Photo: David Palazón

Madeira speaks at opening of *A Dream
Come True*, Hotel Timor, Dili, 2005
Courtesy of the artist

Cover of final report 'Chega! The Report
of the Commission for Reception, Truth
and Reconciliation, (CAVR)', 2013
Courtesy of Balibo Veterans Museum,
Timor-Leste

p. 113
Catalogue cover, *Picturing the Sea*,
Lawrence Wilson Gallery, University of
Western Australia, 2006
Courtesy of Maria Madeira

Poster for *Silent Voices*, Cannery Arts
Centre, Esperance, Western Australia,
2007
Artist's collection

Gazette newspaper 'A Taste of Timor's
Art', 2007
Artist's collection

Newspaper article 'Art lover's dream in
Denmark this Easter', 2008
Artist's collection

Madeira teaching Arte Moris Students,
Dili, 2008
Artist's collection

Madeira with tais weaver in Viqueque,
Timor-Leste, 2009
Artist's collection

Poster art, *Balibo*, directed by Robert
Connolly, 2009
Courtesy of Robert Connolly

Book Cover for Belton et al., *Maternal
Mortality, Unplanned Pregnancy and
Unsafe Abortion in Timor-Leste*, Charles
Darwin University, Sydney, 2009
Courtesy of Maria Madeira

p. 114
Dr Maria Madeira with Dr Zacarias
Albano da Costa, *Quietly Speaking*,
Casa Europa, Dili, 2010
Courtesy of Maria Madeira

Magazine article on *Quietly Speaking*,
May 2010
Artist's collection

Madeira and locals in Dili with *Traveller
(Lao Rai)*, 2010
Installation in collaboration with Matias
Madeira
Mixed materials
80 x 115 x 400 cm
Courtesy of Maria Madeira
Photo: David Palazón

Close-up detail of *Traveller (Lao Rai)*,
2010
Photo: David Palazón

Poster of Madeira for *Smiling Project*,
Macau 2011
Artist's collection

Article in CulturGUIA, *Festival Da
Lusofonia*, Macau, 2011
Artists collection

Madeira at Creative Industries
Conference, Dili, 2011
Artist's collection

Maria Madeira with Narelle Jubelin, Fiona
MacDonald and a local Tais weaver in Ilat
Lau, Bobonaro, Timor-Leste 2012
Artist's collection

Poster for Timor-Leste Mobile residency
from *Elastics/Borracha/Elástico*, (ed.)
Jo Holder, 2012
Courtesy of Maria Madeira

p. 115
Invitation to *Ina Lou*, Galeri Cipta II,
Jakarta, Indonesia, 2014
Artist's collection

Madeira at the opening of *Ina Lou*,
Jakarta Arts Centre, 2014
Artist's collection

Madeira giving guided tour of *Ina Lou*,
Jakarta, Jakarta Arts Centre, 2014
Artist's collection

Madeira with Dona Veronica Pereira
Maia at the opening of *Elastic/Borracha*,
Contemporary Art Space, Darwin 2014
Artist's collection

Madeira presenting talk at Fremantle
Arts Centre, Perth, 2014
Artist's collection

Book cover, *Elastics/Borracha/Elástico*,
(ed.) Jo Holder, Northern Centre for
Contemporary Art, Darwin & The Cross
Art Projects, Sydney, 2016

Madeira receiving Fremantle Arts Centre
Print Award for *Elastic/Borracha/Elastico*,
2015
Artist's collection

Fremantle Arts Centre Print Award, 2015
Artist's collection

Herald Arts 'A Tale of Timor takes out
Print Award', Perth, 2015
Artist's collection

CD album cover, Jen Shyu and Jade
Tongue, *Sounds and Cries of the World*,
2015
Artist's collection

Book cover, (eds.) Jon Alterman and Will
Todman, *Independence Movements
and Their Aftermath: Self-Determination
and the Struggle for Success*, Barnes &
Noble, 2018
Courtesy of Maria Madeira

p. 116
Maria Madeira and Dennis Phillip Irwin,
Curtin University, Western Australia, 2019
Artist's collection

Maria Madeira with Terezinha de Jesus
Madeira and Ohara Madeira Irwin, Curtin
University, Western Australia, 2019
Artist's collection

Columbia University poster 'Art in
Contested Political and Cultural Terrains,
Asia', March 2019 Artist's collection

Book Cover for Hannah Loney, *In
Women's Words: Violence and Everyday
Life during the Indonesian Occupation of
East Timor, 1975-1999*, Sussex Academic,
Liverpool University Press, Liverpool,
2018
Courtesy of Maria Madeira

Invitation to 'ARTFEM, Women Artists
International Biennale in Macau', 2020
Artist's collection

New York Times on Jen Shyu and Jade
Tongue's album *Zero Grasses: Rituals for
the Losse*, Pi Recordings, 2021
Artist's collection

Madeira delivering speech at *Hasoru
Malu, Fundação Oriente*, Dili, 2022
Artist's collection

Madeira with Tony Amaral in front of his
mural work, Dili, 2022
Courtesy of Maria Madeira

Madeira with the Honourable
Administrator of Northern Territory Vicki
O'Halloran, *Hasoru Malu*, Fundação
Oriente, Dili, 2022
Courtesy of Maria Madeira

p. 117
Madeira giving talk, *Hasoru Malu*,
Fundação Oriente, Dili, 2022
Courtesy of Maria Madeira

Madeira giving talk, *A Place in the Sun*,
Fundação Oriente, Dili, 2022
Courtesy of Maria Madeira

Madeira at *Ko'alia Funan-Funan (Flowery
Talk)*, Fundação Oriente, Dili, 2023
Courtesy of Fundação Oriente, Dili and
Anna Schwartz Gallery, Australia

Madeira giving opening speech at *Ko'alia
Funan-Funan (Flowery Talk)*, Fundação
Oriente, Dili, 2023
Courtesy of Fundação Oriente, Dili and
Anna Schwartz Gallery, Australia

Catalogue cover *Ko'alia Funan-Funan
(Flowery Talk)*, Fundação Oriente, Dili,
2023
Courtesy of Fundação Oriente, Dili and
Anna Schwartz Gallery, Australia

Detail of *Grupo Coral Sol Nascente*, 2023
Tais and sunlight
89 x 123 cm
Courtesy of Fundação Oriente, Dili and
Anna Schwartz Gallery, Australia

Madeira on TimorCast Radio, Episode
14, Dili, 2023
Artist's collection

Maria Madeira and Natalie King give
presentation, Dili, 2023
Courtesy of the artist

Maria Madeira with Jorge Soares
Cristovão, Adriano Pedrosa and Roberto
Cicutto, Venice, Italy, 2024
Courtesy of the artist

CONTRIBUTORS

DR MARIA MADEIRA is an artist who lives and works between Dili, Timor-Leste and Perth, Western Australia. She was born in Gleno, in the Ermera region of Timor-Leste. She has a BA Fine Arts (Visual Arts) (1991) and Graduate Diploma of Education majoring in Art (1996) from Curtin University, Western Australia. She has a BA in Political Science from Murdoch University, Western Australia (1996) and a PhD (Doctor of Philosophy) from Curtin University (2019). In 2024 she will be the first artist to represent Timor-Leste at the 60th International Art Exhibition – La Biennale di Venezia. Her solo exhibitions include *Flowery Talk*, Fundação Oriente, Dili, Timor-Leste, 2024; *Mana Maria*, Chiang Mai University, Thailand, 2022; *A Place in the Sun*, Fundação Oriente, Dili, Timor-Leste, 2022; *Timor-Leste: An Artistic Perspective*, University of Colorado, 2019; *Ina Lou (Dear Mother Earth)*, Galeri Cipta II, Jakarta, 2014; *Familiar Steps*, Festival da Lusofonia, Macau, 2011 and *Silent Voices*, Cannery Arts Centre, Esperance, Western Australia, 2007.
www.mariamadeira.art

PROFESSOR NATALIE KING OAM is an Australian curator, editor and arts leader based in Naarm, Melbourne. She is an Enterprise Professor of Visual Arts at the University of Melbourne. In 2022 she was curator of *Paradise Camp: Yuki Kihara*, Aotearoa New Zealand Pavilion at the 59th International Art Exhibition – La Biennale di Venezia, accompanied by an award-winning publication that she edited with Thames & Hudson. In 2022 she also co-curated *Reversible Destiny: Australian and Japanese Contemporary Photography* at the Tokyo Photographic Art Museum as part of the Olympics Cultural Programme. In 2017, she was curator of *Tracey Moffatt: My Horizon*, Australian Pavilion at the 57th Venice Biennale. She has curated exhibitions for the Singapore Art Museum; National Museum of Art, Ōsaka; Tokyo Photographic Art Museum; National Gallery of Indonesia, Jakarta; and Museum of Contemporary Art, Sydney, among others. She is co-Artistic Director, with Sujan Chitrakar, of the Kathmandu Triennale 2026.
www.natalieking.com.au

CRISTINA BALDACCI is Associate Professor of the History of Contemporary Art at the Ca' Foscari University of Venice and coordinator of the Ecological Art Practices research group at THE NEW INSTITUTE Centre for Environmental Humanities (NICHE). The main focus of her research is the archive as metaphor and art form; practices of appropriation, montage and re-enactment in contemporary art; the theory of images and visual culture; the relationship between art and the Anthropocene: all subjects on which she has published extensively. She combines her academic activity with contributions to art magazines and the curating of exhibitions.

LEAH BATTERHAM is a curator and researcher based in Sydney, Australia. Guided by a commitment to opening up spaces for artistic dialogue and learning, she graduated with a Masters of Art Curatorship from the University of Melbourne in 2023 and wrote a thesis research paper on the challenges and opportunities for Australian arts organisations in producing biennials. She assisted with the early stages of exhibition development, writing and research for the Archie Moore, Australia Pavilion at the 60th Venice Biennale. Previously, she has undertaken research for Mosman Art Gallery, Sydney, and worked voluntarily as a visitor experience guide at the Art Gallery of New South Wales.

DR WULAN DIRGANTORO is an art historian and curator based in Melbourne, Australia. She currently holds the position of Lecturer in Contemporary Art at the School of Culture and Communication at the University of Melbourne. Her publications include *Feminisms and Indonesian Contemporary Art: Defining Experiences* (Amsterdam University Press, 2017) and 'After 1965: Historical Violence and Strategies of Representation in Indonesian Visual Arts' in *Living Art: Indonesian Artists Engage Politics, Society and History* (ANU Press, 2022). As a researcher, her writings have also been published in various books, magazines, journals and exhibition catalogues in Indonesia, Australia, England and Japan. Her current research is on the impact of historical violence on aesthetic practice in modern and contemporary art in Indonesia and Timor-Leste.

KAY RALA XANANA GUSMÃO was born on 20 June 1946 in then Portuguese Timor. He was a journalist when his country was invaded by Indonesia in 1975. He joined the Timorese resistance and became leader in 1981. After 17 years as a guerrilla fighter, he was arrested in 1992. Gusmão led the resistance from prison in Jakarta until his release in 1999 after the Timorese people voted in support of independence. Revered as a national hero, he became the first elected President of the Democratic Republic of Timor-Leste in 2002. He served as Prime Minister from 2007 to 2015 with a focus on reconciliation, peace-building, national unity, and economic development. He resigned in 2015 to lead Timor-Leste's maritime boundary negotiations with Australia and maritime and land boundaries with Indonesia. Gusmão was elected for a third term as Prime Minister in May 2023.

DR KIM McGRATH is an Australian writer and researcher who has worked on development and governance issues in Timor-Leste for nearly two decades. She provides strategic advice, research, policy development, writing and editorial services to governments, private companies, universities, and not-for-profit organisations. She was arts advisor to the Victorian Premier from 1999 to 2007. She served on the board of the Melbourne International Film Festival from 2008 to 2018 and Film Victoria from 2010 to 2013. She was an advisor to the Australian Commissioner for the Venice Biennale in 2017. Her book *Crossing the Line, Australia's Secret History in the Timor Sea* was released in August 2017. A Portuguese edition was published in 2019. She was awarded a Doctor of Philosophy from Monash University in 2021.

ANTONIO SAMPAIO is a journalist with more than 30 years of experience. He has written on Timor-Leste since 1990 and covered the pro-independence struggle, the independence referendum and the first steps towards the restoration of independence and most significant events since then. He has won several media awards and was recognized with the Medal of the Order of Timor-Leste for his contributions to the country.

JOANA SARAIVA is the director of Fundação Oriente in Timor-Leste, where she has worked since 2020. With a background in communications, she holds a degree in Social Communication with a Major in Journalism (UFRGS, Brazil), a postgraduate degree in Poverty Reduction (CeDEP/SOAS, University of London) and a Masters in Communication for Development (Malmö University, Sweden). She has worked with a number of national and international institutions in Timor-Leste over the years. In her role at Fundação Oriente, a Portuguese foundation present in Timor-Leste since 2000, she has worked alongside Timorese artists towards enhancing the country's arts scene, with a view to strengthening technical and artistic professional skills within the cultural industry and increasing the quality and quantity of cultural goods and services produced, while forging networks within the international arts scene and promoting the work of Timorese artists and their visibility, both in the country and worldwide.

ARTIST'S ACKNOWLEDGEMENTS

First and foremost, thank you God for the wonders of creativity and for being all that I am.

I thank the Government of Timor-Leste, particularly Prime Minister Xanana Gusmão and the Secretary of State for Arts and Culture and Timor-Leste's Commissioner for the Venice Biennale, Jorge Soares Cristovão, for giving me this extraordinary opportunity.

Thank you also to La Biennale di Venezia for inviting Timor-Leste to participate in the 60th Venice Biennale 2024.

My deepest gratitude to the Timor-Leste Venice Biennale team: curator and editor, Professor Natalie King OAM, and project advisors Anna Schwartz AM, Dr Kim McGrath and Simon Fenby as well as Pavilion Manager, Diego Carpentiero. Your support, advice and encouragement has been invaluable.
Thank you also to the Fundação Oriente and Director Joana Saraiva for giving me opportunities to exhibit in Timor-Leste and to be a part of the growing contemporary artistic language of Timor-Leste.

Thank you to Caitlin Wilson, Australian Ambassador to Timor-Leste, and Australian Volunteers International for giving me the opportunity to interact and work closely with other visual and performance artists in Timor-Leste.

Thank you to the ancestors for showing me my roots. And thank you to the women of Timor-Leste who are the source of our artistic and cultural identity. I acknowledge all female visual artists for having the talent, courage and passion to create, tell stories, and share our reality.

Thank you to my friends and colleagues from Coro Loro Sa'e and to all Timor-Leste artists for their passion and creativity.

My deepest gratitude is extended to the Timorese community of Perth in Western Australia, and to my friends in Timor-Leste for their help, support and encouragement.

Thank you you Uca, Mong, Alfeo, Mariano, Juventino, Adelino, Natercia, Camilio, Dedito, Quico, Vanessa, Marisa, Peter, Thomas, Cidalia, Nino, Fernando, Milena, Zacarias, Tilda, Amo Anibal, Luisa, Jacinta, Benny, Ines and Gonçalo.

My eternal gratitude to my parents, brothers, sisters, nephews, nieces and my extended family for their support, encouragement and inspiration.

Finally, thank you Phillip and Ohara for all your love, patience and understanding. In God's grace I thank you for being all that you are, for I am because we are.

CURATOR'S ACKNOWLEDGEMENTS

On 1 August 2023, my friend and gallerist Anna Schwartz AM left a phone message to call her. Little did I know that this unexpected call would entice me to join Anna, Dr Kim McGrath and Simon Fenby to support Maria Madeira's journey to the Venice Biennale, representing Timor-Leste as the newest country in Asia with their inaugural pavilion.

I thank His Excellency Kay Rala (Xanana) Gusmão, Prime Minister of Timor-Leste, his Chief of Staff Elizabeth Exposto and our Commissioner, Jorge Soares Cristovão for their vision and leadership. I also thank Dr Nidio Pinto and Claudio Marques Cabral for guiding us in Dili and managing many aspects of this complex project.

When I first glimpsed Maria's work, I knew that her story was urgent, uncompromising and profound, further amplified by visiting Maria's exhibition *Flowery Talk* at Fundação Oriente in Dili with Director, Joana Saraiva. Her haunting narrative and lived experience needed to be told in the global arena at the most prestigious and oldest international visual arts event, La Biennale di Venezia. Maria's work has material dexterity and ingenuity but most importantly, it is a story from the heart.

Maria and I share the same year of birth: we are mothers, sisters, partners and daughters from different worlds and we are passionately committed to giving voice to women.

From the outset, I have been swept into Maria's warmth and sincerity, creativity and kindness. I extend my profound thanks to Maria for trusting me to be her curator, for smiling despite the pressures and drawing the entire team into her enchanting orbit. Every step has been a miracle from Peter McMullin AM and Ruth McMullin generously funding our magnificent catalogue with Italian publisher Skira, staff Giulia Rizzuto and Costanza De Bellegarde to filmmaker Robert Connolly directing Maria's performance with his crew and the Melbourne Timorese Community Choir.

I sincerely thank Anna, Kim and Simon for keeping us on track, dreaming big and providing invaluable advice on every aspect of this mammoth project. Our trip to Dili in January 2024, harnessed our deep commitment to realising the Timor-Leste Pavilion. I thank Morry Schwartz for his sage advice on the publication.

Producing an exhibition and publication in a compressed timeframe has been exhilarating and unremitting, only possible with the hard work of a dedicated and talented team often referred to as the 'dream team' including: Pavilion Manager, Diego Carpentiero; Exhibition Manager, Karen Hall; Exhibition Designer, Anita Gigi Budai; Graphic Designer, Andy Warren; Publicist Katrina Hall; Assistant Curator, Leah Batterham and photographers Juventino Madeira, Mariano Gonçalves, Jorge de Aurjo and David Palazón. I am indebted to your collective professionalism, good will and supreme capabilities by working harmoniously and steadily.

I would like to extend my deepest thanks to the contributors of this publication for their illuminating words, poems and reflections especially His Excellency Kay Rala (Xanana) Gusmão, Prime Minister of Timor-Leste, Wulan Dirgantoro, Cristina Baldacci, Antonio Sampaio, Dr Kim McGrath, Joana Saraiva and Leah Batterham.

I thank my colleagues at the Victorian College of the Arts, University of Melbourne for their ongoing support, in particular Professor Emma Redding and Professor Marie Sierra.

My circle of female friends has held me close in particular Christine St Clair, Destiny Deacon, Kimberley Moulton and Liz Nowell. Professor Francesca Tarocco, Director, NICHE: Center for Environmental Humanities, Ca' Foscari, University of Venice has provided invaluable support. Thanks to Chips Mackinolty for kindly providing his wonderful poster image.

Finally, I acknowledge my beloved family for their patience while I have been tethered to a desk over long days and late-night zooms. Thank you for being bystanders to three Venice Biennales and supporting me with unconditional love, especially my husband, David, and children, Lilly, Coco and Woody.

DR MARIA MADEIRA

Maria Madeira is a multi-disciplinary artist who lives and works between Dili, Timor-Leste and Perth, Australia. Her art practice spans a wide range of media, from painting to sculpture, drawing, mixed media collage and installation. Her work has been shown in over 30 exhibitions across Australia, Portugal, Brazil, Macau, United States, Indonesia, and Timor-Leste.

As one of the most prominent artists in Timor-Leste, she recently presented the major solo exhibition *Ko'alia Funan-Funan (Flowery Talk)* at Fundação Oriente, Dili in 2024. In 2005, Madeira was the first Timorese artist to present a solo exhibition in Timor-Leste with *A Dream Come True* in Hotel Timor, Dili, and in 2014 she became the first female Timorese artist to present a solo exhibition in Indonesia with *Ina Lou (Dear Mother Earth)* at Galeri Cipta II in Central Jakarta.

One of her main concerns as an artist, arts educator and cultural adviser is to convey Timor-Leste's culture and traditions to other societies – and vice-versa. It is her strong belief that art and culture are the spirit and soul of a nation. They are a vehicle through which future generations can learn to appreciate the beauty and strength of their own culture – and, in this way, discover who they are in the world.

Born in the Ermera district of Timor-Leste and spending most of her adolescence in a refugee camp in Portugal, Madeira's art is informed by a history of activism for the rights and freedom of people. Her work highlights the role of women in Timor-Leste arts and culture, and uniquely draws together contemporary art and ideas with Timorese material and cultural traditions. In 2019 she was awarded a Doctor of Philosophy from Curtin University, Western Australia, for her thesis titled 'Women's Contribution to Timor-Leste's Art and Culture'.

Madeira's works have been presented at the *Biennale Jogja XVI Equator #6*, Jakarta (2021), ARTFEM, *Women Artists International Biennial of Macau* (2020), *Macau City Fringe Festival* (2011) and *World Expo98* at the University of Lisbon, Portugal (1988).

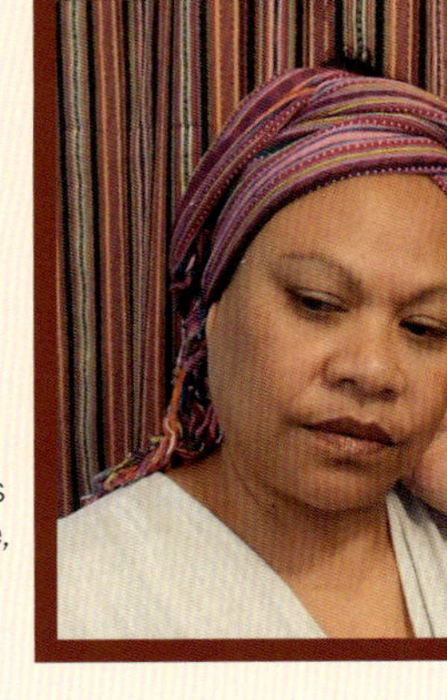

In addition, Madeira has presented her work at the University of Aveiro in Portugal, Galeri Cipta II in Central Jakarta, University of Colorado in New York, Galeria Marta Traba in São Paulo in Brazil, Casa Europa, Galeri Cipta II, Arte Moris, Hotel Timor and Fundação Oriente in Dili, Contemporary Art Space in Darwin, Cannery Arts Centre, Fremantle Arts Centre, Centre for Sustainable Living, Lawrence Wilson Gallery, Kulcha, Kalla Yeedip Gallery, Curtin University School of Fine Arts and Perth Institute of Contemporary Arts in Western Australia. In 2023 she curated the exhibition *Hasoru Malu* at the Fundação Oriente in Dili.

Madeira has presented at conferences and workshops including at Columbia University in New York (2019), University of Colorado in New York (2019), Creative Industries Conference in Dili (2011), University of Western Australia (2008), National Conference 'Different Stories' in Western Australia (2000) and the 'National Convention of East Timorese Abroad' Worldwide Convention in Portugal (1999).

She has been a cultural advisor and researcher for the Western Australian Museum (2012), the mobile research project 'Tatoli ba Kultura' (Messenger for Culture) in Timor-Leste (2010), Deckchair Theatre in Western Australia (2002) and Western Australian Department of Culture & the Arts (1996–2000). In 2004 she worked as an interpreter, translator and cultural adviser for the United Nations Serious Crimes Unit in Timor-Leste, investigating Crimes Against Humanity committed in 1999 and 2000.

www.mariamadeira.art

NATALIE KING

Professor Natalie King OAM is a curator, writer, editor and senior researcher engaged with artists and institutions across the Asia-Pacific region and Europe. King is an Enterprise Professor of Visual Arts, Victoria College of the Arts, University of Melbourne. In 2020, King was awarded the Medal of the Order of Australia (OAM) for 'service to the contemporary visual arts'. She is co-Artistic Director, with Sujan Chitrakar, of the Kathmandu Triennale 2026.

Recent projects include Curator of *Paradise Camp: Yuki Kihara*, Aotearoa New Zealand Pavilion at the 59th Venice Biennale 2022, the first Pacific, transgender and Indigenous artist to be selected by New Zealand and Powerhouse Museum, Sydney 2023. She edited the accompanying book published by Thames & Hudson that won two awards for Best Artist Led Publication and Best Art Writing by an Aotearoa Māori or Pasifika Winner. In 2022, she co-curated *Reversible Destiny: Australian and Japanese Contemporary Photography* at the Tokyo Photographic Art Museum as part of the Olympics Cultural Programme. She is Series Editor of Mini Monographs with Thames & Hudson.

In 2017, King was Curator of *Tracey Moffatt: My Horizon,* Australian Pavilion, the 57th Venice Biennale, the first solo presentation by an Indigenous artist for Australia. She has curated exhibitions for the Singapore Art Museum; the National Museum of Art, Osaka; National Gallery of Indonesia, Jakarta; the Museum of Contemporary Art, Sydney; Kaohsiung Museum of Fine Arts, Taiwan, amongst others. King has realised projects in India, Indonesia, Japan, Korea, Singapore, Taiwan, Italy, Thailand, Bangladesh, New Zealand,

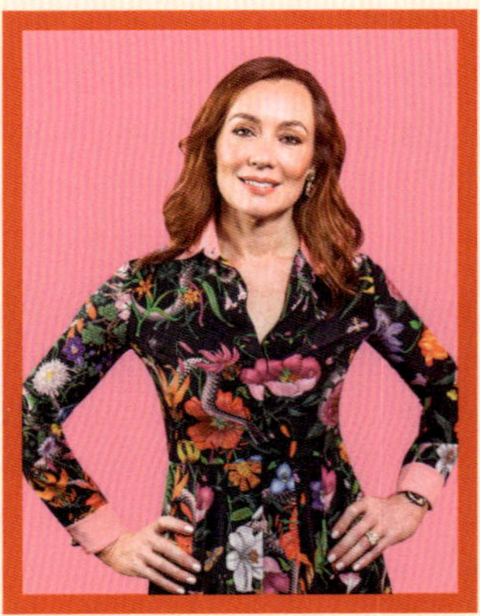

New Caledonia, and Vietnam, where she has explored Indigeneity, intersectionality, feminism and new media.

She is President of AICA-Australia (International Association of Art Critics, Paris); a member of CIMAM (International Committee for Museums and Collections of Modern Art) and Metro Tunnel Arts Advisory Panel; and a mentor for Mentor Walks. In 2021, she was awarded a University of Melbourne Excellence Award: The Patricia Grimshaw Award for Mentor Excellence.

www.natalieking.com.au

TEAM

Commissioner
Jorge Soares Cristovão
Secretary of State for Arts and Culture

Artist
Dr Maria Madeira

Curator
Professor Natalie King OAM

Advisors
Anna Schwartz AM
Dr Kim McGrath
Simon Fenby

Lawyer
Dr Nidio Pinto

Pavilion Manager
Diego Carpentiero

Exhibition Manager
Karen Hall

Exhibition Designer
Anita Gigi Budai

Graphic Designer
Andy Warren Design

Publicist
Katrina Hall

Videographer
Tim Stone

Photographers
Juventino Madeira
Mariano Goncalves
David Palazón
Jorge de Arujo

Professional Support
Claudio Marques Cabral, M.ICP. L.Ed.

Artist's Assistant
Alfeu Sanches Pereira

National Directorate for Arts and Cultural Promotion
Felix Ximenes

Assistant Curator
Leah Batterham

Media
Evangelisto Gandry dos Santos Meilana

Pavilion Attendants
Julianto Pereira
Lourença Francisca Ximenes
Januario Guterres Parada
Grigoriana das Dores Tilman Carvalho
Marcos Maia Sousa da Silva

FILM CREDITS

Production Company
Arenamedia

Director
Robert Connolly

Producer
Kate Laurie

Director of Photography
Alex Cardy

Editor
Maria Papoutsis

1st Assistant Camera
Harrison Byrne

Gaffer
Han Palmer

Best Boy
Caitlin Bryan

3rd Electrics
Coco Mata

Production Manager
Ruby Davis

Grip
Dan Mitton

Sound Recordist
Steve Bond
Tim Smith

Stills Photographer
Jorge de Arujo

The Timor-Leste Government acknowledges the late Harold Mitchell AC Ordem de Timor-Leste for his long-term support for our nation's development and the support of her Excellency Inês Maria de Almeida, Timor-Leste Ambassador to Australia.

MELBOURNE TIMORESE COMMUNITY CHOIR

Choir Co-ordinator
Jose Pires

Conductor
Miguel De Deus

Jacinta Da Costa
Sabina Santos Guterres
Teresa Santos Fraga
Carmelita Lim Gomes
Rosalia Dos Santos
Manuela De Deus
Joaninho Ana De Fatima
Lucia Maria Dos Santos Soares
Celestina De Fatima Soares
Eleonora Cardoso
Virginia Marcal
Deolinda Da Cunha

Tais bags made by Grupo Bobometo, Grupo Linda Hadomi Kultura, Alola Foundation/Alola Esperansa Weavers Group from 13 municipalities.

PROJECT LEADER

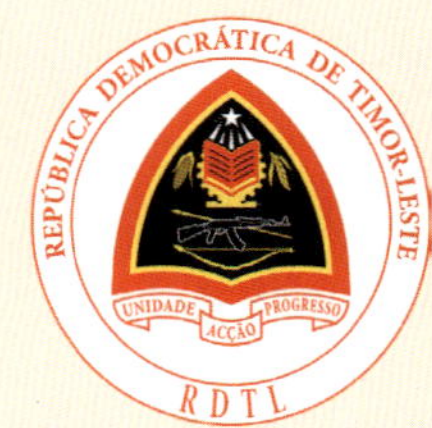
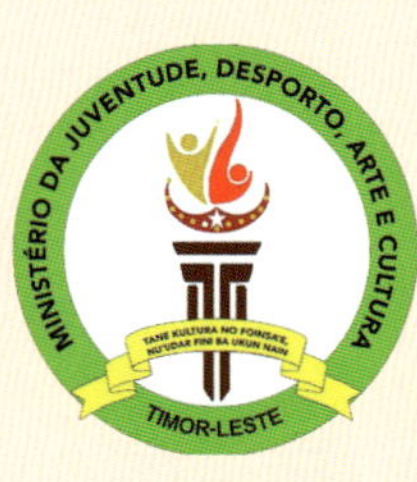

SPONSORS

This publication is generously supported by Peter McMullin AM and Ruth McMullin

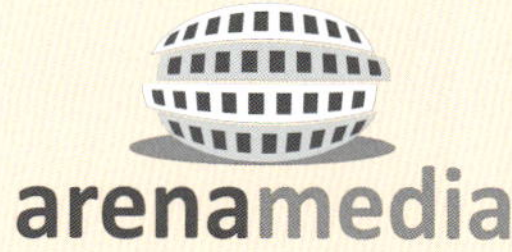

First published on the occasion of the exhibition *Maria Madeira:
Kiss and Don't Tell*, curated by Natalie King, for the Timor-Leste Pavilion
at the 60th International Art Exhibition – La Biennale di Venezia,
20 April – 24 November 2024

COVER & BACK COVER
Kiss and Don't Tell, 2024
Mixed media on canvas: acrylic, gesso, impasto, gel, glue, lipstick, tais, red earth
Courtesy of Maria Madeira and Anna Schwartz Gallery, Australia
Photo: Juventino Madeira

ENDPAPERS
Mama Malus I & II (Chewing Betel Nut I & II), 2009
Mixed media on paper
55 x 36 cm
Courtesy of Maria Madeira and Anna Schwartz Gallery, Australia
Photo: David Palazón

EDITOR
Professor Natalie King OAM

EDITORIAL ASSISTANT
Leah Batterham

DESIGN
Andy Warren Design

COPY EDITING
Andrew Ellis

First published in Italy in 2024 by
Skira editore S.p.A.
Palazzo Casati Stampa
via Torino 61
20123 Milano
Italy
www.skira.net

Printed and bound in Italy. First edition

ISBN: 978-88-572-5277-3 (State Secretariat for Arts and Culture of Timor-Leste)
ISBN: 978-88-572-5276-6 (Skira editore)

Distributed in the world by Thames and Hudson Ltd., 181A High Holborn,
London WC1V 7QX, United Kingdom.

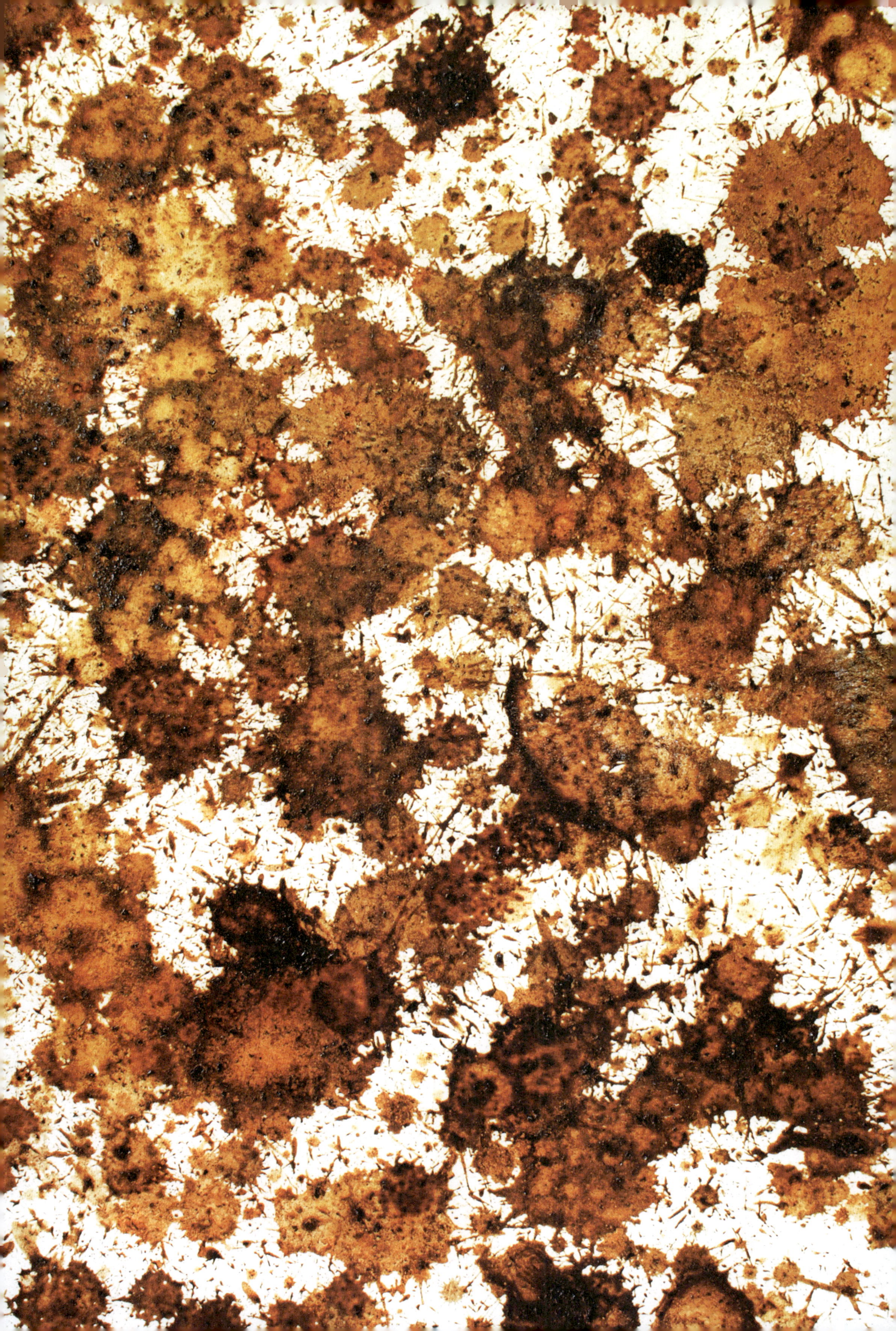

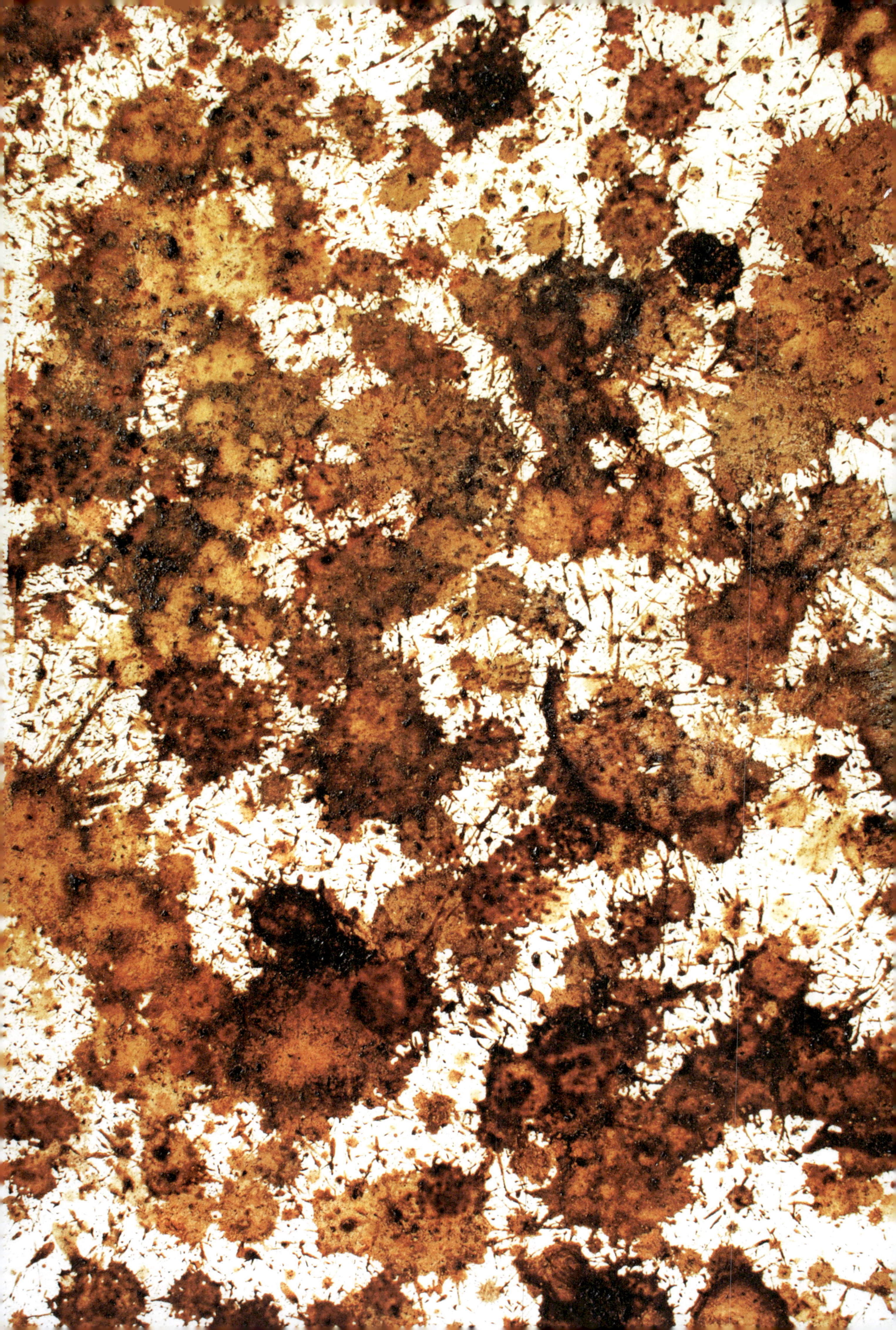